ALGORITHMS AND AUTONOMY

Algorithms influence every facet of modern life: criminal justice, education, housing, entertainment, elections, social media, news feeds, work … the list goes on. Delegating important decisions to machines, however, gives rise to deep moral concerns about responsibility, transparency, freedom, fairness, and democracy. *Algorithms and Autonomy* connects these concerns to the core human value of autonomy in the contexts of algorithmic teacher evaluation, risk assessment in criminal sentencing, predictive policing, background checks, news feeds, ride-sharing platforms, social media, and election interference. Using these case studies, the authors provide a better understanding of machine fairness and algorithmic transparency. They explain why interventions in algorithmic systems are necessary to ensure that algorithms are not used to control citizens' participation in politics and undercut democracy. This title is also available as Open Access on Cambridge Core.

Alan Rubel is an associate professor in the Information School and the Center for Law, Society & Justice at the University of Wisconsin-Madison. He has been a visiting scholar at the 4TU Centre for Ethics & Technology and Delft University of Technology, and a senior advisor to the Presidential Commission for the Study of Bioethical Issues.

Clinton Castro is an assistant professor in the Department of Philosophy at Florida International University.

Adam Pham is a postdoctoral instructor in the Division of the Humanities and Social Sciences at the California Institute of Technology.

T0371454

Algorithms and Autonomy

THE ETHICS OF AUTOMATED DECISION SYSTEMS

ALAN RUBEL
University of Wisconsin-Madison
CLINTON CASTRO
Florida International University
ADAM PHAM
California Institute of Technology

CAMBRIDGE
UNIVERSITY PRESS

CAMBRIDGE
UNIVERSITY PRESS

University Printing House, Cambridge CB2 8BS, United Kingdom

One Liberty Plaza, 20th Floor, New York, NY 10006, USA

477 Williamstown Road, Port Melbourne, VIC 3207, Australia

314–321, 3rd Floor, Plot 3, Splendor Forum, Jasola District Centre, New Delhi – 110025, India

79 Anson Road, #06–04/06, Singapore 079906

Cambridge University Press is part of the University of Cambridge.

It furthers the University's mission by disseminating knowledge in the pursuit of education, learning, and research at the highest international levels of excellence.

www.cambridge.org
Information on this title: www.cambridge.org/9781108841818
DOI: 10.1017/9781108895057

First published 2021

A catalogue record for this publication is available from the British Library.

Library of Congress Cataloging-in-Publication Data
NAMES: Rubel, Alan, author. | Castro, Clinton, author. | Pham, Adam K., author.
TITLE: Algorithms and autonomy : the ethics of automated decision systems / Alan Rubel, University of Wisconsin-Madison; Clinton Castro, Florida International University; Adam Pham, California Institute of Technology.
DESCRIPTION: Cambridge, United Kingdom ; New York, NY : Cambridge University Press, 2021. | Includes index.
IDENTIFIERS: LCCN 2021000620 (print) | LCCN 2021000621 (ebook) | ISBN 9781108841818 (hardback) | ISBN 9781108795395 (paperback) | ISBN 9781108895057 (ebook)
SUBJECTS: LCSH: Artificial intelligence – Law and legislation – Moral and ethical aspects. | Decision support systems – Moral and ethical aspects. | Expert systems (Computer science) – Moral and ethical aspects.
CLASSIFICATION: LCC K564.C6 R829 2021 (print) | LCC K564.C6 (ebook) | DDC 174/.90063–dc23
LC record available at https://lccn.loc.gov/2021000620
LC ebook record available at https://lccn.loc.gov/2021000621

ISBN 978-1-108-84181-8 Hardback
ISBN 978-1-108-79539-5 Paperback

Contents

Acknowledgments

We are enormously grateful for the people, audiences, and institutions that have provided support, feedback, discussion, advice, and criticism along the way. Thanks in particular to Richard Warner, Rob Streiffer, Filippo Santoni De Sio, Sven Nyholm, Ken Fleischmann, Eric Meyers, Bernadette Baker, Marc Alfano, Owen King, Nicole Nelson, Noah Weeth Feinstein, Suresh Venkatasubramanian, Tijn Borghuis, Holly Robbins, Catherine Crump, Helen Nissenbaum, Philip Nickel, Guy Axtell, Amiel Bernal, Adam Moore, Bryce Newell, Jeroen van den Hoven, Jean François Blanchette, Jens-Erik Mai, Kris Unsworth, Ellen LeClere, Anita Mukherjee, Mariah A. Knowles Knowles, Barbara Alvarez, Zhiyan Chen, Kristen Maples, Philip Romero-Masters, Xerxes Minocher, Nikita Shepard, Jerome Hodges, David Grant Gray, Milo Phillips-Brown, and Macy Salzberger.

There are a number of audiences that have provided a place for us to present and receive feedback on earlier versions of our arguments. These include the BIAS Workshop at the iConference at the University of Sheffield; the University of Texas Information School; the Information Ethics Roundtable at the University of Copenhagen; the Amsterdam Privacy Conference; the Computer, Privacy, & Data Protection Conference; the Privacy Law Scholars Conference; the Zicklin Normative Business Ethics Workshop at the Wharton School, University of Pennsylvania; the Eindhoven University of Technology Philosophy Department; the University of Twente Philosophy Department; the Department of Values, Technology & Innovation at Delft University of Technology; the Society for Philosophy and Technology; the Holtz Center for Science, Technology & Society at University of Wisconsin-Madison; the Risk and Insurance Department at UW-Madison Business School; the Bowling Green Philosophy Department; the University of California, San Diego, Philosophy Department; and the Jain Family Institute.

Alan would like to thank the Information School, the Center for Law, Society & Justice, and the Department of Medical History & Bioethics for being wonderful scholarly, educational communities. He would particularly like to thank the members of the 4TU Centre for Ethics & Technology in the Netherlands and the Faculty of Technology, Policy and Management at Delft University of Technology, where he was a visiting scholar in 2018–19. It was wonderful to spend an academic year around so many people doing outstanding work across philosophy, technology, ethics, and policy. Thanks especially to Tijn Borghuis, Ibo van de Poel, Sabine Roeser, and Nathalie van den Heuvel for facilitating the visit and helping make it a fruitful year. He'd also like to thank several people who have been enormously helpful along the way. Claudia Card was an outstanding dissertation advisor, mentor, and friend, and he misses her dearly. Thanks also to Ann Walsh Bradley. The fact that she authored the *Loomis* opinion doesn't affect our analysis here, but her mentorship and example has made his work better in every way. Thanks coauthors Clinton and Adam for the hard work and careful thinking. He is grateful to his family, Peggy and Paul Rubel, Louise Rubel, and Fred Dikeman, for love and patience. And most of all thanks to Kristin Eschenfelder, for everything.

Clinton would like to thank the Departments of Philosophy at Florida International University and University of Wisconsin-Madison – as well as the universities themselves – for supporting his work on this book. He'd like to thank Michael Titelbaum, Sarah Paul, Alan Sidelle, Wayne Wright, and Nellie Wieland for being such excellent teachers. He'd like to thank the McNair Scholars Program, without which he would not have become a professional philosopher. He'd like to thank Alan and Adam for their hard work on this project. Most of all, he'd like to thank Molly and Ray for their love and support.

Adam would like to thank the Division of Humanities and Social Sciences at the California Institute of Technology, as well as the Department of Philosophy at University of Wisconsin-Madison, for supporting his work on this book. He owes special acknowledgments to Dan Hausman and Harry Brighouse, who have been special sources of philosophical guidance and support over the years. He would also like to thank his coauthors, Alan and Clinton, for their diligent work. For all other support, emotional and practical, he owes everything to Emma Prendergast.

We have been able to publish this book Open Access thanks to Sarah M. Pritchard's continued, generous support to the University of Wisconsin Information School and her enthusiasm for making scholarly publications accessible. Thank you! We also wish to thank the University of Wisconsin's Alumni Research Foundation for their financial support of the project.

Some of the material in the book is based on work we have published elsewhere. The rudiments of the arguments in Chapters 3, 4, and 7 first appeared in "Algorithms, Agency, and Respect for Persons," *Social Theory & Practice* 46, no. 3 (July 2020): 547–572. The ideas in Chapter 7 saw light as a conference paper ("Agency Laundering and Algorithmic Decision Systems," in *Information in Contemporary Society (Lecture Notes in Computer Science)* (Proceedings of the 2019 iConference), edited by N. Taylor, C. Christian-Lamb, M. Martin, and B. Nardi, 590–598. *Springer Nature*, 2019). We later developed those preliminary thoughts into the article that is in large part reproduced as Chapter 7 here: "Agency Laundering and Information Technologies," *Ethical Theory & Moral Practice* 22, no. 4 (August 2019): 1017–1041.

The book chapter "Epistemic Paternalism Online" (in *Epistemic Paternalism Reconsidered: Conceptions, Justifications and Implications*, edited by Guy Axtell and Amiel Bernal [Rowman & Littlefield, 2020]) was a launching point for Chapter 6. However, Chapter 6 contains little of the same content and instead begins where the earlier work leaves off.

PART I

Some Cases, Some Ground Clearing

1

Introduction

1.1 THREE CASES

1.1.1 *Big Bars Bad:* Loomis *and* COMPAS

A little after 2 a.m. on February 11, 2013, Michael Vang sat in a stolen car and fired a shotgun twice into a house in La Crosse, Wisconsin. Shortly afterward, Vang and Eric Loomis crashed the car into a snowbank and fled on foot. They were soon caught, and police recovered spent shell casings, live ammunition, and the shotgun from the stolen and abandoned car. Vang pleaded no contest to operating a motor vehicle without the owner's consent, attempting to flee or elude a traffic officer, and possession of methamphetamine. He was sentenced to ten years in prison.[1]

The state of Wisconsin also charged Loomis with five crimes related to the incident. Because Loomis was a repeat offender, he would face a lengthy prison sentence if convicted. Loomis denied being involved in the shooting, and he maintained that he joined Vang in the car only after the shooting. Nonetheless, Loomis waived his right to a jury trial and pleaded guilty to two less severe charges (attempting to flee a traffic officer and operating a motor vehicle without owner consent). The plea agreement dismissed the three most severe charges[2] but stipulated that they would be "read-in" such that the court would consider them at sentencing and would consider the underlying, alleged facts of the case to be true. In determining Loomis's sentence, the circuit judge ordered a presentence investigative report ("PSI" or "presentence report"), using a proprietary risk assessment tool called COMPAS that is developed by Northpointe, Inc.[3]

---

[1] Jungen, "Vang Gets 10 Years in Prison for Drive-by Shooting."

[2] First degree recklessly endangering safety, possession of a firearm by a felon, and possession of a short-barreled shotgun or rifle (all as party to a crime). See *Wisconsin v. Loomis*, 881 N.W.2d paragraph 11.

[3] The tool used is part of a suite of assessment tools developed for use at various stages in the criminal justice system with different algorithms and software packages geared toward (among others) defendants who are recently incarcerated or under state supervision (COMPAS Core), persons who will soon reenter their community after incarceration (COMPAS Reentry), young people (COMPAS Youth), and general case management (Northpointe Suite Case Manager). The tool used in Loomis is COMPAS Core (which we call "COMPAS" for simplicity).

COMPAS takes as inputs a large number of data points about a defendant's criminal behavior, history, beliefs, and job skills, and generates a series of risk scales. These include pretrial release risk (likelihood that a defendant will fail to appear in court or have a new felony arrest if released prior to trial), risk of general recidivism (whether a defendant will have subsequent, new offenses), and risk of violent recidivism.[4] Among the factors that COMPAS uses to assess these risks are current and pending charges, prior arrests, residential stability, employment status, community ties, substance abuse, criminal associates, history of violence, problems in job or educational settings, and age at first arrest.[5] Using information about these factors and a proprietary algorithm, COMPAS generates bar charts corresponding to degree of risk. According to Northpointe, "[b]ig bars, bad—little bars, good," at least as a first gloss.[6] Users can dig deeper, though, to connect particular risk factors to relevant supervisory resources.

Loomis's COMPAS report indicated that he presented a high risk of pretrial recidivism, general recidivism, and violent recidivism.[7] The presentence report recounted Northpointe's warning about the limitations of COMPAS, explaining that its purpose is to identify offenders who could benefit from interventions and to identify risk factors that can be addressed during supervision.[8] Likewise, the presentence report emphasized that COMPAS scores are inappropriate to use in determining sentencing severity.[9] Nonetheless, the prosecution urged the court to use Loomis's risk scores, and the circuit court referenced the scores at sentencing.[10] The presentence and COMPAS reports were not the only bases for the sentence: The other charges (i.e., those to which Loomis did not plead guilty) were read in, meaning that the trial court viewed those charges as a "serious, aggravating factor."[11] The court sentenced Loomis to "within the maximum on the two charges" amounting to two consecutive prison terms, totaling sixteen and a half years.[12]

1.1.2 *School-wide Composite Scoring: Wagner and TVAAS*

In 2010, the state of Tennessee began requiring that school systems evaluate teachers based on value added models (VAMs). VAMs are algorithmic tools used to measure student achievement.[13] They seek to isolate and quantify teachers' individual

---

[4]   Northpointe, Inc., "Practitioner's Guide to COMPAS Core," 27–28.
[5]   Northpointe, Inc., 24.
[6]   Northpointe, Inc., 4.
[7]   *Wisconsin v. Loomis*, 881 N.W.2d paragraph 16.
[8]   *Wisconsin v. Loomis*, 881 N.W.2d paragraph 16.
[9]   *Wisconsin v. Loomis*, 881 N.W.2d paragraph 18.
[10] *Wisconsin v. Loomis*, 881 N.W.2d paragraph 19.
[11] *Wisconsin v. Loomis*, 881 N.W.2d paragraph 20.
[12] *Wisconsin v. Loomis*, 881 N.W.2d paragraph 22.
[13] Walsh and Dotter, "Longitudinal Analysis of the Effectiveness of DCPS Teachers."

contributions to student progress in terms of the influence they have on their students' annual standardized test scores.[14]

One VAM endorsed by the state legislature is the Tennessee Value-Added Assessment System (TVAAS), a proprietary system developed by SAS, a business analytics software and services company. The TVAAS system included standardized tests for students in a variety of subjects, including algebra, English, biology, chemistry, and US history. Roughly half of teachers at the time of the case taught subjects not tested under TVAAS. Nonetheless, because of the law requiring teacher evaluation on the basis of VAMs, teachers of non-tested subjects were evaluated on the basis of a "school-wide composite score," which is the average performance of *all* students on *all* subjects in that school. In other words, it is a score that is identical for all teachers in the school regardless of what subjects and which students they teach.

Teresa Wagner and Jennifer Braeuner teach non-tested subjects (physical education and art, respectively). From 2010 to 2013, each received excellent evaluation scores based on observations of their individual classes combined with their schools' composite scores. In the 2013–14 school year, however, their schools' composite scores dropped from the best possible score to the worst possible score, while their individual classroom observation scores remained excellent. The result was that Wagner's and Braeuner's individual, overall evaluations decreased from the highest possible to middling. This was enough to preclude Wagner from receiving the performance bonus she had received in previous years and to make Braeuner ineligible for consideration for tenure. Moreover, each "suffered harm to her professional reputation, and experienced diminished morale and emotional distress."[15] Nonetheless, the court determined that the teachers' Fourteenth Amendment equal protection rights were not impinged on the grounds that use of TVAAS passed the rational basis test.[16]

1.1.3 *"Exiting" Teachers:* Houston Fed of Teachers *and EVAAS*

In 2012, the Houston Independent School District ("Houston Schools") began using a similar SAS-developed proprietary VAM (EVAAS) to evaluate teachers. Houston Schools had the "aggressive goal of 'exiting' 85% of teachers with 'ineffective' EVAAS ratings."[17] And in the first three years using EVAAS, Houston Schools

---

[14] Isenberg and Hock, "Measuring School and Teacher Value Added in DC, 2011–2012 School Year."

[15] *Wagner v. Haslam*, 112 F. Supp. 3d.

[16] 112 F. Supp. 3d at 698. In reviewing government regulations under the Fourteenth Amendment's Equal Protection Clause, courts apply increasingly stringent levels of scrutiny (and are therefore more likely to find violations of the equal protection clause) based on types of classification used and how fundamental the right affected is. Where government regulation does not use a suspect class or affect a fundamental right, it is subject to the rational basis test. This is the least stringent level of scrutiny, and requires only that the regulation be rationally related to a legitimate government purpose. This is a high bar for plaintiffs to clear. See 16B Am Jur 2d Constitutional Law §§ 847–860.

[17] *Houston Fed of Teachers, Local 2415 v. Houston Ind Sch Dist*, 251 F. Supp. 3d at 1174.

"exited" between 20 percent and 25 percent of the teachers rated ineffective. Moreover, the district court determined that the EVAAS scores were the sole basis for those actions.[18]

As in *Wagner*, the *Houston Schools* court determined that the teachers did not have their substantive due process rights violated because use of EVAAS cleared the low rational basis standard.[19] However, the court determined that the teachers' *procedural* due process rights were infringed. Because the system is proprietary, there was no meaningful way for teachers to ensure that their individual scores were calculated correctly. The court noted that there were apparently no mechanisms to correct basic clerical and coding errors. And where such mistakes did occur in a teacher's score, Houston Schools refused to correct them because the correction process disrupts the analysis. In response to a "frequently asked question," the school district states:

> Once completed, any re-analysis can only occur at the system level. What this means is that if we change information for one teacher, we would have to run the analysis for the entire district, which has two effects: one, this would be very costly for the district, as the analysis itself would have to be paid for again; and two, this re-analysis has the potential to change all other teachers' reports (emphasis in original).[20]

That last point is worth stressing. Each teacher's individual score is dependent on all other teachers' scores. So a mistake for one teacher's score affects all others' scores. As the court states, "[T]his interconnectivity means that the accuracy of one score hinges upon the accuracy of all."[21]

1.1.4 *So What?*

Taking a step back from the specifics of the three cases, it is worth considering the impetus for decision-makers to adopt proprietary, algorithmic systems such as COMPAS, TVAAS, or EVAAS. Using sophisticated algorithms based on large datasets to help anticipate needs and better manage complex organizations like criminal justice systems and school systems makes a certain degree of sense. Human decision-makers have significant epistemic limitations, are prone to many kinds of biases, and at times act arbitrarily. And there are enormous advantages to using data-driven systems in lots of domains, generally. However, such systems have substantial problems.

A best-selling book by Cathy O'Neil describes similar systems as "Weapons of Math Destruction" because they hide harms, biases, and inadequate models behind

[18]   *Houston Fed of Teachers, Local 2415 v. Houston Ind Sch Dist*, 251 F. Supp. 3d at 1175.
[19]   *Houston Fed of Teachers, Local 2415 v. Houston Ind Sch Dist*, 251 F. Supp. 3d at 1183.
[20]   Houston Independent School District, "EVAAS/Value-Added Frequently Asked Questions."
[21]   251 F. Supp. 3d 1168, 1178.

complicated and inscrutable veneers.[22] In another widely popular book, mathematician Hannah Fry offers a series of cautionary tales about over- and misuse of algorithmic systems, even while being optimistic about the power of such systems to do important work.[23] In a series of articles for the news organization *ProPublica*, Julia Angwin and others make the case that risk assessment algorithms used in criminal justice are racially biased.[24] Others have argued that algorithmic systems are harmful, oppressive, opaque, and reflect and perpetuate discrimination.[25]

Despite the growing literature on algorithmic harm, discrimination, and inscrutability, there remain several puzzles related to the cases we have described. Consider, for instance, *Loomis*. It is plausible that Loomis was not harmed in that he received exactly the sentence he would have received without the PSI. After all, he had a violent criminal history; the charges in the case were related to a violent, dangerous crime; and he admitted to the underlying conduct on which the charges were based. The circuit court specifically concluded that he had been driving the car when Vang fired the shotgun, that the shooting might have resulted in killing one or more people, and that Loomis had not taken full responsibility for his role. Moreover, because he is White, and the COMPAS algorithm appears to disadvantage Black[26] defendants (as we will discuss in Chapter 3), the judge's use of the COMPAS report likely did not expose Loomis to racial discrimination. Nonetheless, something seems off about using COMPAS in the case, and we will argue that he was wronged, regardless of whether his sentence was ultimately appropriate. But just how so is a difficult question.

Likewise, something seems off in the *Wagner* and *Houston Schools* cases, but it is not straightforward to pin down whether the teachers were wronged (and, if so, why). It is certainly true that some teachers were harmed in each case, but that is not enough to conclude that they were wronged. After all, any teacher that does not receive a bonus, becomes ineligible for tenure, or is laid off is harmed. But such harms are wrongful only if they are unwarranted. Moreover, it is an open question whether the VAMs used in those cases were either unfair or unjust. We will argue that the use of algorithmic systems in these cases *is* wrongful. But again, that conclusion requires substantial explanation.

[22] O'Neil, *Weapons of Math Destruction: How Big Data Increases Inequality and Threatens Democracy.*
[23] Fry, *Hello World: Being Human in the Age of Algorithms.*
[24] Angwin et al., "Machine Bias," May 23, 2016.
[25] Citron, "Technological Due Process"; Sweeney, "Discrimination in Online Ad Delivery"; Citron and Pasquale, "The Scored Society: Due Process for Automated Predictions"; Sweeney, "Only You, Your Doctor, and Many Others May Know"; Barocas and Selbst, "Big Data's Disparate Impact"; Calo and Rosenblat, "The Taking Economy: Uber, Information, and Power"; Eubanks, *Automating Inequality: How High-Tech Tools Profile, Police, and Punish the Poor;* Pasquale, *The Black Box Society: The Secret Algorithms That Control Money and Information;* Noble, *Algorithms of Oppression;* Rosenblat, *Uberland.*
[26] Regarding capitalization of "Black" and "White," we are persuaded by the arguments in Appiah, "The Case for Capitalizing the 'B' in Black."

Answering these questions is the central task of this book. And our central thesis is that understanding the moral salience of algorithms requires understanding how they relate to the autonomy of persons. Understanding this, in turn, requires that we address three broad issues: what we owe people as autonomous agents (Chapters 3 and 4), how we preserve the conditions under which people are free and autonomous (Chapters 5 and 6), and what the responsibilities of autonomous agents are (Chapters 7 and 8).

Before we go any further, let's clarify our target.

1.2 WHAT IS AN ALGORITHM?

The academic literature and wider public discourse about the sorts of systems we have been discussing involve a constellation of concepts such as "algorithms," "big data," "machine learning," and "predictive analytics."[27] However, there is some ambiguity about these ideas and how they are related, and any discussion of emerging technologies requires some ground-clearing about the key concepts. There are, however, some general points of overlap in the literature. We won't attempt to settle any taxonomical debates here once and for all, but we will fix some of the important concepts for the sake of clarity.

Among the key concepts we will use, "algorithm" is among the most important, but its usage also invites confusion. At its most basic, an algorithm is just an explicit set of instructions for solving a problem. The instructions may be for a digital computer, but not necessarily so: a recipe for chocolate chip cookies, a set of instructions for operating a combination lock, and even the familiar procedure for long division are all algorithms. In contrast to this broad concept, we are considering algorithms in terms of their functional roles in complex technological systems.[28] The term "algorithm" is also ambiguous in this more specific setting. It can be used to refer either to a set of instructions to complete a specific task or to a system that is driven by such algorithms. This distinction makes a difference in patent law. Inventions built upon an abstract mathematical algorithm (such as a special mechanical process for molding synthetic rubber) can be patented, while the algorithm itself (meaning the equations used to guide the process or system) cannot.[29]

Our focus here, however, is algorithms in the more applied, systematic sense. That is, we are concerned with algorithms that are incorporated into decision systems. These systems take a variety of forms. Some are parts of mechanical systems, for example, sensor systems in modern cars that activate warnings (e.g., for obstacles nearby) or control safety features (e.g., emergency brakes). Others are parts of information systems, for example, recommendation systems for videos (e.g.,

[27] Mittelstadt et al., "The Ethics of Algorithms."
[28] Select Committee on Artificial Intelligence, "AI in the UK: Ready, Willing and Able?" 15; Fry, *Hello World: Being Human in the Age of Algorithms.*
[29] See *Diamond v. Diehr*, 450 U.S. 175 (1981).

Netflix, YouTube), music (Spotify, Pandora), books (Amazon, Good Reads), and maps (Google maps). Still others are incorporated into complex social structures (supply chain logistics, benefits services, law enforcement, criminal justice). These systems have become ubiquitous in our lives; everything from border security to party planning is now managed by algorithms of one sort or another. When we discuss COMPAS, EVAAS, and the Facebook News Feed in one breath, we are discussing algorithms in this broad sense. Moreover, algorithms in this sense are best understood as constitutive parts of *socio-technical systems*. They are not purely sets of instructions for carrying out a task and they are not mere technological artifacts. Rather, they are used by individuals and groups and affect other individuals and groups such that they constitute an interrelated system that is both social and technological. For the remainder of the book we will refer to these kinds of systems in several ways, including "automated decision systems," "algorithmic decision systems," and (for the sake of terseness) simply "algorithms."

Another key concept is "big data." This term is often used to describe any data-mining approach to a problem using large datasets, but this washes over much of what makes such datasets a distinctive ingredient of modern technological systems. Datasets that are "big" in the sense of big data are usually enormous and high dimensional; often they consist of hundreds of thousands of rows and thousands of columns. However, a dataset that is merely big in this sense will not render the statistical magic often discussed under the rubric of predictive analytics. Rather, the systems and datasets that underlie algorithmic decision systems also have a number of other special properties.[30] These additional properties are often summarized in terms of the "three V's": *volume, velocity*, and *variety*. In other words, datasets that are big in the relevant sense are not only big in volume. They also have high velocity, meaning that they are often continuously updated or are created in real time, for example, systems offering driving route instructions that are updated to account for traffic conditions. Finally, they are diverse in variety, meaning that they encompass both data that is structured (i.e., organized in a predefined format), in the sense of being organized and comprehensible for analysis, and data that is unstructured (i.e., not organized in a predefined format).

As with the concepts of algorithms and big data, "predictive analytics" is not defined by a well-codified set of rules, systems, or practices. At root, the term describes the application of data-mining techniques in developing predictive models, but it is more than that. Many of the model-building techniques, such as linear regression, are standard statistical methods that have been known for hundreds of years.[31] The characteristic feature of modern predictive analytics is not its use of algorithms or even the size or complexity of its datasets, but rather the analytical possibilities offered by machine learning.

[30] Kitchin, "Big Data, New Epistemologies and Paradigm Shifts."
[31] Finlay, *Predictive Analytics, Data Mining and Big Data*, 3; Sloan and Warner, "Algorithms and Human Freedom."

Machine learning involves training computers to perform tasks according to statistical patterns and inferences rather than according to human-coded logical instructions. This approach incorporates different kinds of processes, the broadest categories of which are "supervised" and "unsupervised" learning. Supervised learning is the more straightforward and familiar of the two forms of machine learning. It involves systems that have been trained on large numbers of examples, either for classification (i.e., for classifying future examples) or for regression (i.e., for performing regression analysis). What makes the computer's learning supervised in these cases is that both classification and regression processes involve a "supervision signal," which is constructed from training on a set of pre-labeled examples and which defines the desired sort of output in advance. Classification, for instance, involves sorting novel examples into a known set of discrete values (e.g., determining whether a given image is of a cat, a dog, or a rabbit), given a set of pre-labeled training examples. Regression involves predicting some real-valued output (e.g., determining the value of a rental property in a complex market), given some set of examples.

In contrast to supervised learning, unsupervised learning involves analysis using large numbers of examples but lacks a supervision signal. Unsupervised learning algorithms, then, are not given right answers in advance for the purposes of future prediction; rather, they are designed to somehow discern or reduce the deep structure of the (often high dimensional) dataset for explanatory purposes. This can take the form of "clustering," in which the data is "naturally" grouped according to the distances between its data points, or "dimensionality reduction," in which the dataset is either compressed or broken down for intuitive visualization. In recent years, these techniques have found applications in data center regulation, social media sentiment analysis, and disease analysis based on patient clustering.

There is widespread recognition that there are ethical issues surrounding complex algorithmic systems and that there is a great deal of work to be done to better understand them. To some extent, concern about these issues is related to beliefs about the potential of unsupervised learning to help realize strong forms of AI.[32] The reality is more pedestrian.[33] Outside of cutting-edge AI labs such as OpenAI or DeepMind, machine learning is mainly a matter of employing familiar techniques such as classification, regression, clustering, or dimensionality reduction, at a big data scale. So rather than grappling with ghosts in machines that have not yet begun to haunt us, we aim to address the practical issues we already face.

---

[32]   On its website, OpenAI describes its mission as "to ensure that artificial general intelligence (AGI) – by which we mean highly autonomous systems that outperform humans at most economically valuable work – benefits all of humanity." OpenAI, "About OpenAI." DeepMind, meanwhile, describes itself as "a team of scientists, engineers, machine learning experts and more, working together to advance the state of the art in artificial intelligence." DeepMind, "About DeepMind." For a somewhat recent book-length analysis of these issues, see Bostrom, *Superintelligence*.

[33]   Marcus, "Deep Learning."

1.3 ALGORITHMS, ETHICS, AND AUTONOMY

We began this introduction by describing several recent legal disputes. *Loomis*, *Wagner*, and *Houston Teachers* will be polestar cases throughout the book. But at root, this book addresses *moral* questions surrounding algorithmic decision systems. Whether use of COMPAS violates legal rights is a distinct (though related) question from whether it impinges moral claims. Moreover, the proper scope of legal claims and how the law and legal systems ought to treat algorithmic systems are moral questions. Concerns about algorithmic systems have come from a range of sectors and include guidance from nongovernmental organizations, government agencies, legislators, and academics. For example, the UK's Nuffield Foundation published a road map for research on ethical and societal implications of algorithmic systems. They argue that there are important conceptual gaps that need to be facilitated by philosophical analysis. In their canvas of various sets of AI principles offered by scientific, engineering, corporate, and government groups, "most of the principles prosed for AI ethics are not specific enough to be action guiding."[34] Likewise, they point to a gap in the philosophical literature on ethics in algorithms, data, and AI.[35]

Government entities have also recognized moral concerns and the need for greater research on these issues as well. The US President's National Science and Technology Council's 2016 report, "Preparing for the Future of Artificial Intelligence," outlined a number of ethical concerns surrounding AI and algorithmic systems.[36] While the report focuses on transparency and fairness, the issues it raises have autonomy implications as well. The Ethics Advisory Group to the European Data Protection Supervisor (EDPS-EAG) issued a report in 2018 outlining a slate of ethical concerns surrounding digital technologies, including algorithmic decision systems. In particular, the advisory group explained the importance of linking foundational values – among them autonomy, freedom, and democracy – to digital technologies. The UK parliament appointed a Lords Select Committee on Artificial Intelligence in 2017 to examine a handful of issues in development and adoption of AI (within which they include algorithmic systems), one of which is "What are the ethical issues presented by the development and use of artificial intelligence?"[37] Among their recommendations are principles protecting "fairness and intelligibility" and prohibiting automated systems from having the power to "hurt, destroy, or deceive human beings."[38] Members of both houses of the U.S. Congress have introduced an Algorithmic

---

[34] Whittlestone et al., "Ethical and Societal Implications of Algorithms, Data, and Artificial Intelligence: A Roadmap for Research," 11.

[35] Whittlestone et al., 46–47.

[36] National Science and Technology Council, "Preparing for the Future of Artificial Intelligence."

[37] Select Committee on Artificial Intelligence, "AI in the UK: Ready, Willing and Able?" 12.

[38] Select Committee on Artificial Intelligence, 125. Related reports and recommendations have come from Japanese Society for Artificial Intelligence, "Ethical Guidelines"; Association for Computing Machinery, US Public Policy Council, "Statement on Algorithmic Transparency and Accountability"; Campolo et al., "AI Now 2017 Report."

Accountability Act that would impose requirements to create impact assessments and address bias and security issues.[39]

The academic literature is also expanding in its criticism of algorithmic systems. Kirsten Martin, for instance, argues that big data generates negative externalities in the form of additional surveillance, which she calls "surveillance as pollution."[40] Tal Zarsky argues that automated decision-making introduces both efficiency- and fairness-based problems.[41] Danielle Citron and Frank Pasquale argue for imposing auditing procedures on the process of algorithmic development on the basis of those problems.[42] Karen Yeung argues that the inoffensive practice of nudging, which classically involves only subtle forms of behavioral modification through manipulation of "choice architectures," can be galvanized by predictive analytics to produce "hypernudging" platforms whose effects at scale wind up being radically paternalistic.[43] Cathy O'Neil groups such systems under the banner of "weapons of math destruction,"[44] arguing that they enjoy an aura of epistemic respectability that encourages us to use them beyond their actual capacities. Citron argues that addressing these problems requires nothing short of a new constitutional paradigm – a new "technological due process."[45]

Algorithmic systems (including both predictive systems and digital platforms) have come under substantial economic, political, and philosophical criticism. We agree with much of it. However, for a few reasons we do not defend any overall moral or ethical conclusion about the technologies themselves. First, the fact that they are rapidly advancing as part of an ongoing process means that the horizon for productive commentary on current technology is time delimited. Second, we acknowledge that these technologies – whatever their life spans might be – can be employed for useful aims as well as for pernicious ones. There are few global, all-things-considered moral judgments that can be made about, for instance, the governance of Facebook's News Feed or use of risk assessment algorithms. Third, we acknowledge that the algorithmic landscape of predictive analytics and digital platforms is here to stay in some form or other. It is possible to exert some influence on how these systems are employed and perhaps even develop new conceptions of fair play to cope with these changes, but predictive analytics and digital platforms will not be eliminated altogether.

For those reasons we aim to look beyond the particular features of the technologies as much as possible, treating the technologies themselves as case studies that are useful for making certain moral and social issues vivid and concrete, rather than as the sources of ontologically distinctive philosophical issues. In many cases, the philosophical issues have more to do with our psychological features and our social

---

[39] Algorithmic Accountability Act of 2019, H.R. 2231; Algorithmic Accountability Act of 2019, S. 1108.
[40] Martin, "Ethical Issues in the Big Data Industry," 75.
[41] Zarsky, "The Trouble with Algorithmic Decisions."
[42] Citron and Pasquale, "The Scored Society: Due Process for Automated Predictions."
[43] Yeung, "'Hypernudge': Big Data as a Mode of Regulation by Design." See also Lanier, *Ten Arguments for Deleting Your Social Media Accounts Right Now.*
[44] O'Neil, *Weapons of Math Destruction: How Big Data Increases Inequality and Threatens Democracy.*
[45] Citron, "Technological Due Process."

structures than with the inherent hazards of technological systems considered abstractly. Hence, what unifies the systems discussed in the book is not strictly about the technologies per se, but rather about the human values that are implicated by the designs and modes of operation of all of those socio-technical systems. All these systems, we argue, raise philosophical issues about *autonomy*.

Focusing on autonomy is important for several reasons. Primarily, it connects unease about algorithmic systems to a good that has deep, stable, and plausible moral value. This is a rich seam to mine in the same way that autonomy issues have been fundamentally important in other domains of applied ethics. Arguments grounded in autonomy connect concerns about algorithmic systems to an area with a broad and well-developed philosophical literature.

Moreover, by drawing out the importance of autonomy, our account can address concerns about algorithmic decision systems that are not captured by accounts that focus on fairness, harm, and bias. Algorithmic systems often reflect, harden, and create unfair structures; this is an enormous moral concern. However, that is only part of the moral importance of algorithmic systems. *Loomis* shows why: Loomis was plausibly wronged, but it is not clear that he has been treated unfairly (at least in the sense that COMPAS treats him differently from other, similarly situated defendants) and it does not appear that he has been materially harmed by use of COMPAS. Note, too, that while there are some scholars who have addressed whether certain kinds of algorithmic systems conflict with autonomy via manipulation,[46] our view is that autonomy is grounds for a much broader evaluation of algorithmic systems. *Loomis*, *Wagner*, and *Houston Schools* do not appear to involve manipulation in any strong sense.

Our focus on autonomy also provides a foundation for moral concerns that are often under-explained (e.g., transparency, filter bubbles). Specifically, a focus on autonomy can serve to route around at least some disputes about bias and fairness. It has become clear that there are different ways that a single system can be plausibly unfair to members of different groups.[47] Determining which facets of fairness matter the most requires considering different values. We will argue that an appeal to autonomy can help in that regard. Finally, note that our approach is consistent with other important critiques; that is, a concern about autonomy for the most part *adds to* rather than contradicts extant critiques.

---

[46] For accounts addressing algorithmic systems and autonomy, see Yeung, "'Hypernudge': Big Data as a Mode of Regulation by Design"; Lanzing, "'Strongly Recommended' Revisiting Decisional Privacy to Judge Hypernudging in Self-Tracking Technologies"; Danaher, "The Threat of Algocracy: Reality, Resistance and Accommodation"; Danaher, "Toward an Ethics of AI Assistants"; Susser, Roessler, and Nissenbaum, "Online Manipulation: Hidden Influences in a Digital World." They most often address direct effects of automated systems on individuals' decision procedures. Certainly, such cases are important from the standpoint of autonomy. However, our aim here is to address a broader range of issues surrounding autonomy. We address this issue further in Chapter 5.

[47] Binns, "Fairness in Machine Learning: Lessons from Political Philosophy"; Binns, "Algorithmic Accountability and Public Reason"; Corbett-Davies and Goel, "The Measure and Mismeasure of Fairness."

1.4 OVERVIEW OF THE BOOK

To get at the different ways in which algorithmic systems bear upon autonomy, we have divided the book into four main parts. Part I is introductory and ground-clearing. Chapters 1 and 2 serve as introductory chapters, outlining the conceptual foundations and philosophical commitments that ground our arguments throughout the book. The primary task of Chapter 2 is providing an account of autonomy and its importance. It begins with a high-level explanation of autonomy itself and then canvasses several key conceptions of autonomy and the philosophical concerns underlying them. We then advance our ecumenical account of autonomy. Specifically, we draw on procedural, psychological accounts of autonomy as well as social accounts of personal autonomy. We argue that while they have important differences in how they explain key facets of autonomy, in practice they are substantially overlapping. Hence, we can draw on both as a foundation for the arguments we make in the book. That is because fully realized autonomy demands both procedural independence (which includes both epistemic competence conditions and authenticity conditions) and substantive independence (which includes conditions of reciprocal support and non-domination from society more broadly).

Part II builds upon our account of autonomy and our polestar cases to address the kinds of moral claims and the nature of the respect that persons are owed in virtue of their autonomy. In Chapter 3 we argue that people are owed systems of rules and practices that they can reasonably endorse. We begin the chapter with a closer consideration of VAMs used for K-12 teacher assessment. We argue that the problem with such tools cannot be reduced to concerns about their reliability or their potential for bias. Rather, teachers have a claim to incorporate their values into their lives as they see fit. And respecting teachers requires recognizing them as value-determiners, neither thwarting nor circumventing their ability to act according to those values without good reason. Moreover, as agents they are capable of abiding fair terms of social agreement (so long as others do too), and hence "good reasons" will be reasons that they can abide as fair terms of cooperation. Teachers can endorse those reasons either as consistent with their own values or as a manifestation of fair social agreement.

We argue that VAMs fail to respect teachers as agents because they are used in a way that teachers cannot reasonably endorse, for four interrelated reasons. First is their reliability, which many have questioned. Second is that their results can be based on factors for which teachers are not morally responsible (e.g., student performance may correlate with teachers' age, ethnicity, or gender). Third is stakes. The fact that an algorithmic system is unreliable or measures factors for which persons are not responsible is important primarily as a function of the stakes involved. Fourth is the relative burdens placed upon people subject to them. We conclude by applying our framework to our polestar cases (*Loomis*, *Wagner*, and *Houston Schools*).

One important, oft-cited criticism of algorithmic systems is that they lack transparency. Such systems can be opaque because they are complex, protected by patent or trade secret, or deliberately obscure. In the EU, there is a debate about whether the General Data Protection Regulation (GDPR) contains a "right to explanation," and if so what such a right entails. Our task in Chapter 4 is to address this informational component of algorithmic systems. We argue that information access is integral for respecting autonomy, and transparency policies should be tailored to advance autonomy.

To make this argument we distinguish two facets of agency (i.e., capacity to act). The first is *practical* agency or the ability to act effectively according to one's values. The second is what we call *cognitive* agency, which is the ability to exercise what Pamela Hieronymi calls "evaluative control" (i.e., the ability to control our affective states such as beliefs, desires, and attitudes). We argue that respecting autonomy requires providing persons sufficient information to exercise evaluative control and properly interpret the world and one's place in it. We draw this distinction out by considering algorithmic systems used in background checks, and we apply the view to our polestar cases.

While Part II of the book considers what we owe people *given that they have autonomy*, Part III addresses our responsibility to secure the conditions under which people can *act autonomously*. Chapter 5 considers the relationship between algorithmic systems and freedom. There is substantial dispute about the concept and moral value of freedom. A key area of dispute is whether freedom is best understood in terms of negative, positive, or republican freedom. We offer an account according to which freedom is *ecological* and includes both republican freedom (which is to say, freedom from others' exercise of arbitrary power) and positive freedom, properly understood (i.e., where positive freedom is a function of quality of agency). We argue that algorithmic systems in several ways conflict with ecological freedom.

Chapter 6 addresses a specific condition of autonomy from Chapter 2, viz., epistemic competence. It has been clear since the early 2000s that internet communication technologies generally and algorithmically driven information systems in particular create epistemically noxious environments. These include phenomena like filter bubbles and echo chambers as well as more insidious phenomena like toxic recommendation systems.[48] Most every media platform now employs content moderation systems to screen for the truly awful content that would make sites like YouTube, Facebook, Reddit, and others unnavigable.[49] That practice is relatively

---

[48] Among the most odious of these are YouTube algorithmic recommendation systems that serve disturbing (including violent and sexualized) content on channels specifically designed and marketed for children. See Maheshwari, "On YouTube Kids, Startling Videos Slip Past Filters"; Orphanides, "Children's YouTube Is Still Churning out Blood, Suicide and Cannibalism."

[49] For an overview of the enormous labor and the labor practices involved in content moderation, see Roberts, *Behind the Screen*.

uncontroversial. We argue that there are further obligations on sites to exercise a kind of epistemic paternalism.

While Parts II and III begin from the premise that people have certain claims as agents (specifically, claims to the conditions that foster autonomy), Part IV shifts focus to the obligations *of* agents. Chapter 7 considers the autonomy and responsibility of those who deploy information technologies (as collectors of big data, users of algorithmic decision systems, developers of social media sites, and so on). Specifically, we argue that there is a type of wrong that arises when autonomous agents obscure responsibility for their actions, which we call "agency laundering." At root, agency laundering involves a failure to meet one's moral responsibility for an outcome by attributing causal responsibility to another person, group, process, or technology, and it does so by undermining a key component of responsibility itself, viz., accountability. We apply our conception of agency laundering to a series of examples, including Facebook-automated advertising suggestions, Uber driver interfaces, as well as to our polestar cases.

We then turn to the ways in which autonomy underwrites democratic governance. Political authority, which is to say the ability of a government to exercise power, may be justifiable or not. Whether it is justified and how it can come to be justified is a question of political *legitimacy*. In Chapter 8 we consider several views of legitimacy and argue for a hybrid version of normative legitimacy based on one recently offered by Fabienne Peter.[50] We explain that each facet of the hybrid requires a legitimation process that is itself grounded in autonomy. We argue that the autonomy view is a basis for criticism of the legitimation processes related to a predictive policing technology and to actions of Cambridge Analytica and the Internet Research Agency in recent elections. In Chapter 9 we offer some conclusions and caveats.

1.5 A HEURISTIC

It is worth stepping back for a moment before launching into the main substance of the book's arguments in order to explain its purpose and approach. This book is about ethics and algorithmic decision systems, such as COMPAS, EVAAS, YouTube and other recommendation systems, Facebook Ad services, and others. Its aim is to better understand moral concerns about those systems. So we will consider questions such as the following: Is it morally justifiable for a court to use an algorithmic system such as COMPAS in determining whether, and if so for how long, to sentence a defendant to incarceration? Should school systems use algorithmic systems such as EVAAS to promote, reward, and fire teachers? Does YouTube have an obligation to better police the videos that are suggested to viewers?

[50] Peter, "The Grounds of Political Legitimacy."

These questions are multifaceted, and there are lots of different ways we might construe them. There is a meta-ethical issue of what the "should" and "justifiable" in the questions mean or refer to.[51] There are questions of legal doctrine such as whether the use of a system like COMPAS impinges upon due process rights and whether algorithmic systems violate contract terms or statutory protections. Those kinds of questions have ethical implications and will come up now and again in the book, but they are not the focus.

Instead we will focus on ethics (which we use interchangeably with "morals"). How, though, does one do that? There is no univocal recipe for answering moral questions. However, we can offer a heuristic for evaluating moral questions.[52] It is not the only way to think through problems, and it is useful in part because it shows just how difficult resolving some moral problems actually is. Nonetheless, it is a way to keep oneself in check and (perhaps more importantly) letting others understand what exactly one is doing. The hope is that following this kind of heuristic will help readers recognize what (if anything!) an ethical argument contributes and what its limitations are.

The first step is clarifying relevant concepts. In considering whether it is justifiable to use algorithmic systems in criminal justice decisions, for example, we will need to specify a number of concepts in order to make progress. An obvious one is "algorithmic system," which we have tried to clarify in Section 1.2. Do we mean literally *any* algorithm, including an ink-and-paper set of sentencing guidelines? Or are we talking about only sophisticated, big data–driven systems? Or even machine learning–based systems? Another concept to clarify is "criminal justice decisions." That could mean decisions about sentencing, supervision, early release, or something else altogether. As we will see in our discussion of COMPAS throughout the book, those issues matter. We will also spend substantial time working to clarify moral concepts. These include "autonomy," "agency," "fairness," "freedom," "legitimacy," and others.

The next step is to get one's empirical facts[53] straight. Of course, this is easier said than done. If we want to address the question of whether some use of algorithmic

---

[51] For example, one might ask whether the claim that X should happen is merely expressive of support for a view, or whether it seeks to say something true about the world, but is mistaken because there are no such facts, or the like. We won't take up that debate here, though we invite anyone who *would* like to have that debate to attend the Madison Metaethics Workshop at the University of Wisconsin-Madison each fall.

[52] Here, we offer a modified version of one Tom Regan outlines in Regan, "Introduction to Moral Reasoning." He offers what he calls a process for "ideal moral judgment," which strikes us as overly optimistic. We'll call it instead a "heuristic for better moral judgment." That may also be overly optimistic, even if substantially less so than Regan.

[53] One might call these "non-moral facts," though that has the potential to derail us. At least one of the authors is adamant that all facts are non-moral. At least one tentatively believes that moral facts are types of natural facts. And at least one has argued that there are moral facts and those facts are nonnatural. It is possible that some of these describe multiple authors and that some authors are described by more than one of these sentences. What matters for our purposes here is that there are

systems in criminal justice decisions is justifiable or not, we will want to know something about how such systems operate, what effects they have, and what the underlying picture of the criminal justice system looks like. We might want to know something about how people are likely to use such systems; how those systems interact with social structures like courts, prisons, parole boards, and the like. There is a world of facts surrounding any moral question, some of which are contested, some of which are unknowable, and some of which people get wrong. Regardless, any moral claim will rest on some understanding of the facts on the ground, and getting those straight, getting a clear-eyed view of what facts are tenuous and unknown, and having a sense of what we would *like* to know is vital in addressing moral questions.

Step three is discerning and applying the correct moral theory to the questions at hand. A few thousand years of religious and philosophical disputes have not answered the question of which moral theories are correct. It is debatable as to whether (and to what extent and by what metric) there has been progress, and there is an important debate about the degree of cultural convergence and divergence on fundamental questions of right and wrong. However, the entire premise of the project of debating the justifiability of anything – using animals for food, abortion, policing, capital punishment, universal suffrage, civil disobedience, mandating vaccinations, and, our topic, applying algorithmic systems in various contexts – is that there can be better and worse (i.e., more and less morally justifiable) answers. And hence, we need some basis on which to find our way on these kinds of questions.

Of course, the question of *which* moral theory is correct comprises its own, vast area of inquiry. Among the possibilities are consequentialism, deontology, virtue ethics, and contractarianism, each of which has myriad versions. And even once one has some set of moral values one believes to be correct, it is yet another daunting task to figure out just how to apply them. If one is a thorough-going consequentialist who believes that an action is right just in case that act leads to the best overall consequences, it remains an open question of how to figure out how to apply that to actions on the ground.

There are, however, a number of views of morality that are critical of the notion that there are moral principles to apply in the first place, even while accepting that actions can be more or less justified. Some of these views are forms of pragmatism, holding that the practice of theorizing is inseparable from practical consideration. Others adhere to "casuistry," according to which one can find justification by comparing contested situations to similar "paradigmatic" cases. Still others are forms of moral particularism, according to which general moral principles (e.g., "lying is bad," "killing is wrong," "people should be treated equally") carry no moral weight and provide no role in explaining why actions are right or wrong. Rather,

---

issues about metaethics that lurk underneath the surface of any project in applied ethics. Nonetheless, we can make progress without resolving those underlying questions.

particular acts are right or wrong, and any generalities we draw from particular acts are neither explanatory nor applicable to other cases. But even these "anti-theory" positions continue to insist that there is an account of moral justification (even if it is not one based on explanatorily prior moral principles). And so, if you are searching for the answer, as we are, to the question of whether using algorithmic systems under certain conditions is right or wrong, then you are committed at some level (and perhaps only implicitly) to there being better and worse accounts of moral justifiability on which to base such judgments. We should therefore understand "moral theory" in this third step of the heuristic (i.e., discern and apply the correct moral theory) to be quite broad. It is not only the discernment and application of moral principles but also (or, on the anti-theory views, rather) the discernment and application of the correct understanding of moral justification.

The final part of the heuristic is to apply principles of critical reflection to the concepts, empirical claims, and moral theories one has at one's disposal. This does *not* imply that one can simply apply rote, bloodless, "pure" reason to problems. That would be impossible, and it would be unwarranted in light of the inevitable conceptual questions, factual lacunae, and steep burdens of determining the correct moral theories. Rather, it requires a much more limited (but no less important) set of constraints. One should follow one's reasons where they lead. If the concepts, empirical claims, and moral theory entail that some action is impermissible, one should recognize that entailment and either accept the conclusion or aim to look for the flaw in the premises that led one there. Another element of good reasoning is to recognize just how fallible reasoning is; in other words, one should avoid dogmatism. Related is to accept that one's conceptual apparatus, understanding of facts, and moral theory are revisable. That's a good thing. After all, we are bound to have mistaken beliefs and commitments.

This is a project in applied moral philosophy and it aims to use the heuristic we have outlined. It considers some questions that are legal, and it adopts some factual claims. Its contribution comes in several parts. First, it clarifies some relevant concepts, including (among others) autonomy, agency, freedom, paternalism, responsibility, and legitimacy. Second, as to the empirical facts, we largely take our cues from others, drawing on court cases and related documents, other academics' empirical work on algorithmic systems, and journalists' investigations on related issues. Third, we advance some claims of normative moral theory. Most of these are grounded in autonomy. However, we do not advance the view that autonomy is the only moral value relevant to analyzing and evaluating algorithmic systems. Rather, our view is that autonomy is an important value, and many moral concerns about algorithmic systems are best understood as, at bottom, issues of autonomy.

Put slightly differently, our project is based on the premise that people are, to some degree, and within important limitations, able to govern themselves. They can determine what kinds of things matter to them, how to use those values to order their lives, and come to agreements with others about how to navigate differences in belief about values. The capacity for autonomy, we argue, gives rise to moral claims that others respect (to some degree and within important limits) persons' decisions about self-government. Our task, then, is to craft a set of considerations surrounding algorithmic systems based on autonomy. There are many other considerations. Some involve consequences. Some are about the law, including to what extent the law itself provides moral reasons. Yet another is virtue. There are also deeper questions of justice. Still others involve religious and quasi-religious issues. Others involve the proper scope of freedom for technologists to develop and implement systems. Still others involve trade secrets and capitalism. There is no way to adequately address all of these in a volume like this. But we submit that many potential readers will agree with our rock-bottom premise that autonomy matters. So we will start there, clarifying the concept and positing some moral principles that rest on it. On to Chapter 2.

2

Autonomy, Agency, and Responsibility

The central claim of this book is that understanding the moral salience of algorithmic systems requires understanding how they bear upon the autonomy of persons. In Parts II through IV of the book, we explain in detail several different ways in which algorithmic systems are important in relation to autonomy and agency. But before we can do that, we have the basic ground-clearing task of providing an account of autonomy and its value. The discussion in this chapter will set out the basics of our view. However, autonomy is a foundation for many of the concepts and arguments we develop in later chapters, such as responsibility, liberty, paternalism, and democratic legitimacy. We will explain these concepts in more detail in the chapters that draw on them.

We begin by setting out some basics of autonomy, including some key distinctions. Then we explain two broad categories of competing views, focusing on exemplars of each. We offer an ecumenical account of autonomy that incorporates features of both psychological autonomy and personal autonomy, and which requires both procedural and substantive independence. The chapter concludes with an explanation of some of the ways that considerations of autonomy bear upon our arguments in later chapters.

2.1 AUTONOMY BASICS

Autonomy is at root self-government. Individuals can (to some degree and with more or less success) develop their own sense of value, make decisions about what matters most to them, and act accordingly. But just below the surface of that general statement is a rich, complex, and deeply contested set of questions about the scope, nature, and moral importance of autonomy. Our task in this chapter is to offer an account that shows our philosophical commitments, positions itself within some of the weightiest philosophical debates about autonomy, and explains where (and why) we decide not to make stands. The account we offer here is lightweight and ecumenical. It is lightweight because it takes on minimal commitments. It is ecumenical in that it is compatible with a broad range of views. This approach can go a long way in helping understand the moral importance of algorithmic systems without having to resolve some of the deepest and most vexing disputes about the nature and scope of autonomy.

We can get a sense of the basic contours of autonomy by considering some archetypical ways that autonomy can be undermined.[1] For one, a person's actions and preferences are not autonomous to the extent that they are the result of coercion or deceit. Where an employer gives an employee the option of working after they have clocked out or being fired, the employee's choice to keep their job is of course their genuine preference. However, that choice is not autonomous because it is constrained in an illegitimate and coercive way. Suppose instead that the employer constrains the employee's options through deceit. The employer lies to the employee that the company will fail if the employee does not put in extra, unpaid hours after they have clocked out. Again, the employee's choice to do unpaid work is based on their genuine desire to keep the company afloat and retain their job. It is not, however, an autonomous choice because they have been deliberately deceived.

A more subtle type of case concerns adaptive preferences. Suppose that the employer continuously asks the employee to work extra, unpaid hours in order for their business to thrive. The employee believes that other employment options are limited and fears losing their job if they do not do the unpaid work. Although it is a burden, the employee does indeed want the business to thrive. They may consciously embrace the practice to make the burden seem manageable. This would seem to conflict with their autonomy in that they formed their preference to work extra, unpaid hours in response to illegitimate pressure from the employer and their belief that other alternatives were bad. Finally, suppose the employer comes to rely on the employee in a close working relationship, provides appropriate encouragement, and genuinely values the employee's skill and professionalism. Indeed, the employer values it so much that they regularly promote other, similarly qualified employees to better-paid, management positions so that they can keep drawing on the employee's talents directly. The employee may come to think that the management positions are not really attractive anyway, as they involve a steep learning curve, increased time demands, and working with people they do not know. These are, in the employee's mind, grapes that are out of reach and probably sour anyway. What the employee prefers conflicts with their autonomy in that they formed their preferences in response to their limited opportunity.[2]

---

[1]   Following Brighouse, *School Choice and Social Justice*, 66.

[2]   Note that the third and fourth cases are ones in which the person's preferences and values are not autonomous. It is a further question as to whether the employee is *globally* autonomous and a further question still whether the employer undermined, infringed, or failed to respect their autonomy. Our task in this chapter is get a handle on the concept of autonomy. We take up questions about the moral demands of autonomy in subsequent chapters.

The key to each of these examples is that just what it means for individuals to develop their own sense of value, the conditions under which individuals' decisions are their own, and precisely when people act according to their own preferences is itself a nuanced question. Hence, it is not enough to say that autonomy is simply a matter of people being able to do what they want. Rather, the deeper question is this: Under what conditions are people and their choices, preferences, and values properly understood as autonomous?

The view that we will advocate here is that although autonomy of preference and choice is important, this sort of autonomy is limited. A fuller understanding of autonomy will focus on autonomy of *persons*, which is to say the social conditions under which a person is autonomous. Our view, though, is ecumenical in that it incorporates both psychological views and personal autonomy views. The reason is that the normative considerations substantially overlap, as we explain in Section 2.4.

2.2 SOME DISTINCTIONS

With our first gloss in mind and having described several ways in which persons' autonomy may be impinged, it will be useful to make a few distinctions. After doing so, we can fill out our conception.

2.2.1 *Global versus Local*

Autonomy can apply to a relatively narrower or wider range of circumstances. For example, a person may be autonomous with respect to local decisions. That is, they may be able to make decisions about actions with immediate effect and may be able to ensure that those decisions comport with their values. Suppose, for example, that Ali exercises substantial control over most aspects of her life and is able to do more or less as she pleases. However, suppose that her employer routinely assigns her to projects that she does not like. When Ali asks for different responsibilities, the employer ignores her. This is a case in which Ali lacks local autonomy over the circumstances of her employment, and that is true regardless of whether she could find another job relatively quickly and regardless of whether she can effectively govern other facets of her life. In other words, her global autonomy is consistent with her lack of local autonomy.[3]

It is also true that a person may be locally autonomous but lack global autonomy. Suppose that Bari lacks financial resources, lives in an isolated community, and has had little opportunity to develop her talents. And suppose that her family and community expect her to fulfill a strict set of social obligations: care for her siblings and older relatives, cook for the family, and obey her husband. However, she has a great deal of latitude in *how* she fulfills those expectations. Bari, in this case, lacks

---

[3] Meyers, *Self, Society, and Personal Choice*, 48.

global autonomy even while being able to exercise local autonomy. Notice that Bari may lack global autonomy either because the social expectations placed upon her are strictly enforced or because she has internalized those expectations and formed adaptive preferences favoring her actual circumstances.

Distinguishing local and global autonomy matters in two ways. First, particular cases of coercion and manipulation are wrong (when they are wrong) at least in part because they involve failures to treat people as autonomous, but they need not be so substantial as to undermine a person's overall ability to govern their life. Second, the fact (if it is a fact) that some groups of people are not currently the subject of manipulation and coercion is not enough to ensure that their autonomy is respected globally. They may have developed values and preferences under oppressive or otherwise limiting circumstances, or their circumstances may be constrained overall.

2.2.2 *Capacity, Exercise, Successful Self-government*

Closely related to the distinction between global and local autonomy are a number of different meanings for autonomy that are relevant in moral and political philosophy. Joel Feinberg, for one, distinguishes the capacity to govern oneself, successful self-government, the personal ideal of self-government, and moral claims that one might assert that reflect a person's sovereignty over theirself. [4]

The first meaning of autonomy is the capacity for (global) self-government. There are a number of rock-bottom, baseline capacities that a person must have to self-govern. They must be able to consider the world and make rational assessments and decisions. "Rational" here means only that there is a close connection between facts and inferences, and a person's decisions either line up with well-enough ordered assessments of facts and reasons, or they make decisions fully aware that they do not line up. The second issue of capacity is that a person must not be so profoundly damaged, and must not have had their world so dramatically circumscribed, that their understanding of it prevents well-enough ordered assessments of facts and reasons. Capacity autonomy does not require much; it is a bar low enough that adults can generally clear it. Note that "capacity" is distinct from "potential." Infants and young children lack the (present) capacity to be autonomous, but they have the potential to develop that capacity. So the "capacity for autonomy," we might say, refers to the current state of a person and whether they can exercise self-government at this moment so long as the situation in which they are placed is conducive to that exercise. A person held hostage has the capacity for autonomy, should they escape or be released. A disenfranchised person in an apartheid state has the capacity for autonomy, should the governing regime change.

---

[4] Feinberg, "Autonomy," 28.

Contrast capacity autonomy with the successful *exercise* of autonomy, which Feinberg calls "autonomy as condition."[5] A person with the capacity to govern themselves may be constrained by circumstances, hindered by other people, or fail to use their capacity. Autonomy in this sense involves several things. It includes subjecting one's values to scrutiny, that is, exercising the capacity to self-scrutinize. It also involves engaging in some degree of self-determination, which is to say one must act on their values, principles, beliefs, and so forth to steer their course. Feinberg suggests that it also involves a degree of self-legislation by adopting moral principles and holding oneself to those principles. This way of conceptualizing autonomy owes a great deal to Kant. The third ("autonomy") formulation of the Categorical Imperative is "the idea of the will of every rational being as a will giving universal law" and requires a person act according to a maxim of one's will and such that their will "could at the same time have as its object itself as giving universal law."[6] Maxims are compelling, and one acts autonomously in following universal maxims, in that one both sets and follows them.

Successful exercise of autonomy does not require that one make up this self-legislation whole cloth; one will invariably adopt principles that are based on one's community. The capacity to self-govern, the values an agent develops, and the ways in which they incorporate those values into their life are socially situated.[7] Moreover, developing one's sense of what is important depends on social conditions that nurture the ability to do so.[8] Social structures may delimit the conceptions of value that are available for a person to draw upon in developing their own principles and their own sense of value. Persons' abilities to incorporate their values into their important decisions will depend on the prevailing "social forms" and the opportunities that exist in the broader social context.[9] Nonetheless, holding oneself to their principles autonomously requires that one adhere to them because they are principles, not merely because others happen to adhere to those principles. This in turn requires authenticity, self-control, and taking moral responsibility for one's actions.

Such conditions form the basis of a third conception: autonomy as ideal. The successful-exercise conception outlines important component parts of autonomy. However, people are not isolated, wholly self-legislating individuals. Rather, they are parts of families, communities, and other social groups, and exercising autonomy must be compatible with being parts of social groups. Moreover, the elements of successfully exercising autonomy (self-determination, authenticity, self-control, integrity) can be used to bad ends. Autonomy is not the only relevant value, and it is a mistake to elevate it above the social and historical context of human life.

[5] Feinberg, "Autonomy," 30.
[6] Kant, *Groundwork of the Metaphysics of Morals*, sec. 4:432.
[7] Mackenzie and Stoljar, *Relational Autonomy: Feminist Perspectives on Autonomy, Agency, and the Social Self*, 4.
[8] Oshana, *Personal Autonomy in Society*, 90.
[9] Raz, *The Morality of Freedom*; Mackenzie, "Relational Autonomy, Normative Authority and Perfectionism."

Abstracting autonomy away from humans' social nature altogether, Feinberg explains, ignores the fact that no one selects "his country, his language, his social community and traditions. No individual invents afresh his tools, his technology, his public institutions and procedures [*sic*]."[10] Moreover, all of those things (country, language, tradition, etc.) are key parts of being human, and we all become self-aware within those contexts and "as part of ongoing social processes."[11] Hence, a person's successful exercise of their capacity to self-govern according to their individual preferences may not be ideal, in part because it risks ignoring one's social circumstances and it may conflict with one's responsibilities to other community members.

Lastly, we may understand autonomy as a *right*. Individuals with the capacity for autonomy have certain valid claims and others have correlative obligations. One is that individuals have a claim to be recognized as having the capacity to govern themselves. Related to recognition is that individuals have decisional prerogatives; where others interfere with a person's decisions, that interference is a limitation on autonomy (though it may well be justifiable). The extent of those claims is a further question we return to throughout the book. What matters here, though, is that the notion of autonomy as a right is distinct from the notions of autonomy as a capacity, a condition, or an ideal.

2.3 THE KEY SPLIT

These distinctions are important and useful, but we still owe our own account. The view we advance in this book incorporates two different conceptions of autonomy. The first focuses on the relationship between a person and their motives, intentions, values, and preferences; that is, it holds that autonomy is primarily understood in terms of how an individual's desires, preferences, and actions relate to their history and psychology. For lack of a better term, we will call this "psychological autonomy." A different way of understanding autonomy focuses on an individual's social conditions, relationships to other people, status within a community and polity, and the range of options and opportunities in which one develops a sense of self and others. Following Marina Oshana, we will call this "autonomy of persons" or "personal autonomy."[12] The boundaries between these two ways of understanding autonomy are blurry, as a person's social circumstances are closely related to their desires, values, and preferences. Nonetheless, both facets are important in understanding the relationship between algorithmic decision systems and autonomy. We will argue that both components are morally important, and the conceptual differences between them matter less than the fact that both conceptions can underwrite similar social, moral, political, and legal claims.

[10]   Feinberg, "Autonomy," 45.
[11]   Feinberg, 45.
[12]   Oshana, *Personal Autonomy in Society*, 49.

To explain the two different ways of understanding autonomy, we will examine an exemplar of each.

2.3.1 *Psychological Autonomy*

There are different ways to characterize psychological conceptions of autonomy. Oshana emphasizes that such views are fundamentally concerned with psychological authenticity.[13] Perhaps the best, most succinct characterization of this set of views is that they are "accounts of the autonomous agent's special relation to her own motives."[14] Another fruitful way to understand such views is that they are *procedural* accounts, which is to say that autonomy does not turn on a person's particular desires, preferences, and beliefs.[15] Rather, what matters is whether their motivations and actions stand in the right relation to their psychology.[16]

An important objection to procedural views is that focusing on the individual and their psychology may not adequately account for the ways individuals are fundamentally social, embedded within relationships, embodied, and historical. Those social and relational facts are inextricable from how a person develops values, preferences, and desires. A view of autonomy whereby a person is autonomous just in case their actions comport with their higher-order preferences[17] will miss the fact that a person's highest-order preferences may be formed in oppressive (or otherwise severely delimited) circumstances and hence are themselves suspect.[18] We address this concern in our discussion of personal autonomy in Section 2.3.2.

Nonetheless, autonomy must have at least some procedural, psychological component, and such views need not be so narrowly constructed that they recognize only lone individuals, independent of their social relations and historical selves. Consider

---

[13] Oshana, 21–46.
[14] Buss and Westlund, "Personal Autonomy," sec. 2.
[15] "Procedural" does not quite capture the difference, though. That is because procedural accounts are typically contrasted with "perfectionist" views, which maintain that there are certain values that are intrinsically part of autonomy. However, there are perfectionist accounts of a person's relation to their own motives. Benson, "Taking Ownership: Authority and Voice in Autonomous Agency."
[16] There is a wide range of autonomy views with varied accounts of the relation between an agent and his or her motives and intentions. Some focus on the relationship between motivational structure and desires. Frankfurt, "Freedom of the Will and the Concept of a Person"; Dworkin, *The Theory and Practice of Autonomy*; Buss and Westlund, "Personal Autonomy." Some views are *internalist* in that they consider only how facts internal to an agent (e.g., motives, desires, intentions) relate to one another. Others index autonomy to some external standard; Fischer and Ravizza argue that autonomy requires an agent to be responsive to reasons (which are extrinsic to a person's psychology). Fischer and Ravizza, *Responsibility and Control: A Theory of Moral Responsibility*. What is important for our account, though, is that each of these accounts relies on *some* feature(s) of a person's psychology as a condition for autonomy, and those features can be understood in terms of competence or authenticity.
[17] Frankfurt, "Freedom of the Will and the Concept of a Person"; Dworkin, *The Theory and Practice of Autonomy*.
[18] Meyers, "Personal Autonomy and the Paradox of Feminine Socialization"; Meyers, *Self, Society, and Personal Choice*.

John Christman's account, which places individuals' social and historical contexts at
the center of autonomy.

Christman argues that individual autonomy has two key requirements: *competence* and *authenticity*.[19] Each is necessary and both are jointly sufficient for a person
to be autonomous. The competence conditions Christman describes are similar to
baseline autonomy requirements in other accounts. First, a person must have some
set of fundamental values and commitments and the ability to "effectively form
intentions" to act on the basis of those values and commitments.[20] Second, they
must have the capacity to critically reflect on their basic values and commitments,
their motivations, and other facets of their decision-making abilities. In other words,
autonomy requires that a person have the capacities to form, develop, and critically
reflect on their values and to intentionally and effectively act in accord with those
values. That's the easy part.

More controversial, and more difficult to reckon, is the authenticity requirement.
This is a conditional requirement that a person would not be *alienated* from their
basic values and commitments were they to "engage in sustained critical reflection"
on them.[21] By "alienated," Christman just means that the person would believe that
their values and commitments were incompatible with their sense of themselves and
their practical identity over time. As Christman puts it, those values and commitments could "not be sustained as part of an acceptable autobiographical narrative
organized by her diachronic [i.e., existing over time] practical identity."[22] For the
critical reflection to be adequate to ensure autonomy, it must be sustained over time,
occur in a range of conditions, consider processes that affected how the person came
to form their values and commitments, and not be distorted by other factors.[23]

There are three key features of Christman's account that will help as we develop
our own view. The first is that the view is proceduralist; it is based on the mechanisms and processes by which persons come to have values and commitments and
how they incorporate those into beliefs and actions. Procedural accounts do not
depend on the content of persons' values. An advantage to procedural views is that
they do not presume that any particular values, commitments, and beliefs are
inconsistent with autonomy. Procedural views contrast with perfectionist views,
which build into their conceptions of autonomy at least some requirements for
the content of persons' values and commitments.

Second, Christman develops his account with an eye to addressing important
lines of criticism of psychological autonomy views. These criticisms are (1) that
selves are decentered and historical (i.e., there is no isolated, asocial self that is cut

[19]   Christman, *The Politics of Persons: Individual Autonomy and Socio-Historical Selves.*
[20]   Christman, 154.
[21]   Christman, 155.
[22]   Christman, 155.
[23]   Marilyn Friedman offers a related view, positing that an agent is autonomous when the "agent chooses
        or acts in accord with wants or desires that she has self-reflectively endorsed." See Friedman,
        Autonomy, Gender, Politics, 5.

off from the circumstances that form one's sense of self) and (2) that values and commitments form in social contexts and in relation to other people and communities.[24] Third, Christman's view is internalist, which is to say that the criteria for autonomy are indexed only to a person's own psychology.

2.3.2 *Personal Autonomy*

Christman's understanding, like those of Frankfurt, Dworkin, Fischer and Ravizza, and others, is that the relation between a person and their intentions (in Christman's case, whether the competence conditions and the authenticity conditions obtain) forms sufficient conditions for a person to be autonomous. Such accounts have received substantial criticism in recent years because of their focus on individuals rather than their social connections, communities, structures, physical embodiment, emotion, and so forth. We return to some of these critiques in Section 2.6.

To capture this separate family of conceptions of autonomy, consider Marina Oshana's thoroughly social and relational account. Oshana's starting point is that views like Christman's, which center on an agent's relation to his or her values and preferences, are at root about persons' psychologies. However, Oshana argues, people are not reducible to their psychological states, and an adequate account of personal autonomy must involve more than a person's psychological history, competency, and authenticity.[25] Autonomy should instead be understood primarily as a characteristic of *persons*, and personal autonomy is inherently a social phenomenon: "Autonomy is not a phenomenon merely enhanced or lessened by [social relations]. Social relations do not just causally facilitate or impair the exercise of autonomy. Rather, appropriate social relations form an *inherent part* of what it means to be self-directed."[26]

Oshana's argument draws on several cases in which agents fully accept and internalize values that subordinate their own interests: a person raised in oppressive circumstances who embraces the subservience their community demands, a person who voluntarily becomes a part of a total institution in which they commit to serving the institution and its hierarchy, and so on. Among Oshana's examples is a woman who chooses and values being subservient in a marriage and being the "angel of the house." She has no say in important facets of family financial and life decisions, and she develops none of the professional and educational skill and social capital that would allow her to change her situation. In Oshana's conception, the woman's reasons for her choice are consistent with her values, she is reflective about those values, she finds the life wholly gratifying, and her values are not based on social conditions that established or reinforced a belief in her inferiority. In other words, Oshana's conception is of a person who meets both a competence condition and

---

[24] See also Sandel, *Liberalism and the Limits of Justice.*
[25] Oshana, *Personal Autonomy in Society*, 46.
[26] Oshana, 49 (emphasis added).

authenticity condition. Nonetheless, Oshana argues that the "angel of the house" lacks autonomy *precisely because* of her social status and her personal relationships, regardless of whether she is the architect of both. Similarly, Oshana argues, a person who surrenders to the strictures of a monastic religious order such that the order controls all facets of their life lacks autonomy regardless of whether doing so was a choice that comports with their deepest values.

The point of Oshana's examples is that there are plausibly individuals who do not have the power to manage important aspects of their lives because of restrictive or oppressive social circumstances, and yet their situations may be consistent with their authentic values. Nonetheless, persons' de facto ability to manage important facets of their lives is "tantamount to governance over their selves."[27] And because self-governance *just is* autonomy, the lack of de facto power is incompatible with autonomy.

To sharpen her argument, Oshana contrasts the angel of the house case with the "would-be surrendered woman," who has a great deal of financial, social, and educational independence, is professionally very successful, and can exercise a great deal of global and local control over the course of her life.[28] However, her values and self-conception are to live like the angel of the house, deferential to a controlling partner. In other words, her actions and motivations in navigating life are inauthentic (at least in Christman's sense). Oshana maintains that she is nonetheless autonomous precisely because her social and relational circumstances allow her to govern herself, even if she has not been able to do so in a way that satisfies her deeper value commitments.

There are several important consequences of Oshana's conception. One is that it de-emphasizes autonomy with respect to preferences and values and instead emphasizes autonomy of persons. On Oshana's view a person can be autonomous with respect to their desires, preferences, and values, but still not be autonomous in a morally important sense.

Another feature is that Oshana's view is weakly perfectionist. Her view is that autonomy requires that a person recognize themselves as the person with primary authority over their life; that is a substantive, non-proceduralist value and her view is hence perfectionist. It is only *weakly* perfectionist because recognizing oneself as having authority over their life is a relatively nondemanding requirement. Many different conceptions of value will be compatible with it.[29]

Third, which is related to the first consequence and is perhaps most controversial, is that authenticity (in Christman's sense, in Frankfurt's sense, or anyone else's) is neither necessary *nor* sufficient for a person to be autonomous. On Oshana's view a person can be autonomous even if they are, upon reflection, alienated from their desires, motivations, and aspects of their character. However, if they have latitude to

---

[27]   Oshana, 67.
[28]   Oshana, 64–65.
[29]   See also Benson, "Taking Ownership: Authority and Voice in Autonomous Agency."

change that desire and to act on an alienating desire, Oshana's view is that they are still autonomous.

Fourth is that social conditions are key for autonomy in multiple ways. They may be causally important. Christman agrees on this point – indeed, it is hard to see how it could be otherwise. Social conditions are also at least partially *constitutive* of autonomy. Regardless of the connection between a person's values and preferences and one's psychology, one cannot be autonomous on Oshana's view if others fail to foster, support, and respect their self-governance.

The fundamental difference between Christman's and Oshana's accounts concerns whether autonomy properly applies to one's psychology (including its contents over time and the social and historic processes affecting it) or to one's person (including one's de facto power to determine their affairs). This difference entails that the conditions of autonomy are different on the two accounts. Whereas Christman's view demands only competence and authenticity, which are procedural requirements, Oshana's view also includes additional requirements that are associated with appropriately conducive social conditions and choice architectures.

The conditions for personal autonomy on Oshana's account do have some points of contact with Christman's. In particular, she argues that personal autonomy requires a kind of procedural independence, which in turn includes a number of competence conditions. Foremost among these is *epistemic* competence. A person must be self-reflective and self-aware, and they must conceive of themself as a person "who can affect the world in light of a perspective and plan for life that is of her making."[30] Related is that a person must be rational. Again, this is not the caricature of "rational" in the sense of being coldly calculating. Rather, one must be attuned to their environment and understand the world around them. They must be able to develop and be disposed to follow through with plans based on their own ends and their sense of value. Furthermore, they must be able to distinguish choices, actions, and relationships that are conducive and not conducive to self-governance.

Another condition that is compatible with Christman's view is that agents must have self-respect. Respect involves recognizing the inherent worth of a person and treating them accordingly. To respect another person, one cannot understand that person's value as deriving solely from their usefulness to oneself. That, in turn, demands recognizing them as autonomous and not "treating [them] in a manner that makes light of [their] autonomy."[31] Likewise, respecting oneself demands that one understand one's value (and the value of one's commitments) as inherently valuable.[32] Christman's view would account for self-respect under non-alienation.[33]

What is most distinctive of Oshana's account is that it posits conditions that go beyond an agent's relationship to their own intentions and preferences. One of these

---

[30] Oshana, *Personal Autonomy in Society*, 77.
[31] Oshana, 81.
[32] See also Hill, Jr., "The Kantian Conception of Autonomy."
[33] Christman, *The Politics of Persons: Individual Autonomy and Socio-Historical Selves*, 182.

involves an agent's control. The view that autonomy requires an agent have control over their actions is familiar in accounts of psychological autonomy. For example, Fischer and Ravizza argue that autonomy demands that agents exercise a kind of "guidance control," such that the source of actions is the agent themself.[34] However, guidance control can be understood as *local* guidance: Is *this* action something over which the agent exercises guidance? Oshana's view is that personal autonomy requires a more global control over his or her ability to determine how they live. Can one, in other words, effectively act to advance their interests and satisfy their commitments, or do their social circumstances allow others to severely limit their ability to exercise control (if they choose to do so). Oshana writes:

> Autonomy necessitates a fairly robust variety of control of a sort that must be effective within a person's social situation … . We cannot claim a person is autonomous if she is party to social relations or institutions that would enfeeble her ability to determine how she will live if it were the will of others that they do so.[35]

It is neither possible nor necessary for autonomy that an agent be able to exercise control over all aspects of their life. Just how much control autonomy demands, though, is a vexing question. Here Oshana's conception follows closely Joseph Raz's view that mere choice and control over that choice is insufficient. Rather, autonomy requires an agent have access to a variety of relevant, attractive options. A person with the choice of whether to eat bland food now or eat it later does not have autonomy over their diet, and a person having to constantly make decisions that affect their very survival may have a variety of options, but they are not attractive, and the person is therefore not autonomous with respect to their life's course.[36]

The crux of Oshana's account, and another reason it is distinctive, is her argument that autonomy demands *substantive* independence. For a person to be substantively independent they must have sufficient social and relational support, and they must not have such substantial social and relational impediments that prevent them from enjoying de facto ability to determine their life course.

Substantive independence is itself multifaceted. First it involves social conditions that afford a person some baseline level of social and psychological security. A person with very little such security is vulnerable to arbitrary actions by others and hence will lack the de facto power necessary for global autonomy. Second, substantive independence requires that a person be able to have values and pursue interests that are different from those of people with relatively greater power and influence, and to do so without risk of reprisal. The idea here is that if others use one's values and interests as a reason to exact a toll on the person, then they are dependent on others' forbearance of their values and interests. But one cannot be self-governing when they depend on that forbearance.

---

[34] Fischer and Ravizza, *Responsibility and Control: A Theory of Moral Responsibility.*
[35] Oshana, *Personal Autonomy in Society*, 83.
[36] Raz, *The Morality of Freedom*, 373–376.

Substantive independence also requires a degree of financial self-sufficiency. That simply means that one is not subject to the control of others through financial means. And if, for example, one is dependent on a state or employer for financial support, the terms of that support or employment cannot be contingent on inappropriate conditions or subject to arbitrary termination.[37] Further, substantive independence requires that a person not be subject to misinformation that curtails their ability to exercise their agency over facets of their life.

Oshana summarizes her understanding of substantive independence by drawing on Philip Pettit's work on republican freedom. Specifically, she argues (following Pettit) that understanding freedom as merely freedom of choice misses the mark. The idea, which we address at length in Chapter 5, is that many accounts of freedom (or liberty) focus on negative liberty or whether a person is subject to external constraints, imposed by others, which prevent them from engaging in the activities that they wish to pursue. Other accounts address *positive* liberty, which is to say persons' de facto ability to engage in the activities they wish. A person might be free of others' constraints to, for example, produce a movie yet might not have the financial or social wherewithal to actually do so. In that case they would have negative liberty but lack positive liberty. Both of those facets of liberty focus on freedom of *choice*.

Oshana thinks these conceptions leave out the fundamental importance of freedom of the *chooser*. A person may be fortunate enough that others do not interfere with their actions, and they may have resources to act more or less according to their values. However, if other people have social power to interfere with them and constrain their ability to function, or if they have to negotiate obstacles and order their life to make such interference less likely, their freedom is nonetheless constrained. Specifically, their *social* freedom is diminished.

Consider, for example, a series of lawsuits concerning "stop-and-frisk" policies in New York City.[38] From 2004 through 2012, New York City police conducted over 4.4 million *"Terry"* stops of people in the streets. *Terry* stops are short, informational police stops that do not rise to the level of a full search. Because they are limited in scope, the legal requirement for conducting a *Terry* stop is lower than the "probable cause" standard required under the Fourth Amendment of the U.S. Constitution. Specifically, police may stop people under the Terry standard if they have "specific and articulable facts which, taken together with rational inferences from those facts, reasonably warrant that intrusion."[39] Hence, police may stop persons if they have reasonable suspicion that "criminal activity may be afoot" and may conduct a brief frisk for weapons so long as it is based on a reasonable suspicion that the person is armed and dangerous. Fifty-two percent of the Terry stops conducted during this period included a frisk for weapons, though 98.5 percent of the frisks turned up no weapon. A very small percentage of the stops resulted in either arrest (6 percent) or

---

[37] Oshana, *Personal Autonomy in Society*, 87; see also Meyers, *Self, Society, and Personal Choice*, 12.
[38] *Floyd v. City of New York*, 959 F. Supp. 2d.
[39] *Terry v. Ohio*, 392 U.S.

summons (6 percent). The overwhelming majority of the persons stopped were Black (52 percent) or Hispanic (31 percent); 10 percent of the people stopped were White (the population of New York City at the time was 23 percent Black, 29 percent Hispanic, and 33 percent White). Police used some kind of physical force in 23 percent of stops of Black people, 24 percent of stops of Hispanic people, and 17 percent of stops of White people. Finally, despite the fact that the *Terry* standard is a low hurdle, police conducting stop-and-frisks often did not state a specific crime they suspected to be afoot (in 2004, police failed to state a specific crime for only 1 percent of stops, but by 2009 police failed to state a specific crime for 36 percent of stops).[40] Moreover, data collected from the forms that police filled out after stops indicated that many more stops were "apparently unjustified," as officers often simply checked boxes to justify stops post hoc (e.g., checking boxes indicating persons stopped had made "furtive movements" or made "furtive movements" along with having a "suspicious bulge" in their clothing).[41] This pattern led to a series of lawsuits, and the U.S. District Court determined that the city had violated persons' Fourth and Fourteenth Amendment rights by acting with deliberate indifference to unconstitutional police stops.[42]

What is important for our purposes is how they illustrate Oshana's conception of substantive independence and its relation to republican freedom. The idea is this: Considered in isolation, any particular stop-and-frisk event constitutes a relatively small imposition of freedom. It does not take a long time and hence in most cases will not prevent one from going about their business shortly. And, hence, the mere fact of being subject to a stop-and-frisk does not undermine one's substantive independence. However, stopping the analysis there omits the overweening and arbitrary nature of the New York City stop-and-frisk program in practice at scale. Because the stops were so frequent, often failed to meet even the low Terry hurdle, and were so divorced from actual criminal conduct and from actual weapons possession, they infected the daily lives of residents (and in particular Black and Hispanic residents) with persistent exposure to arbitrary power. The ability to go about one's life free from being stopped was, in effect, at the whim of the police. It is in *that* way that people's freedom was impinged, and it is in *that* way that their substantive independence was reduced. And, hence, their personal autonomy was diminished.

2.4 RECONCILING PSYCHOLOGICAL AND PERSONAL AUTONOMY

In the previous sections we described two categories of autonomy views. The first, which focuses on an individual's special relationship to their values, intentions, and motivations, is exemplified by John Christman's account. Christman's view is

---

[40]   All the statistics in this paragraph are from "Overview of Uncontested Statistics," in *Floyd v. City of New York*, 959 F. Supp. 2d at 572–575.

[41]   *Floyd v. City of New York*, 959 F. Supp. 2d at 559–560.

[42]   *Floyd v. City of New York*, 959 F. Supp. 2d at 562.

procedural in that it does not index autonomy to the content of an individual's values and motivations. The view is relational in that it understands the importance of a person's history and social circumstances in supporting values and preferences from which a person would not be alienated. As noted in Section 2.3.1, there are numerous competing views of autonomy in this category, articulating different kinds of procedural conditions necessary for persons to be autonomous. The second category, exemplified by Marina Oshana's view, understands psychological autonomy as an insufficient account of what matters morally, which is *personal* autonomy. Oshana's view is that while elements of psychological autonomy are important, they are neither necessary nor sufficient for personal autonomy. Personal autonomy demands more, including substantive independence.

This split seems wide at first blush, one focusing on a person's psychology and its history, the other focusing instead on facts about a person's place in the social, material world (and in a weakly perfectionist way at that). However, for several reasons, we need not draw a conclusion about which family of views is better supported. To begin, our project is different from the projects of Christman, Oshana, Buss, Frankfurt, Dworkin, and others. We are not aiming at a new, comprehensive account of autonomy and its importance. Rather, we are beginning with the premise that autonomy is important, adopting a minimal, ecumenical approach to the existing accounts, and developing an understanding of the moral salience of automated decision systems from the account built from convergence among the other accounts. Hence, differences in the families of views matter here only to the extent that they affect an analysis of autonomy-based moral claims.

And when we look at *that* set of issues, the categories of accounts of autonomy (including Christman's and Oshana's) converge. Both types of account can agree about many of the conditions that are important for individuals' autonomy. Consider Oshana's example of the woman raised in oppressive circumstances. She argues that the woman in that case lacks autonomy because the social conditions necessary for her to act with substantive independence are lacking, regardless of whether her (current, local) values and beliefs are procedurally independent. Christman agrees that the woman lacks autonomy, but he argues that this is because, in all likelihood, she would experience alienation if she were to reflect on her values and preferences in light of the oppressive processes affecting their formation.[43] What's important for our account, though, is that Oshana and Christman agree that she lacks autonomy, it is the result of a moral wrong, and the lack of autonomy is a key part of the explanation for why her treatment is morally wrong.

Oshana's would-be surrendered woman case is a bit more difficult. Oshana, recall, argues that this person *is* autonomous because she is procedurally and substantively independent. She has the social wherewithal to act differently than she does, regardless of whether her current actions are ones from which she would be

---

[43]   Christman, *The Politics of Persons: Individual Autonomy and Socio-Historical Selves*, 172–177.

alienated (if she were to critically reflect upon them). Christman's view is that the would-be surrendered woman lacks autonomy precisely because her actions do not meet the authenticity conditions. However, as Oshana has constructed the case, Christman would not be able to point to a moral wrong undermining her autonomy. Instead, Christman could argue that a more thoroughgoing examination of a person's history and the social structures in which a person's values are formed are likely to uncover limitations rooted in competence conditions or authenticity conditions. However, if there are no such limitations, Christman would allow that she lacks autonomy.[44]

What is important, though, is that Christman and Oshana's positions about what is morally relevant are compatible. What matters to each is that the would-be surrendered woman's social and relational circumstances are not particularly constrained and that she *does* experience alienation. The difference is whether that alienation is incompatible with the best-supported conception of autonomy, *not* whether there is a moral infirmity, and not what the source of such an infirmity might be.

Moreover, even in the relatively narrow range of cases in which Oshana and Christman would disagree about whether a person is autonomous, they can agree that there are autonomy-based wrongs. Consider instead a case in which a person is raised in oppressive circumstances, internalizes facets of that oppression, and in which they come to have values, motivations, and preferences that reflect that oppression. And suppose that even with sufficient opportunity to critically reflect on those values, motivations, and preferences and their genealogy, they would experience no alienation. Christman would have to conclude that the person is autonomous (after all, they meet his competence and authenticity conditions). Oshana would conclude that they lack autonomy only if they lack sufficient social opportunity to change their views and act accordingly. She would disagree that the person is autonomous only if their current social circumstances reinforce the values, motivations, and preferences formed under limited conditions. But Christman and Oshana could agree that there is an autonomy-based wrong in their limited circumstances. Christman could argue that those circumstances are unjust because they *tend* to be wrongs that lead to alienation. Oshana's view is that the wrong is based on the fact of social limitation per se. In other words, the precise explanation of the wrong will vary. However, the views overlap in the cases of moral wrongs and the type of wrongs, while differing in the explanation of them.

There is also the possibility of an account of autonomy that bridges the psychological authenticity, procedural accounts with social-relational accounts. Recently, Zi Lin has argued that instead of self-rule, autonomy should be understood as independence from other-rule.[45] Her idea is that psychological authenticity requires

---

[44]   In his response, Christman questions whether a richer account of specific cases would reveal ways in which their subjects would be alienated. Christman, 168–169.

[45]   Lin, "New Perspectives on the Moral Significance of Coercion, Manipulation, and Bodily Violence," 50–59.

something other than non-alienation or confluence with higher-order values. Those accounts index authenticity solely to a person's psychology (and in Christman's view, their diachronic psychology). Such views have some well-known conceptual problems, including the problem of regress and problem of problematic influencers. Both of these, Lin argues, can be resolved by building autonomy around independence from other-rule. Hence, on Lin's view, psychological autonomy has a relational component that is constitutive of autonomy, rather than merely being causally relevant.

2.5 AN ECUMENICAL VIEW

There are plenty of disputes about the nature of autonomy: whether it describes a person's relation to his or her values, motivations, and intentions or describes a person's social and relational circumstances; whether competence and authenticity conditions are necessary or sufficient for a person to be autonomous; whether social conditions are constitutive of autonomy or merely causally relevant to whether one is autonomous. But, as we explain in the previous section, the different views can agree that certain things matter because of autonomy. That is the basis of our ecumenical view of autonomy in which we distill a number of key points about autonomy and its value from different conceptions.

To begin, any plausible view of autonomy will recognize the importance of procedural independence (though they may disagree about whether procedural independence is necessary for autonomy, sufficient for autonomy, or merely important for autonomy). Procedural independence requires several things. One is epistemic competence, which is to say one must be to some degree self-reflective, self-aware, and understand themself as able to actualize a life plan. Respecting people as autonomous demands fostering epistemic competence.

Notice, though, that affording people the circumstances in which they can exercise their epistemic competence is a facet of *personal* autonomy. Hence, severely or deliberately constrained information environments are ways in which an epistemically competent person will fail to have personal autonomy because they lack substantive independence.

Another component of psychological autonomy is rationality, or the ability to understand the world around oneself, to make close connections between facts and inferences, and to make decisions that line up with well-enough ordered assessments of facts and reasons. As noted, this is a low bar. Rationality is also related to personal autonomy. Constraints on a person's ability to reason clearly can come from poor informational environments or from psychological stressors that thwart their ability to think clearly, hence inducing poor decisions.

Procedural independence also includes some degree of authenticity. Oshana argues that authenticity is not required, and this is a key difference between her and Christman. Our view, however, is not that authenticity is necessary or sufficient for autonomy. Rather, authenticity is important for two reasons. One is that authenticity is *evidence* of personal autonomy. The ability to reflect on one's values and preferences and to recognize them as compatible with one's sense of self and practical identity over time is an important test of the degree to which one's values and preferences are one's own, and (hence) that one self-governs. Likewise, lack of authenticity – that is, where a person would be alienated from their preferences and values upon reflection – is defeasible evidence that one's personal or social autonomy is compromised. And fostering authenticity is itself morally important in that individuals are morally valuable in part because individuals are capable of determining for themselves what is of value in their lives, and they are (hence) the source of that value.[46] In other words, structures that make it likely that individuals would experience alienation from their desires and values (in Christman's conception, where structures make it likely that a person will have inauthentic preferences and motivations) are in all likelihood antithetical to *personal* autonomy. Those structures may be morally justifiable overall, but that would be in spite of their relationship to autonomy.

Beyond procedural independence and its competence and authenticity components, autonomy requires substantive independence. Whether one is personally autonomous turns on their circumstances and their environment.[47] This includes social conditions such as choice among a range of attractive options (per Raz), control over meaningful facets of life, conditions of self-respect, relative financial independence, and so forth. In this we follow Oshana's conception closely. There are, however, a few ways in which substantive independence is insufficient in ensuring autonomy overall. A person can be substantively independent (in terms of having financial wherewithal, not subject to others' arbitrary power) but can have competence conditions undermined. Likewise, one can have local substantive independence but have been subject to conditions that make it difficult to have authentic preferences and desires (we will return to this in Chapters 4, 5, and 6). Of course, those limitations may be understood in terms of more global substantive independence.

We can summarize our view and provide a foundation for the arguments in the remainder of the book with a few primary propositions.

The first set of these concerns Feinberg's distinctions between the various meanings of "autonomy." First, autonomy as a capacity predominantly grafts onto psychological autonomy; it is entirely possible for a person to have a capacity for autonomy, but be prevented from exercising it (i.e., being denied *personal* autonomy). Second, successful exercise of autonomy in Feinberg's sense demands substantive independence; however, the autonomy one exercises in that sense is psychological. Third, autonomy as ideal (which is to say that individual autonomy properly integrated into a larger

---

[46]   cf. Korsgaard et al., *The Sources of Normativity*.

[47]   Indeed, some scholars refer to "environmental" conditions of autonomy to refer to components that are extrinsic to one's psychology. See Piper, "Autonomy: Normative." See also Chapter 5, where we describe the concept of ecological freedom.

matrix of values, including one's responsibilities and community concerns) reflects persons' obligations to respect others' psychological autonomy and ensure the conditions of personal autonomy. Fourth, the idea that autonomy is a right should be understood in the sense that persons have claim-rights grounded in their autonomy.

The next propositions reflect the fact that both psychological and personal autonomy are important and (hence) that both procedural and substantive independence are valuable.

To begin, procedural independence is morally important, but limitations on a person's procedural independence are important in large part because of conditions that impose such limitations (including limitations placed by other people, by organizations, by social structures, by natural causes, and so forth). Fostering conditions that promote procedural independence is the crucial part. It is similarly important that others respect the actions of those who lack procedural independence. They may have capacity autonomy, after all, even if it is unsuccessfully exercised.

Substantive independence is important beyond its role in fostering psychological autonomy. It does not require that one can literally do without others – business partners may need each other's expertise and efforts, but that does not undermine their substantive independence. Rather, what matters is whether others make demands that are arbitrary, demand inauthentic or epistemically unjustifiable actions, or undermine one's ability to act for one's own reasons. That does not mean any kind of compromise is antithetical to respecting autonomy. What matters is whether agreements and dependence are such that one could agree to them as part of valuable social relationships and other goods. It also matters how global those contradictions are.

2.6 OBJECTIONS

So far, we have considered a few different conceptions of autonomy and offered the account we will use to ground the arguments in the remainder of the book. There are, however, important critiques of autonomy, both as a concept and as a basic value. One family of criticism is that autonomy-based moral theories (and deontological theories generally) are simply mistaken about what matters. Consequentialists and virtue ethicists (among others) might argue that other values are the proper measure of moral value. As important as those criticisms are, we won't offer a defense here. Rather, we will simply confirm that a rock-bottom assumption of this project is that autonomy is morally valuable, and it is an important enough (and rich enough) value that it can ground the arguments we offer throughout. If one disagrees with that assumption, this project probably won't be persuasive.

Much more important in our view are criticisms levied against the very concept of autonomy and its value. Feminists, for instance, have critiqued autonomy-based theories as atomistic, divorced from social responsibilities, unmindful of the importance of relationships in identity formation, hyperrational, and disembodied. These criticisms have provided a compelling corrective to major strains of autonomy scholarship. The principal views that we have drawn on for our account are sensitive to these concerns and explicitly incorporate the critiques into their accounts. Indeed, the critiques are so clearly correct that any plausible contemporary account of autonomy will be explicitly relational. Nonetheless, it is worth canvassing a few of the critiques here.[48]

One set of critiques Mackenzie and Stoljar characterize as "metaphysical." Specifically, such critiques reject autonomy views on the grounds that autonomy attributions assume that agents are atomistic. That, in turn, can mean several things. One possibility is that individuals are *causally* independent or isolated from others; that is, individuals are self-creating sources of values and desires. Of course, that is false; one can discern autonomy in some sense even while recognizing that people's understandings are caused by their social milieu.[49] A different possibility is that agents are atomistic in the sense that they are independent of social and family relationships or that persons have intrinsic properties that do not depend on how they relate to others. Again, individuals are not like this at all. First, as a matter of empirical fact humans are hyper-social. Second, people's identities and values do not cohere with absent relationships with others. Nonetheless, autonomy remains conceptually coherent so long as we allow there are important ways in which an individual can form their values under competence and authenticity conditions and has some claim to avoiding arbitrary interference.[50] A final way of understanding atomistic individualism is that persons are metaphysically distinct. Mackenzie and Stoljar point out that this is not so much a critique as an obvious fact.[51]

A related set of critiques are based on conceptions of *care*. The idea is that traditional understandings of autonomy have under- or devalued women's perspectives and traditional, gendered social roles. Hence, relationships of care have been systematically excluded from autonomy conceptions. But those roles are of fundamental human value, and ignoring their centrality is a mark against any view. Mackenzie and Stoljar point out, though, that a number of feminist scholars, such as Jennifer Nedelsky and Evelyn Fox Keller, incorporate understandings of care into conceptions of autonomy. Acting as an agent in the world – a constitutive part of autonomy – should involve interdependence, nurturing, and care. And such capacities are indeed types of competence conditions for autonomy.[52]

The upshot of these critiques is that while traditional conceptions of autonomy are cramped and implausible, more capacious understandings can address some of

---

[48] Here we follow Mackenzie and Stoljar, *Relational Autonomy: Feminist Perspectives on Autonomy, Agency, and the Social Self*, chapter 1.

[49] Mackenzie and Stoljar, 8; See also Baier, *Postures of the Mind: Essays on Mind and Morals*.

[50] Mackenzie and Stoljar, *Relational Autonomy: Feminist Perspectives on Autonomy, Agency, and the Social Self*, 8.

[51] Mackenzie and Stoljar, 8.

[52] Mackenzie and Stoljar, 9–10; see also Nedelsky, "Reconceiving Autonomy: Sources, Thoughts and Possibilities," 7–36; Keller, *Reflections on Gender and Science*, chapter 5.

those shortcomings. Specifically, any reasonable account of autonomy will recognize that the sources of self, meaning, and value will be intimately bound up with one's social, community, and family relationships. We are not self-executing sources of value; rather, we are sources of value within social, relational contexts. Moreover, the competencies of autonomy will involve one's ability to enter and foster those relations. And lastly, the procedural and substantive independence conditions (e.g., those articulated by Christman and Oshana, and upon which we draw heavily) provide an explanation for why oppressive conditions (based on gender, or race, or ethnicity, or class, or happenstance) *conflict* with autonomy.[53]

2.7 CONCLUSION: RELATED CONCEPTS AND MORAL SALIENCE OF AUTONOMY

In this chapter we have made some basic distinctions about autonomy and canvassed two important, representative views (each exemplifying a different family of conceptions of autonomy). We have argued that those groups of views have substantial normative overlap, and we have used that overlap to advance an ecumenical view of autonomy. That conception provides a foundation for the arguments in the rest of this book. Before turning to those arguments, though, it is worth briefly describing why autonomy matters and how it grounds other concepts that will figure into the chapters that follow.

One way that autonomy matters morally is built into our account. People are capable of determining their values, desires, and preferences, and they can use those values, desires, and preferences to guide their decisions and steer their lives. They are, in other words, a source of value. To the extent that others severely constrain individuals' ability to form their own sense of value (e.g., by limiting their procedural or substantive independence), they stifle the degree to which individuals' values are their own. Moreover, thwarting persons' abilities to act on their own values by coercion, deception, or severely constrained choice architecture is a way of circumventing autonomy and an affront to persons as choosers and self-governors.

However, the moral salience of autonomy goes well beyond limitations on persons' abilities to act on their own desires and values. Consider again the distinctions we set out at the beginning of this chapter. The ability to act on one's own desires and values is a matter of successfully exercising one's capacity for autonomy. That assumes that people *have* the capacity to autonomous. It may not be enough, though, to simply assume people have that capacity. Rather, it is plausible that there is a social responsibility to promote that capacity. Indeed, that is an important justification for education.[54]

---

[53] For further discussions of these and related criticisms of autonomy, and for feminist "rehabilitations" of autonomy, see Stoljar, "Feminist Perspectives on Autonomy."
[54] Brighouse, *School Choice and Social Justice*; Gutmann, *Democratic Education*.

Throughout the book, we consider different kinds of moral concerns about automated systems, all of which are rooted in autonomy. In Chapter 3, we address broader *social* claims regarding use of algorithmic systems. The systems we discuss in that chapter – K-12 teacher evaluation systems and criminal justice risk assessment tools – do not directly limit autonomous individuals' choices via deception, coercion, or manipulation, and they do not obviously undermine substantive independence. Rather, we argue that autonomy is a foundation for a claim that persons be subject only to social systems that they could reasonably endorse. In Chapter 4, we make the case that autonomy includes more than the ability to act on one's values and preferences. It also has an important informational component. That informational component is vital regardless of whether a person is able to put information into practice. Autonomy demands, in our view, the ability to exercise both practical agency (the ability to function effectively in important arenas) and cognitive agency (the ability to exercise a kind of evaluative control and understand one's place in the world, regardless of one's ability to affect it).

Later, we will expand our discussion of the social conditions of freedom. We have already discussed how Oshana's account incorporates facets of Philip Pettit's understanding of republican freedom into her understanding of personal autonomy. Our task in Chapter 5 is to draw out the autonomy- and agency-based conditions of freedom. In Chapter 6, we argue that successful exercise of autonomy may in many cases demand a degree of epistemic paternalism. That is, given the competence and authenticity requirements for autonomy, certain kinds of media entities may be permitted (or even *obligated*) to exert a degree of editorial control over the content posted on their platforms. In Chapter 7 we explain the moral requirements of autonomous agents. That is, autonomous persons are capable of legislating and following moral principles. That capacity creates obligations to act responsibly. Obfuscating that responsibility will in many cases be a distinct kind of wrong. Finally, in Chapter 8, we will consider how autonomy plays a crucial role in underwriting political legitimacy.

Having introduced our polestar cases, situated concerns about algorithmic systems in a broader discourse, and explained our strategy in Chapter 1, and having provided our catholic conception of autonomy here, we can begin directly addressing the autonomy-grounded moral concerns in algorithmic systems. Next stop: Chapter 3.

PART II

Respecting Persons, What We Owe Them

3

What Can Agents Reasonably Endorse?

In Chapter 2, we offered an account of autonomy that is both compatible with a broad range of views and ecumenical in that it incorporates important facets of competing views. The key features of our account are that autonomy demands both procedural independence (i.e., competence and authenticity) and substantive independence (i.e., social and relational conditions that nurture and support persons in acting according to their values as they see fit, without overweening conditions on acting in accord with those values). Our next task is to draw on that conception of autonomy to better understand and evaluate algorithmic decision systems. Among those that we will consider are ones we introduced in Chapter 1, including risk assessment algorithms such as COMPAS and K-12 teaching evaluation systems such as EVAAS.

How, though, do we get from an account of an important moral value such as autonomy to an evaluation of complex socio-technical systems? We will do that by offering a view of what it takes to respect autonomy and to respect persons in virtue of their autonomy, drawing on a number of different normative moral theories. Our argument will proceed as follows. We start with a description of another K-12 teacher evaluation case – this one from Washington, DC. We then consider several puzzles about the case. Next, we provide our account of respecting autonomy and what that means for individuals' moral claims. We will explain how that conception can help us understand the DC case, and we will offer a *general* account of the moral requirements of algorithmic systems.[1] Finally, we will explain how our view sheds light on our foundational cases (i.e., *Loomis*, *Wagner*, and *Houston*).

3.1 IMPACT: NOT AN ACRONYM

In 2007, Washington, DC sought to improve its public school system ("DC schools") by implementing an algorithmic teacher assessment tool, IMPACT, the aim of which is to identify and remove ineffective teachers. In 2010, teachers with

---

[1]   This argument originated in Rubel, Castro, and Pham, "Algorithms, Agency, and Respect for Persons."

IMPACT scores in approximately the bottom 2 percent were fired; in 2011, teachers with IMPACT scores in approximately the bottom 5 percent were fired.[2]

There is a plausible argument for DC schools using IMPACT. The algorithm uses complex, data-driven methods to find and eliminate inefficiencies, and it purports to do this in an objective manner. Its inputs are measurements of performance and its outputs are a function of those measurements. Whether teachers have, say, ingratiated themselves to administrators would carry little weight in the decision as to whether to fire them. Rather, it is (ostensibly) their effectiveness as teachers that grounds the decision. Using performance measures and diminishing the degree to which personal favor and disfavor affect evaluation could plausibly generate better educational outcomes.

Nonetheless, DC schools' use of IMPACT was problematic. This is in part because IMPACT's conclusions were epistemically flawed. A large portion of a teacher's score is based on VAM that seeks to isolate and quantify a teacher's individual contribution to student achievement on the basis of annual standardized tests.[3] However, VAMs are poorly suited for this measurement task.[4] DC teachers work in schools with a high proportion of low-income students. At the time IMPACT was implemented, even in the wealthiest of the city's eight wards (Ward 3) nearly a quarter of students were from low-income families, and in the poorest ward (Ward 8), 88 percent of students were from low income families.[5] As one commentary on IMPACT notes, low-income students face a number of challenges that influence their ability to learn:

> These schools' student bodies are full of kids dealing with the toxic stress of poverty, leaving many of them homeless, hungry, or sick due to limited access to quality healthcare. The students are more likely to have an incarcerated parent, to be deprived of fresh or healthy food, to have spotty or no internet access in their homes, or to live in housing where it is nearly impossible to find a quiet place to study.[6]

Given the challenges of their students, it is not surprising that fewer teachers in Ward 8 than Ward 3 are identified by IMPACT as "high performing."[7]

The effects of poverty are confounding variables that affect student performance on standardized tests. For this reason, we cannot expect VAMs – which use only annual test scores to assess a teacher's individual contribution to student achievement – to reliably find the signal of bad teaching through the noise of student poverty. Indeed, the American Statistical Association warns that studies on VAMs

---

[2] O'Neil, *Weapons of Math Destruction: How Big Data Increases Inequality and Threatens Democracy*; Turque, "More than 200 D.C. Teachers Fired."
[3] Isenberg and Hock, "Measuring School and Teacher Value Added in DC, 2011–2012 School Year"; see also Walsh and Dotter, "Longitudinal Analysis of the Effectiveness of DCPS Teachers."
[4] For extensive discussion, see Amrein-Beardsley, *Rethinking Value-Added Models in Education.*
[5] Quick, "The Unfair Effects of IMPACT on Teachers with the Toughest Jobs."
[6] Quick.
[7] Quick.

"find that teachers account for about 1% to 14% of the variability in test scores, and that the majority of opportunities for quality improvement are found in the system-level conditions."[8] The American Statistical Association also notes that "[VAMs] have large standard errors, even when calculated using several years of data. These large standard errors make rankings [of teachers] unstable, even under the best scenarios for modeling."[9]

So IMPACT suffers from an *epistemic* shortcoming. Is there also a *moral* problem? One possibility is that IMPACT poses a moral problem in that it harms teachers; it is harmful for teachers to lose their jobs, and IMPACT scores are the basis for that loss and harm. This, however, is not enough to conclude that there is moral wrong. Firing teachers can be justified (e.g., for cause), though it harms them, and use of IMPACT may create enough student benefit to risk some harm to teachers. Moreover, IMPACT is not obviously unfair; its epistemic flaws may be evenly distributed among teachers.

If there is something wrong about using IMPACT, what does that have to do with the epistemic problem, and what does it have to do with autonomy? We will argue that a teacher who is fired is *wronged* when that firing is based on a system that they could not reasonably endorse. We explain the general argument in the next section. We then apply that argument to IMPACT and our other polestar cases in the remainder of the chapter.

3.2 AUTONOMY, KANTIAN RESPECT, AND REASONABLE ENDORSEMENT

In Chapter 2, we explained that autonomy and self-governance involve (among other things) the capacity to develop one's own conception of value and sense of what matters, and the ability to realize those values by guiding one's actions and decisions according to one's sense of value. We explained the relationship of this conception to Kantian views.[10]

---

[8] American Statistical Association, "ASA Statement on Using Value-Added Models for Educational Assessment: Executive Summary," 2; see also, Morganstein and Wasserstein, "ASA Statement on Value-Added Models."

[9] American Statistical Association, 7; see also, Morganstein and Wasserstein.

[10] It is worth reiterating several points from Chapter 2 to emphasize the limits of this Kantian formulation. The capacity to self-govern, the values agents develop, and the ways in which they incorporate those values into their lives are socially situated. See Mackenzie and Stoljar, *Relational Autonomy: Feminist Perspectives on Autonomy, Agency, and the Social Self*, 4. Developing one's sense of what is important depends on social conditions that nurture the ability to do so. See Oshana, *Personal Autonomy in Society*, 90. Social structures may delimit the conceptions of value that are available for persons to draw upon in developing their sense of value. Persons' abilities to incorporate their values into their important decisions will depend on what opportunities exist in the broader social context. See Raz, *The Morality of Freedom*; Mackenzie, "Relational Autonomy, Normative Authority and Perfectionism." The fact that self-governance is socially situated, however, does not undermine the importance of autonomy and agency. Rather, failures to nurture persons' abilities to develop their

The issue we are addressing here, though, is what kinds of moral requirements are grounded in autonomy. How, in other words, does autonomy ground persons' moral claims? There are a number of different ways to address this question.

Let's begin with a prominent account by Christine Korsgaard.[11] The basic idea of autonomy – that is, that each of us in our capacity as autonomous beings develop conceptions of value for ourselves and act on those conceptions – is that people are self-legislators. By engaging in self-legislation, we understand our capacity to determine what matters for ourselves as a source of value. If we treat this capacity as a source of value, then it is the capacity itself (not, say, our own egoism) that must be valuable. Hence, any instances of that capacity (not just our own) must also be a source of value. So, because we are autonomous, we must value (which is to say, respect) autonomy *generally*. In other words, the premise that the capacity to self-legislate grounds value in one's own case entails a conclusion that a similar capacity to self-legislate must also ground value in others' cases.

A different way to ground the value of autonomy is its connection to well-being. Individuals have the capacity to develop their own sense of value; they are generally well positioned to understand how to advance that value, and the ability to do so (within reasonable parameters) is an important facet of their well-being. Because we have good reasons to promote well-being in ourselves and others, we therefore have good reasons to respect autonomy in ourselves and others. This is the line of reasoning that a utilitarian, for example, John Stuart Mill, can use in support of respecting autonomy.[12]

Views like these link the concept of autonomy to the moral value of respecting autonomy. But what does respect for autonomy require? Returning to Kant, there are different but (roughly) equivalent ways to spell this out. One way to respect autonomy is to abide by the second, Humanity Formulation of the Categorical Imperative:

> **Humanity Formulation:** So act that you use humanity, whether in your own person or in the person of any other, always at the same time as an end, never merely as a means.[13]

Treating something as an end requires treating it as something that is valuable in its own right; treating something "merely" as a means involves treating it as solely an instrument for the promotion of an end, without also treating it as an end itself.

agency and substantial constraints on options available for incorporating values into persons' lives are moral problems in part because of the importance of autonomy. See, for instance, Superson, "Deformed Desires and Informed Desire Tests"; Meyers, "Personal Autonomy and the Paradox of Feminine Socialization." Hence, even though our conception of autonomy echoes Kantian views, it would be a mistake to conclude that autonomy in this sense assumes that individuals are separable from their social, familial, and relational lives.

[11]   Korsgaard et al., *The Sources of Normativity*.
[12]   Mill, *On Liberty*, chapter 3.
[13]   Kant, *Groundwork of the Metaphysics of Morals*, sec. 4:429.

Treating someone as an end-in-themselves requires that we take seriously their ability to make sense of the world and their place in it, to determine what matters to them, and to act according to their own understanding and values (to the extent that they see fit). They may not be considered solely in terms of how they advance values of others.

The Humanity Formula is, of course, vague and has long been the subject of dispute. Derek Parfit can provide some help in specifying it. He offers the following principle as the core idea of the Humanity Formula:

> **Consent Principle:** It is wrong to treat anyone in any way to which this person could not rationally consent.[14]

Famously, Kant gave several formulations of the Categorical Imperative, of which the Humanity Formula is just one. According to another formulation,

> **Formula of Universal Law:** Act only in accordance with that maxim through which you can at the same time will that it become a universal law.[15]

A "maxim" is a principle that connects an act to the reasons for its performance. Suppose one makes a donation to Oxfam. Their maxim might be, "In order to help reduce world hunger, I will contribute fifty dollars a month to Oxfam." An act is morally permissible when its maxim is universalizable, that is, if (and only if) every rational person can consistently act on it.

The Formula of Universal Law is often compared to the Golden Rule. This is a comparison Kant would be loath to accept since he rejected the Golden Rule as a moral principle. Parfit, in his inimitable style, thinks that "Kant's contempt for the Golden Rule is not justified."[16] And indeed, Parfit offers a reconstruction of the Golden Rule that incorporates the core ideas of the Formula of Universal Law as follows:

> **Golden Rule:** We ought to treat *everyone* as we would rationally be willing to be treated if we were going to be in all of these people's positions, and would be relevantly like them.[17]

As consideration of the Humanity Formula, the Consent Principle, the Formula of Universal Law, and the Golden Rule help to lay bare, respecting autonomy involves both an element of treating others in ways to which they can agree (because it aligns with their ends, for example) and an element of understanding how others' positions are relevant to which ends one adopts as one's own.

Hence, there are two facets to this "golden rule" style formulation. The first has to do with a person's ability to develop and endorse their sense of value and act

---

[14] Parfit, *On What Matters*, 181.
[15] Kant, 4:421.
[16] Parfit, 19.
[17] Parfit, 327.

accordingly, including what treatment would they willingly subject themselves to. This facet of the rule explains wrongs that are associated with deception. Deception is wrong (when it is) in part because it circumvents an agent's ability to make decisions according to their own reasons. Likewise, paternalism is an affront (when it is) because it supplants a person's ability to act on their own reasons based on a degree of distrust of their agency.[18]

The second facet of the Golden Rule has to do with the treatment of others. Autonomy can underwrite moral claims only to the extent that it is used to ends that are compatible with others' reasonable interests. The requirement that we consider how we would be rationally willing to be treated if we were relevantly similar to, and in similar circumstances as others is a way of making vivid others' reasonable interests. It also echoes Joel Feinberg's understanding of "autonomy as ideal" (as we discussed in Section 2.2.2). Autonomy as ideal recognizes that people can exercise autonomy badly (such that facets of autonomy are not necessarily virtues) and that people are parts of larger communities. Hence, Feinberg explains, the ideal of an autonomous person requires that their self-governance be consistent with the autonomy of others in their community.[19] This, in turn, reflects Kant's understanding that morally right action requires that the action can coexist with everyone else's ability to exercise freedom under universal moral law.[20]

Feinberg's understanding of autonomy as ideal is reflected in two other conceptions of respecting autonomy that are useful in developing our view. The first comes from John Rawls. In developing his understanding of just political and social systems, Rawls describes people as having two moral powers. The idea is that any person in the original position – which is to say anyone deciding on the basic structure of the society in which they will live, but knowing nothing of their place in it and nothing about their particular characteristics – must possess two powers for their choices to make sense. First, they must be rational. As in our discussion in Chapter 2, "rational" here just means the ability to engage in basic reasoning about means and ends, coupled with some set of basic values and motivations. The idea is that for a person to prefer one social and political structure over another, they must have some basic motivations to ground that preference. If literally nothing mattered to an individual, there would be no basis for their choices. Second, persons must be reasonable. This simply means that they are willing to abide fair terms of social cooperation, so long as others do too. It requires neither subordinating one's reasonable interests to others nor accepting outlandish demands from others.

Rawls's view is that people with these two powers in the original position would, for reasons having to do with nothing more than their own self-interest, accept certain social structures as binding. They will advance ends that people endorse (after all, those ends might be their own) and will establish fair terms of social

[18]   Shiffrin, "Paternalism, Unconscionability Doctrine, and Accommodation."
[19]   Feinberg, "Autonomy," 44–45.
[20]   Kant, *Groundwork of the Metaphysics of Morals*, sec. 6:230.

cooperation because they will be in a position where they will have to abide those terms. Now, there are myriad criticisms and limitations of Rawls's view, but his conception is useful in that it connects procedural autonomy (or psychological autonomy, as we described it in Chapter 2) to respect and social cooperation. Following Kant, Rawls's view is that persons' exercise of their own autonomy is important, but justifiable only to the extent that it is compatible with others'. And, hence, principles *limiting* autonomy can be grounded in fair terms of social cooperation.

A different view comes from Scanlon. Both Scanlon and Rawls are grounded in social contract theories. However, Rawls's target is society's basic structure while Scanlon's main concern is to articulate basic moral principles governing social interaction. Moreover, while Rawls derives principles based on people rationally advancing their own self-interest, Scanlon aims to derive principles based on an account of the reasons one can offer to others to justify conduct. Specifically, Scanlon argues that "[a]n act is wrong if its performance under the circumstances would be disallowed by any set of principles for the general regulation of behavior that no one could reasonably reject as a basis for informed, unforced, general agreement."[21] Parfit distills this view into what we might call the "reasonable rejection" criterion: "Everyone ought to follow the principles that no one could reasonably reject."[22] This criterion holds the linchpin of morality to be the strength of people's reasons: If one has good reasons against some principle and actions based on it, but others have weightier reasons *for* that principle and actions based on it, those weightier reasons should prevail on the grounds that one cannot reasonably reject them.

Rahul Kumar characterizes Scanlon's contractualism as grounding persons' legitimate expectations and demands of one another concerning conduct and consideration "as a matter of basic mutual respect for one another's value as rational self-governors."[23] A key facet of Scanlon's approach, and one that unites the respect-for-persons views we are drawing on here, is that each requires paying attention to individuals and to the separateness of persons.[24] To understand this, contrast the requirement that actions be based on principles no one could reasonably reject with aggregating views such as some forms of consequentialism (i.e., those that are concerned with aggregated welfare).

As Kumar notes, consequentialist concerns with our actions are subordinate to (i.e., only matter in light of) the results of those actions. However, contractualism (and autonomy-respecting theories *generally*) focuses on how our actions reflect our relationships with others directly. Consequences, on this view, matter only insofar as they reflect respect for other persons. That is,

> [Consequentialism is] concerned with what we do, but only because what we do affects what happens. The primary concern in [consequentialism] is with the promotion of well-being. Contractualism is concerned with what we do in a more basic

---

21 Scanlon, *What We Owe to Each Other*, 153.
22 Parfit, *On What Matters*, 360.
23 Kumar, "Reasonable Reasons in Contractualist Moral Argument," 10.
24 Rawls, A *Theory of Justice*, sec. 5.

sense, since the reasons for which we act express an attitude toward others, where what is of concern is that our actions express an attitude of respect for others as persons.[25]

Respecting others as having their own sense of value and being able to order their lives accordingly also makes it the case that their expectations should matter to us, and mutual respect entails that people have legitimate expectations for what they can expect of others. People have good reason to expect that others will respect them as having their own ends and as being capable of abiding fair terms of social cooperation. Treatment that frustrates that expectation is a failure of respect. As Kumar puts it,

> Disappointments of such expectation are (at least *prima facie*) valid grounds for various appropriate reactive attitudes toward one another. Resentment, moral indignation, forgiveness, betrayal, gratitude – the range and subtlety of reactions we have toward others with whom we are involved in some kind of interpersonal relationship is inexhaustible – all presuppose beliefs about what we can reasonably expect from others.[26]

We will return to the issue of reactive attitudes in Chapter 7, where we examine automated decision systems and responsibility.

So what is the upshot?

Recall that the purpose of this section is to move from an understanding of autonomy (from Chapter 2) and explain some moral claims that are grounded in respecting autonomy. We have drawn on several views about respecting autonomy, each of which attends to the importance of the principles one wills for oneself and to the incontrovertible fact that humans are social beings, and hence, to the fact that human moral principles require broad and deep social cooperation. Respecting autonomy, in other words, requires both attention to individuals' conceptions of their own good *and* some broad conception of social cooperation. Notice, though, that the views we have drawn on have substantial overlap. They may entail some differences in application (though that is an open question and would merit an argument), and they may have slightly different normative grounds for principles. But our project is deliberately ecumenical, and for our purposes the most important thing is the similarity across these views. They all point in the same direction, and they each provide a foundation on which to articulate the following, which captures their key elements, at least to a first approximation.

> **Reasonable Endorsement Test:** An action is morally permissible only if it would be allowed by principles that each person subject to it could reasonably endorse.

According to this test, then, subjecting a person to an algorithmic decision system is morally permissible only if it would be allowed by principles that everyone could reasonably endorse.

It's worth clarifying a couple of points about the Reasonable Endorsement Test. It differs from the articulations given by Scanlon and Rawls. One reason that Scanlon uses

[25] Kumar, "Defending the Moral Moderate: Contractualism and Common Sense," 285.
[26] Kumar, 286.

"reasonably reject" is to emphasize that persons must compare the burdens that they must endure under some state of affairs with others' burdens under that state of affairs. Hence, if a person would reject a social arrangement as burdensome, but their burden is less than others, there are substantial benefits to the arrangement, the alternatives are at least as burdensome to others, and the overall consequences are not substantially better, then the person's rejection of the arrangement would be unreasonable.

Our use of "could reasonably endorse" does similar work, as we make clear in our discussion of IMPACT later. However, by focusing on endorsement it leans closer to Parfit's reformulation of the Golden Rule. Specifically, people can reasonably endorse (i.e., can be rationally willing to be treated according to) principles as either consistent with their own sense of value *or* as fair terms of social cooperation. Note, too, that actions and principles that do not affect an individual's personal interests are nonetheless candidates for reasonable endorsement because those individuals can evaluate them as fair terms of social cooperation.

Another thing to note is that each of the formulations we have drawn on, as well as our Reasonable Endorsement Test, will inevitably have important limitations. Recall that each is trying to provide a framework for guiding actions based on a more basic moral value (autonomy). Hence, what matters for each principle is the extent to which it recognizes and respects persons' autonomy. For the reasons we outlined earlier, we think that the reasonable endorsement principle does at least as well in capturing respect for autonomy as the other formulations.

Finally, even if another principle does a better job reflecting the nature and value of autonomy and providing guidance, our sense is that those views, when applied, will converge with ours (at least in the cases that are of interest here). And in any case, objecting to our larger project on the grounds that a different kind of social agreement principle better captures autonomy and social cooperation warrants an argument for why it would better explain concerns in the context of algorithmic systems.

3.3 TEACHERS, VAMS, AND REASONABLE ENDORSEMENT

To sum up our view so far: teachers are autonomous persons, and hence they have a claim to incorporate their values into their lives as they see fit. And *respecting* them requires recognizing them as value-determiners, neither thwarting nor circumventing their ability to act according to those values without good reason. They are also capable of abiding fair terms of social agreement (so long as others do too), and hence "good reasons" for them will be reasons they can endorse as fair terms of social cooperation, which means they can endorse those reasons as either consistent with their own values or as a manifestation of fair social agreement.

Now, what is it to thwart an agent's ability to act according to their values? One example, discussed earlier, is deceit, in which one precludes an agent's ability to understand circumstances relevant to their actions. Another way to thwart agency is to create conditions in which agents are not treated according to reasons that they could reasonably endorse, were they given the opportunity to choose how to be treated. That is, precluding persons from acting according to their values (e.g., by deceit) or placing them in circumstances that they cannot endorse as fair is a failure of recognition of them as value-determiners and a form of disrespect.

IMPACT fails to respect teachers in exactly this way (i.e., placing them in circumstances they cannot endorse), for several interrelated reasons.[27] The reasons are reliability, responsibility, stakes, and relative burden, and they work as general criteria for when people can reasonably endorse algorithmic systems.

Reliability. For the purposes of this project, we will understand reliability in its colloquial sense; that is, as consistent (though not necessarily infallible) accuracy.[28] We have provided some reasons for why IMPACT is an unreliable tool for the evaluation of teacher efficacy. Now, teachers, like any professionals, can reasonably endorse a system in which they are evaluated based on their efficacy. Moreover, through their training and professionalization, they have endorsed the value of educating students, and fair terms of social cooperation would require that truly ineffective teachers be identified for this reason. But because IMPACT is unreliable, there is some reason to think that it misidentifies teachers as ineffective. Hence, teachers should be loath to endorse being evaluated by IMPACT.

Responsibility. IMPACT's lack of reliability is not the only way it fails to respect autonomy. Imagine a case where a teacher evaluation system reliably measures student learning. Two teachers score poorly in this year's assessment. One scores poorly because she did not assign curriculum-appropriate activities, while the other scores poorly because her classroom lacks air-conditioning. Only the first teacher is responsible for her poor scores. The second teacher's scores are based on factors for which she is not responsible. Teachers could not reasonably endorse such a system.[29]

Given the population many DC teachers were working with – underserved students – IMPACT cannot be understood as tracking only factors for which teachers are responsible. The effects of poverty, abuse, bullying, illness, undiagnosed

---

[27]   To be clear, we think that each of these dimensions is relevant in determining whether use of an algorithm is morally problematic. However, we do not think that the dimensions we outline are exhaustive; this list is not meant to be comprehensive. There may be other considerations, such as consideration of desert or other facets of fairness which can play an important role in assessing the appropriateness of the use of an algorithm.

[28]   Because we are using "reliability" in its colloquial sense, we will *not* be using the term in the statistical (and more captious) sense of being free from random error; our use of reliability will more closely align with the statistical sense of "validity," that is, accuracy borne from use of a (statistically) reliable method. We refrain from using the term "validity" to avoid confusion with the philosophical sense of the term, that is, premises entailing the conclusion of an argument. For more on the statistical senses of reliability and validity and an appraisal of value-added models in those terms, see Amrein-Beardsley, *Rethinking Value-Added Models in Education*, chapter 6.

[29]   Notice that in this example responsibility and reliability are both relevant. Teachers could reasonably endorse a system in which their jobs depend on factors for which they are not responsible – e.g., population decline. However, firing teachers whose scores suffer because of exogenous factors (lack of air-conditioning) involves criteria that are not teachers' responsibilities and which are unreliable in making teaching better (though perhaps reliable in achieving better learning outcomes).

learning disabilities (resources for addressing these are much more limited in underserved districts), and so on plausibly undermine teacher efficacy. Yet teachers bear no responsibility for those impediments. So, even if the VAMs were reliable, teachers could not reasonably endorse their implementation.

Note that the dimension of responsibility not only covers the factors that teachers *can't* be responsible for (e.g., children's circumstances outside of school), but also factors they *shouldn't* be held responsible for. It is not impossible to imagine, for instance, that teachers who bring snacks to every session could motivate their students to get higher test scores. Or, that teachers who repair air-conditioners themselves do. Teachers who do (or do not) bring snacks, fix air-conditioners, etc., *can* be responsible for engaging in (or refraining from) those activities, in the sense that they have the power to engage in (or refrain from) those activities. However, they *shouldn't* be held responsible for refraining from the activities mentioned here, as this is not a reasonable ask.

Now, what exactly makes for a reasonable ask? That is a question that we cannot give an informative general account of, as it will vary greatly from domain to domain. We simply introduce the dimension of responsibility to our criterion to highlight the fact that algorithmic systems can affect persons for factors they either cannot or should not be responsible for, and that one factor relevant to the question of whether someone *may* be affected for partaking in (or refraining from) an activity is whether asking them to partake in (or refrain from) that activity is itself reasonable.

Stakes. Perhaps the most important factor in determining whether agents can reasonably endorse an algorithmic decision system is the stakes involved. Suppose that a VAM is set up to provide teachers with lots of information about their own practices but is not used for comparative assessment. The scores are shared with teachers privately and are not used for promotion and firing. Such a system might not be very reliable, or it might measure factors for which teachers are not responsible. Nonetheless, teachers might endorse it despite its limitations because the stakes are low. But if the stakes are higher (work assignments, bonuses, promotions), it is reasonable for the employees to want the system to track factors which can be reliably measured and for which they are responsible.

DC schools' use of IMPACT is high stakes. Teachers rely on their teaching for a paycheck, and many take pride in what they do. They have sought substantial training and often regard educating students as key to their identities. Having a low IMPACT score might cost a teacher their job and career, and it may well undermine their self-worth. By agreeing to work in particular settings they have formed reasonable expectations that they can continue to incorporate those values into their lives, subject to fair terms of cooperation (e.g., that they do their work responsibly and well, that demand for their services continues, that funding remains available, etc.).

IMPACT does poorly on our analysis. It is not reliable, it evaluates teachers based on factors for which they are not responsible, and it is used for high-stakes decisions. These points are reflected in teacher reactions to IMPACT. For example, Alyson

Perschke – a fourth-grade teacher in DC schools – alleged in a letter to Chancellor Kaya Henderson that VAMs are "unreliable and insubstantial."[30] Perschke did so well in her in-class observations that her administrators and evaluators asked if she could be videotaped as "an exemplar."[31] Yet the same year her VAM dragged her otherwise-flawless overall evaluation down to average. Remarking on this, she says, "I am baffled how I teach every day with talent, commitment, and vigor to surpass the standards set for me, yet this is not reflected in my final IMPACT score."[32]

Relative Burden. Another factor that is relevant in determining whether persons subject to an algorithmic system can reasonably endorse it is what we will call "relative burden." It is plausible that IMPACT disproportionately negatively affects teachers from underrepresented groups:

> [T]he scarcely mentioned, uglier impact of IMPACT is disproportionately felt by teachers in DC's poorest wards – at schools toward which minority teachers tend to gravitate. In seeking to improve the quality of teachers, IMPACT manages to simultaneously perpetuate stubborn workforce inequalities and exacerbate an already alarming shortage of teachers of color.[33]

So IMPACT might impose more burdens on members of underrepresented groups. This is another reason – independent of reasons grounded in reliability, responsibility, and stakes – that teachers should refrain from endorsing IMPACT.

There has been a great deal of discussion about how algorithmic systems may be *biased* or *unfair*. However, precisely what those concepts amount to and the degree to which they create moral problems are often unclear. Indeed, different conceptions of fairness can lead to different conclusions about whether a particular system is unfair (cf. Section 3.5).[34]

The problem, stated generally, is that there are many ways in which a decision system can represent subpopulations differently. The data on which a system is built and trained may under- or overrepresent a group. The system may make predictions

---

[30] Strauss, "D.C. Teacher Tells Chancellor Why IMPACT Evaluation Is Unfair."
[31] Strauss.
[32] Strauss. There is another autonomy-related issue here. In Chapter 2, we explained the importance of social and relational facets of autonomy. One way to understand the relationship between autonomy and facts about persons' social circumstances and relationships is that social and relational facts are *causally* important in fostering persons' autonomy. Another way is to understand social and relational facts as *constitutive* of autonomy. See Mackenzie and Stoljar, *Relational Autonomy: Feminist Perspectives on Autonomy, Agency, and the Social Self*, chapter 1. That is, being a part of supportive and meaningful social groups and relationships is (1) a necessary condition for developing the competences and authenticity necessary for psychological autonomy and (2) an inherent part of being a person incorporating values into their life. Teacher-student and teacher-community relationships are deeply important and constitutive of the lives that many teachers value and have cultivated so as to realize their sense of value. Subjecting those relationships to unreliable, high-stakes processes that measure things for which teachers are not responsible conflicts with *that* facet of autonomy as well. Note that this is distinct from the reasonable endorsement argument.
[33] Quick, "The Unfair Effects of IMPACT on Teachers with the Toughest Jobs."
[34] Corbett-Davies and Goel, "The Measure and Mismeasure of Fairness."

about facts that have different incidence rates in populations, leading to different false-positive and false-negative rates. It is plausible to describe each of these cases of difference as in some sense "unfair." But we cannot know as a general matter *which conception* of fairness is appropriately applied across all cases. Thus, we will need an argument for applying any particular conception. In other words, even once we have determined that an algorithmic system is in some sense unfair, there is a further question as to whether (and *why*) it is morally problematic.

Put another way, one could frame our argument about the conditions under which agents can reasonably endorse algorithmic systems as an argument about the conditions under which such systems *are fair* (if everyone could reasonably endorse a system, that system is ipso facto fair). On that framing, fairness is the conclusion of our analysis, so including fairness as a general criterion for whether agents could reasonably endorse a system would make our argument circular.[35] Simply pointing out differences in treatment and concluding that those differences are unfair is not enough to move our argument forward. Rather, our task here is to identify factors that matter in determining whether people can reasonably endorse a decision system independently of whether they can be characterized as unfair. Among those is relative burden.

All automated systems will distribute benefits and burdens in some way or another.[36] Smart recommender systems for music, for example, will favor some artists over others and some users' musical tastes over others. Of course, what matters for our view here is whether they can reasonably endorse such a system. Relative burden matters if that burden either (a) is arbitrary, such that it has nothing to do with the system in the first place, (b) reflects otherwise morally unjustifiable distinctions, or (c) is a *compound* burden, which reflects or exacerbates an existing burden on a group.

An example of an arbitrary burden (a) would be a test that systematically scored English teachers more poorly overall than teachers of other subjects and thereby created some social or professional consequences for those teachers. An example of (b) would be a test that, let's suppose, systematically scored kindergarten teachers who are men lower than others. Perhaps kindergarteners respond less well to even very well-qualified men than they do to women; it would be morally unjustifiable, though, to have evaluation systems reflect that (at least if the stakes are significant). The unjustifiability in that case, though, is not related to some other significant social disadvantage. An example of (c) would be a case where an automated system imposes a burden that correlates with some other significant social burden (in many cases race, ethnicity, gender, or socioeconomic position).

---

[35] To be clear, we are not arguing that fairness analyses are mistaken. Rather, there are many conceptions of fairness that focus on different values. These may conflict, and many are mutually incompatible. Hence, there is a great deal of work to do in working out fairness issues even once one determines that a system is in some sense fair or unfair. We take this issue up again in Section 3.5.

[36] Note that the relationships between system burden and social circumstances need not be causal.

3.4 APPLYING THE REASONABLE ENDORSEMENT TEST

So far, we have argued that for an algorithmic system to respect autonomy in the relevant way, those who are subject to the system must be able to reasonably endorse it. And whether people can reasonably endorse a given system will be a function of its reliability, the extent to which it measures outcomes for which its subjects are responsible, the stakes at hand, and the relative burden imposed by the system's use. We illustrated our framework by analyzing DC Schools' use of IMPACT. Here, we turn back to our polestar cases to help make sense of the moral issues underlying them.

3.4.1 Wagner v. Haslam

Recall from Chapter 1 that the plaintiffs in this case (Teresa Wagner and Jennifer Braeuner) were teachers who challenged the Tennessee Value-Added Assessment System (TVAAS), which is a proprietary system similar to IMPACT. Because TVAAS did not test the subjects Wagner and Braeuner taught, they were evaluated based on a school-wide composite score, combined with their (excellent) scores from in-person teaching observations. This composite score dragged their individual evaluations from the highest possible score (as they had received in previous years) to middling scores. As a result, Wagner did not receive a performance bonus and Braeuner was ineligible for consideration for tenure. Moreover, each "suffered harm to her professional reputation, and experienced diminished morale and emotional distress."[37]

There is a deeper moral issue grounding the legal case. Wagner and Braeuner frame their case in terms of harms (losing a bonus, precluding tenure consideration, and so forth), but those harms matter only because they are wrongful. They are wrongful because TVAAS is an evaluation system that teachers could not reasonably endorse. Wagner and Braeuner's scores did not reliably track their performances nor did the scores reflect factors for which they were responsible, as the scores were based on the performance in subjects Wagner and Braeuner did not teach. And the stakes in the case are fairly high (there were financial repercussions for Wagner and job security for Braeuner). So, per our account, they were wronged.

There may also be a relative burden issue with TVAAS, though it is not discussed explicitly in the *Wagner* opinion. A 2015 study of TVAAS found that mathematics teachers across Tennessee were, overall, found to be more effective by TVAAS than their colleagues in English/language arts.[38] This finding supports two hypotheses: Tennessee's math teachers are more effective than its English/language arts teachers, and TVAAS is systematically biased in favor of math teachers.[39] If the

---

[37] *Wagner v. Haslam*, 112 F. Supp. 3d at 690.
[38] Holloway, "Evidence of Grade and Subject-Level Bias in Value-Added Measures."
[39] Amrein-Beardsley, "Evidence of Grade and Subject-Level Bias in Value-Added Measures: Article Published in TCR"; Spears, "Bias Confirmed – Tennessee Education Report."

latter hypothesis is true – and we suspect that it is – then, there are teachers, specifically Tennessee's English/language arts teachers, who have an additional complaint against TVAAS: It imposes a higher relative burden on them because it arbitrarily returns lower scores for non-math teachers. They could not reasonably endorse this arrangement.

3.4.2 Houston Fed of Teachers v. Houston Ind Sch Dist

The *Houston Schools* case is superficially similar to *Wagner* in that it involves a similar proprietary VAM (EVAAS) to evaluate teachers. The school system used EVAAS scores as the sole basis for "exiting" teachers.[40] The primary concern for our purposes is that Houston Schools did not have a mechanism for ensuring against basic coding and clerical errors. They refused to correct errors on the grounds that doing so would require them to rerun their analysis of the entire school district. That, in turn, would have two consequences. First, it would be costly; second, it would "change all other teachers' reports."[41]

The moral foundations of the teachers' complaints should by now be clear. The stakes here – i.e., losing one's job and having one's professional image tarnished – are high. EVAAS is unreliable, having what the court called a "house-of-cards fragility."[42] And that unreliability is due to factors for which teachers are not responsible, "ranging from data-entry mistakes to glitches in the code itself."[43] Hence, teachers could not reasonably endorse being evaluated under such a system.

We can add a complaint about relative burden, at least for some teachers. EVAAS, like IMPACT, gives lower scores to teachers working in poorer schools. To see this, consider an analysis of EVAAS's use in Ohio (in 2011–12) conducted by The Plain Dealer and State Impact Ohio, which found the following:

- Value-added scores were 2½ times higher on average for districts where the median family income is above $35,000 than for districts with income below that amount.
- For low-poverty school districts, two-thirds had positive value-added scores – scores indicating students made more than a year's worth of progress.
- For high-poverty school districts, two-thirds had negative value-added scores – scores indicating that students made less than a year's progress.
- Almost 40 percent of low-poverty schools scored "Above" the state's value-added target, compared with 20 percent of high-poverty schools.
- At the same time, 25 percent of high-poverty schools scored "Below" state value-added targets while low-poverty schools were half as likely to score "Below."[44]

---

[40] *Houston Fed of Teachers, Local 2415 v. Houston Ind Sch Dist*, 251 F. Supp. 3d at 1175.
[41] Houston Independent School District, "EVAAS/Value-Added Frequently Asked Questions."
[42] *Houston Fed of Teachers, Local 2415 v. Houston Ind Sch Dist*, 251 F. Supp. 3d at 1178.
[43] *Houston Fed of Teachers, Local 2415 v. Houston Ind Sch Dist*, 251 F. Supp. 3d at 1177.
[44] Ideastream, "Grading the Teachers."

In virtue of these findings, it is plausible that – in addition to complaints grounded in reliability, responsibility, and stakes – teachers in low-income schools have a complaint grounded in the uneven distribution of burdens.

And, hence, use of EVAAS is not something teachers subject to it could reasonably endorse.

3.4.3 Wisconsin v. Loomis

Our framework for understanding algorithmic systems and autonomy applies equally well to risk assessment tools like COMPAS.

To begin, COMPAS is moderately reliable. Researchers associated with Northpointe assessed COMPAS as being accurate in about 68 percent of cases.[45] More important is that COMPAS incorporates numerous factors for which defendants are not responsible. Recall that among the data points that COMPAS takes into account in generating risk scores are prior arrests, residential stability, employment status, community ties, substance abuse, criminal associates, history of violence, problems in job or educational settings, and age at first arrest.[46] Regardless of how well COMPAS's big and little bars reliably reflect reoffense risk, defendants are not responsible for some of the factors that affect those bars. So, while Loomis did commit the underlying conduct and was convicted of prior crimes, COMPAS incorporates factors for which defendants are not responsible.[47] For example, the questionnaire asks about the age at which one's parents separated (if they did); whether one was raised by biological, adoptive, or foster parents; whether a parent or sibling was ever arrested, jailed, or imprisoned; whether a parent or parent-figure ever had a drug or alcohol problem; and whether one's neighborhood friends or family have been crime victims.[48] Moreover, even if some factors (e.g., residential

---

[45] Brennan, Dieterich, and Ehret, "Evaluating the Predictive Validity of the COMPAS Risk and Needs Assessment System." We should note that how we apply the concept of reliability could itself be a matter of dispute. The study by Northpointe-affiliated researchers considers how well calibrated COMPAS is; that is, how likely COMPAS is to predict individual defendants' reoffense. However, there are other relevant measures for which COMPAS could be more or less reliable. A study by ProPublica found that prediction failure was different for White and Black defendants such that White defendants labeled lower risk were more likely to reoffend than Black defendants with a similar label, and Black defendants labeled higher risk were less likely to reoffend than White defendants labeled higher risk. See Angwin et al., "Machine Bias," May 23, 2016. These results call into question COMPAS's reliability in avoiding false positives and false negatives. We address this issue in more detail in the next section.

[46] Northpointe, Inc., "Practitioner's Guide to COMPAS Core," 24.

[47] Drawing on factors for which one is not responsible is compatible with a range of theories of punishment. Such factors may help determine a sentence – whether one is even arrested, moral luck, how well punishment deters crime, and so forth. But our view is not that only factors for which one is responsible may contribute to sentencing decisions. Rather, our view is that, as such factors increase, it becomes more difficult for an agent to abide such a system.

[48] Other questions pertain to matters for which defendants' responsibility is less clear: how often one has had barely enough money to get by, whether one's friends use drugs, how often one has moved in the last year, and whether one has ever been suspended from school.

stability, employment status, and community ties) are things over which individuals *can* exercise a degree of control, they are matters for which we *shouldn't* attribute responsibility in determining sentencing for offenses.

Further, the use of COMPAS in *Loomis* is high stakes. Incarceration is the harshest form of punishment that the state of Wisconsin can impose. This is made vivid by comparing the use of COMPAS in *Loomis* with its specified purposes. COMPAS is built to be applied to decisions about the type of institution in which an offender will serve a sentence (e.g., lower or higher security), the degree of supervision (e.g., from probation officers or social workers), and what systems and resources are appropriate (e.g., drug and alcohol treatment, housing, and so forth). Indeed, Northpointe warns against using COMPAS for sentencing, and Loomis's presentence investigation report specifically stated the COMPAS report should be used "to identify offenders who could *benefit from interventions and to target risk factors that should be addressed during supervision.*"[49] When the system is used for its intended purposes – identifying ways to mitigate risk of reoffense of persons under state supervision – the stakes are much lower.[50] Hence, it is more plausible that someone subject to its use could reasonably endorse it in those cases.

One of Loomis's complaints about COMPAS is that it took his gender into account. The court found that COMPAS's use of gender was not discriminatory because it served the purpose of promoting accuracy. So Loomis's claim that he shouldered a higher relative burden under this system was undercut, and the court was – in our opinion – correct in their response to his claim. Because men do commit certain crimes more often than women, removing gender as a factor could result in the systematic overestimation of women's risk scores.[51] This does not, however, mean that COMPAS has no issues with respect to the question of relative burden.

To introduce the relative burden issue, let's turn to a related controversy surrounding COMPAS. In May 2016, ProPublica reported that COMPAS was biased against Black defendants.[52] Specifically, ProPublica found that COMPAS misidentified Black defendants as high risk twice as often as it did White defendants. Northpointe, the company that developed COMPAS, released a technical report

---

49 *Wisconsin v. Loomis*, 881 N.W.2d paragraph 16 (emphasis added).
50 Northpointe describes COMPAS's scope as follows: "Criminal justice agencies across the nation use COMPAS to inform decisions regarding the placement, supervision and case management of offenders." Northpointe, Inc., "Practitioner's Guide to COMPAS Core," 1.
51 Skeem, Monahan, and Lowenkamp, "Gender, Risk Assessment, and Sanctioning"; DeMichele et al., "The Public Safety Assessment"; Corbett-Davies and Goel, "The Measure and Mismeasure of Fairness." Note here that there is another potential issue of responsibility and stakes and of what we will call "substantive fairness" in Section 3.5. It is indeed the case that men are much more likely to reoffend and to commit violent offenses than women, though one's gender is not a factor for which one should be held responsible. Moreover, whether gender is justifiably a difference-maker in determining *sentencing* (as opposed to, say, job training, drug and alcohol counseling, or supportive intervention) will turn on a normative theory of criminal law.
52 Angwin et al., "Machine Bias," May 23, 2016.

that was critical of ProPublica's reporting.[53] They claimed that despite its misidentifying Black defendants as high risk at a higher rate, COMPAS was unbiased. This is because the defendants within risk categories reoffended at the same rates, regardless of whether they are Black or White.

The back and forth between Northpointe and ProPublica is at the center of a dispute over how to measure fairness in algorithmic systems. Northpointe's standard of fairness is known as "calibration," which requires that outcomes (in this case reoffense) are probabilistically independent of protected attributes (especially race and ethnicity), given one's risk score (in this case high risk of reoffense and low risk of reoffense).[54] In this context, calibration requires that knowing a defendant's risk score *and race* should provide the same amount of information with respect to their chances of reoffending as *just* knowing their score. ProPublica's standard of fairness, on the other hand, is "classification parity," which requires that classification error is equal across groups, defined by protected attributes.[55] As the dispute between ProPublica and Northpointe shows, you cannot always satisfy both standards of fairness.

This might be counterintuitive. ProPublica's conclusions about COMPAS are a result of the fact that Black defendants and White defendants are arrested and rearrested at different rates, and hence Black and White defendants are counted as "re-offending" at different rates. To better understand how COMPAS can satisfy calibration but violate classification parity, it will be helpful to substitute a version of COMPAS with simplified numbers, which we will call "SIMPLE COMPAS." Note that we choose the numbers here because they loosely approximate ProPublica's analysis of COMPAS, which included larger numbers of Black defendants counted as reoffending.

> **SIMPLE COMPAS.** SIMPLE COMPAS sorts defendants into two risk groups: high and low. Within each group, defendants reoffend at the same rates, regardless of race. In the low-risk group, defendants reoffend about 20 percent of the time. In the high, about 80 percent. The high-risk group is overwhelmingly (but not entirely) Black, and the low-risk group is overwhelmingly (but not entirely) White. Its results are summarized by the following bar chart (Figure 3.1).[56]

Now consider three questions about SIMPLE COMPAS.

First, if you randomly select a defendant, not knowing whether they are from the high- or low-risk group, would learning their race warrant suspicion that their chance of reoffending is higher (or lower) than others from the risk group they are

---

53 Dieterich, Mendoza, and Brennan, "COMPAS Risk Scales: Demonstrating Accuracy Equity and Predictive Parity."

54 Corbett-Davies and Goel, "The Measure and Mismeasure of Fairness."

55 Corbett-Davies and Goel.

56 We borrow the idea of using this kind of chart to relay the difference between calibration and classification parity from Corbett-Davies et al., "Algorithmic Decision Making and the Cost of Fairness." The image itself is similar to one used in Castro, "Just Machines."

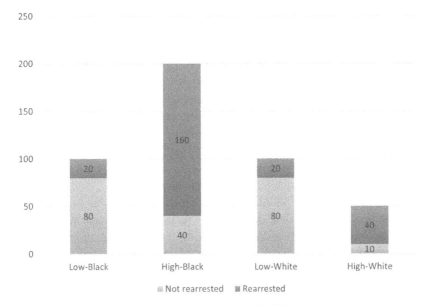

FIGURE 3.1 SIMPLE COMPAS

in? No. As we have stipulated, defendants within a risk group reoffend at similar rates regardless of race, and this is reflected in the bar chart, where the *proportion* of reoffenders to non-reoffenders in "Low – Black" is the same as "Low – White": one in five. Similarly, the proportion of reoffenders to non-reoffenders in "High – Black" is the same as "High – White": four in five. In virtue of this, SIMPLE COMPAS satisfies the calibration standard of fairness.

Second, if you randomly select a defendant, not knowing whether they are from the high- or low-risk group, would learning their race warrant increasing or decreasing your confidence that they are in the high-risk group? Yes. We have stipulated (tracking the analysis of COMPAS from ProPublica) that the high-risk group is predominantly Black and that the low-risk group is predominantly White (80 percent). If the randomly selected defendant is Black, you should increase your confidence that they are from the high-risk group, from about 55 percent (since five out nine total defendants – 250/450 – are high risk) to about 66 percent (since six out of nine Black defendants – 200/300 – are high risk). If, on the other hand, the randomly selected defendant is White, you should increase your confidence that they are from the low-risk group, from about 44 percent (since four out of nine defendants – 200/ 450 – are low risk) to about 66 percent (since six out of nine White defendants – 100/ 150 – are low risk).

Third, if you randomly select a defendant, not knowing whether they are from the high- or low-risk group, should learning their race affect your confidence that they are non-reoffending high-risk (i.e., misidentified as high-risk)? Yes. To see this, just look back to the previous question. If you learn the defendant is Black, you should increase your confidence that they are from the high-risk group. In virtue of this, your confidence that they are in the *non-reoffending* high-risk group should increase too, from about 11 percent (since one out of nine defendants – 50/450 – are non-reoffending high risk) to about 13 percent (since two out of fifteen Black defendants – 40/300 – are non-reoffending high risk). This may not seem like much, unless we appreciate that learning that a defendant is White should drive your confidence that they are non-reoffending high risk down to about 6.6 percent (since one out of fifteen White defendants – 10/150 – are non-reoffending high risk). This means that, in SIMPLE COMPAS, Black defendants are *twice as likely as White defendants to be misidentified as high-risk*, which violates classification parity. And this is what ProPublica found: COMPAS misidentifies Black defendants as high risk about twice as often as it does White defendants.[57] As this should make clear, violating classification parity is one way that an algorithmic system can impose an undue relative burden.

Analyzing SIMPLE COMPAS further shows why this is a matter of relative burden and why this sort of issue is distinct from issues of reliability, responsibility, and stakes. Suppose that in the world of SIMPLE COMPAS, Black and White citizens use illicit drugs at similar rates. However, Black citizens are disproportionately charged with drug crimes because they are more likely to get stopped and searched. Because of this correlation, SIMPLE COMPAS (which does not directly take race into account) is more likely to identify Black defendants as high risk.

If we assume further that the justice system that SIMPLE COMPAS is embedded in has sensible penalties,[58] then the shortcomings of SIMPLE COMPAS defy the categories of responsibility, reliability, and stakes. SIMPLE COMPAS does not hold defendants responsible for factors not under their control: The vast majority of those tagged as high risk are in fact likely to reoffend, and they are being held responsible for breaking laws that they in fact broke. Similarly, we can't complain that SIMPLE COMPAS is unreliable; it is well calibrated and predicts future arrests very reliably. Finally, we cannot complain from the perspective of stakes, because – as we have stipulated – the justice system SIMPLE COMPAS is embedded in has sensible penalties. Yet something is wrong with the use of SIMPLE COMPAS, and the problem has to do with relative burden.

To see this, compare SIMPLE COMPAS with EVEN COMPAS.

EVEN COMPAS. EVEN COMPAS sorts defendants into two risk groups: high and low. Within each group, defendants reoffend at the same rates, regardless of race. In the low-risk group, defendants reoffend about 20 percent of the time. In the high-risk group, about 80 percent . The high-risk group and low-risk group are each

---

[57] Angwin et al., "Machine Bias," May 23, 2016.
[58] Of course, it may well be unjust to impose criminal penalties for many kinds of drug possession and use in the first place. We will leave that issue aside for this project.

50 percent White and 50 percent Black. The sizes of the low- and high-risk groups are such that EVEN COMPAS misclassifies all defendants at the same (low) rate that SIMPLE COMPAS misclassifies Black defendants.

Suppose that EVEN COMPAS, like SIMPLE COMPAS, is embedded in a system that has sensible penalties. The only difference is that the EVEN COMPAS police force does not discriminate, and so EVEN COMPAS does not learn to identify Black defendants as high risk more often than White defendants.

Let us now make two observations. First, note that EVEN COMPAS might not be problematic. That is, given the details of the case, it does not seem like there are obvious objections to its use that we can make: It is an accurate and equitable device. It does misclassify some non-reoffending defendants as high risk, but unless we abandon pretrial risk assessment altogether or achieve clairvoyance, this is unavoidable.

Second, note that SIMPLE COMPAS is intuitively problematic even though – from defendants' points of view – EVEN COMPAS treats them worse on the whole (i.e., compared to SIMPLE COMPAS, EVEN COMPAS is worse for White defendants and it is not better for Black defendants). What could explain SIMPLE COMPAS being problematic while EVEN COMPAS is not? It cannot be an issue of reliability, responsibility, or stakes. Rather, it is the fact that SIMPLE COMPAS imposes its burdens unevenly: It is systematically worse for Black defendants. Hence, relative burden is a factor in whether people could (or could not) reasonably endorse a system that is distinct from reliability, responsibility, and stakes.

Let's return to *Loomis*. COMPAS – like the fictional SIMPLE COMPAS – does have an issue with high relative burden. The burden does not happen to be one that negatively affects Loomis. He does not have an individual complaint that he has endured a burden that is relatively higher than other people subject to it. However, it does not follow that COMPAS is a system that *any* person subject to it can reasonably endorse. Rather, because it imposes a greater relative burden to Black defendants than to White defendants, it is one that at least some defendants cannot reasonably endorse.

3.5 WHY NOT FAIRNESS?

None of the top-line criticisms of algorithmic systems that we offer in this book are that such systems are unfair or biased. This might be surprising, considering the gigantic and expanding literature on algorithmic fairness and bias. It is certainly true that decision systems are in many cases biased and (hence) unfair, and it is also true that unfairness is an extremely important issue in the justifiability of those systems. There are several, related reasons we do not primarily lean on fairness. First is that whether something is fair is often best understood as the conclusion of an argument. As we note in Section 3.3, whether people can reasonably endorse a system to which they are subject can be understood as a criterion for whether that system is fair. Likewise, the component parts of our reasonable endorsement argument can be understood as questions of fairness. So whether a system imposes a relative burden that is arbitrary, compound, or otherwise unjustifiable is a way in which a system can be unfair.

The second reason that we don't lead with fairness is that there is an important ambiguity in conceptions of fairness. The issue is that fairness is a concept that can in some senses be formalized, but in other senses serves as an umbrella concept for lots of more specific moral values. To see why this is important, and why we think it is fruitful not to deploy fairness as a marquee concern, we need to distinguish two broad conceptions of fairness. First is,

Formal fairness: the equal and impartial application of rules.[59]

Formal fairness contrasts with

Substantive fairness: the satisfaction of a certain subset of applicable moral reasons (such as desert, agreements, needs, and side-constraints).[60]

This distinction is straightforward. Any system of rules can be applied equally in a rote or mechanical way and, thus, can arrive at outcomes that are in some sense "fair" so long as those rules are applied without deviation. The rule that deli customers must collect a ticket upon entry and will be served in the order of the ticket numbers is a rule that can be applied in a formally fair way. However, if it is easy to steal tickets, if some tickets are not sequentially numbered, or if some people are unable to stand in line, the rule will be substantively unfair because it fails to satisfy important, applicable moral reasons that the rule does not cover. One might add all kinds of more complicated rules (people may move to the front if they need to, there will be no secondary market in low numbered tickets, people may only buy a defined, reasonable amount, etc.). Each of those additional rules may be applied in a formally fair way. Nonetheless, we cannot ensure substantive fairness by ensuring formal fairness, regardless of how exacting, equal, and impartial an application of rules is. That is because substantive fairness itself *just is* a conclusion about (a) which moral reasons are applicable and (b) whether those reasons have been proportionally satisfied. And (a) and (b) cannot be answered by an appeal to *formal* fairness without assuming the answer to the question at hand, viz., what moral reasons ought to apply.

Moreover, it might be logically impossible to simultaneously maximize different facets of substantive fairness. In other words, even if we could agree on a set of substantive moral criteria that are relevant in determining whether a given algorithmic system is fair, it may not be possible to take those substantive criteria and render a formally fair application of rules that satisfies those criteria. To understand why, consider recent work by Sam Corbett-Davies and Sharad Goel.[61]

In the literature on fairness in machine learning, there are three predominant conceptions of fairness. Corbett-Davies and Goel argue that each one is inadequate

---

[59]   Hooker, "Fairness." See also Castro, "Just Machines."
[60]   Hooker. See also Castro, "Just Machines."
[61]   Corbett-Davies and Goel, "The Measure and Mismeasure of Fairness."

and that it is impossible to satisfy them all at once. The first is "anti-classification," according to which algorithms do not take into consideration protected characteristics (race, gender, or close approximations). They argue that anti-classification is an inadequate principle of fairness, on the grounds that it can harm people. For example, because women are much less likely than men to commit violent crimes, "gender-neutral risk scores can systematically overestimate a woman's recidivism risk, and can in turn encourage unnecessarily harsh judicial decisions."[62] Notice that their argument implicitly incorporates a substantive moral theory about punishment, namely that justification for punishment for violent crimes depends on the likelihood of the criminal committing future offenses. Hence, the question of whether "anti-classification" is the right measure of fairness requires addressing a further question of substantive fairness.

The second main conception of fairness in machine learning Corbett-Davies and Goel describe is "classification parity," which requires that predictive performance of an algorithm "be equal across groups defined by . . . protected attributes."[63] We explained earlier how ProPublica's examination of COMPAS showed that it violates classification parity. The problem is that when distributions of risk *actually* vary across groups, achieving classification parity will "often require implicitly or explicitly misclassifying low-risk members of one group as high-risk, and high-risk members of another as low risk, potentially harming members of all groups in the process."[64]

The third conception, calibration, requires that results are "independent of protected attributes after controlling for estimated risk." One problem with calibration is the reverse of classification parity. Where there are different underlying rates across groups, calibration will conflict with classification parity (as we discussed earlier). In addition, Corbett-Davies and Goel argue that coarse measures that are well calibrated can be used in discriminatory ways (e.g., by using neighborhood as a proxy for credit-worthiness without taking into account income and credit history).[65]

The upshot of the Corbett-Davies and Goel paper is that the results of using each of the formal definitions of fairness are in some way harmful, discriminatory, or otherwise unjustifiable. But that is simply another way of saying that there are some relevant, applicable moral claims that would not be proportionally addressed in each. In other words, there may be substantive reasons that measures of formal fairness are good. However, because substantive fairness is multifaceted, no single measure of formal fairness can capture it.

Another line of literature attends to the fact that there are different conceptions of substantive fairness in the philosophical literature, each of which has different

---

[62] Corbett-Davies and Goel, 2.
[63] Corbett-Davies and Goel, 2.
[64] Corbett-Davies and Goel, 2.
[65] Corbett-Davies and Goel, 2–3.

implications for uses of algorithmic systems.[66] The fact that there are different conceptions of fairness and that those different conceptions prescribe different uses and constraints for algorithmic systems is largely a function of the scope of substantive fairness. That is, substantive fairness is capacious, and different conceptions of fairness, discrimination, egalitarianism, and the like are component parts of it.

Finally, a conclusion that a system is fair will often be tenuous. That is because a system that renders outcomes that are formally and substantively fair in one context may be rendered substantively unfair when the context changes.[67] Consider our discussion of COMPAS. We can imagine a risk assessment tool that is strictly used for interventions meant to prevent violence and reoffense with, for example, drug and alcohol treatment, housing, job training, and so forth. Such a system could (let's suppose) be formally fair and proportionally address relevant moral reasons. However, if that same system is deployed in a *punitive* way, then a different relevant moral reason is applicable, namely that it is substantively unfair to punish people based on facts for which they are not blameworthy. Addictions, housing insecurity, and unemployment are not conditions for which people are blameworthy. Hence, the new application of the risk algorithm would be substantively unfair, even if the original application is not.

To sum up, substantive fairness is broad and includes a range of relevant moral reasons. The purpose of this project is to examine one important component of relevant moral reasons. Thus, we don't begin with fairness.

3.6 CONCLUSION

Our task in this chapter has been to link our conception of autonomy and its value to moral principles that can serve as a framework for when using algorithmic systems is justifiable. We did so by arguing for the Reasonable Endorsement Test, according to which an action is morally permissible only if it would be allowed by principles that each person subject to it could reasonably endorse. In the context of algorithmic systems, that principle is that subjecting a person to an algorithmic decision system is morally permissible only if it would be allowed by principles that everyone could reasonably endorse. From there, we offered several factors for when algorithmic systems are such that people subject to them can reasonably endorse them. Specifically, reasonable endorsement is a function of whether systems are reliable, whether they turn on factors for which subjects are responsible, the stakes involved, and whether they impose unjustified relative burdens on persons.

[66]   Binns, "Fairness in Machine Learning: Lessons from Political Philosophy."
[67]   Herington, "Measuring Fairness in an Unfair World."

Notice, though, that these criteria are merely *necessary* conditions for permissibility based on respect for persons. They are not sufficient. For example, use of algorithmic systems may meet these criteria but will not be justifiable for other reasons. Indeed, one common criticism of algorithmic systems is that they are inscrutable (either because the technology is complex or because access is protected by intellectual property laws). We consider that in Chapter 4.

4

What We Informationally Owe Each Other

In Chapter 2, we articulated our conception of autonomy. We argued for a lightweight, ecumenical approach that encompasses both psychological and personal autonomy. In Chapter 3, we drew on this account to set out conditions that are crucial in determining whether algorithmic decision systems respect persons' autonomy. Specifically, we argued that algorithmic decision systems are justifiable to the extent that people subject to them can reasonably endorse them. Whether people can reasonably endorse those systems turns on conditions of reliability, responsibility, stakes, and relative burden.

Notice, though, that the conditions set out in Chapter 3 are primarily about how those systems threaten persons' material conditions, such as whether teachers are fired based on evaluation systems and whether defendants are subject to more stringent conditions based on risk assessment systems. But people are not just passive subjects of algorithmic systems – or at least they ought not to be – and whether use of a system is justifiable overall turns on more than the material consequences of its use.

In this chapter we argue that there is a distinct *informational* component to respecting autonomy. Specifically, we owe people certain kinds of information and informational control. To get a basic sense of why, consider our understanding of autonomy from Chapter 2, which has two broad facets. Psychological autonomy includes conditions of competence (including epistemic competence) and authenticity. Personal autonomy includes procedural and substantive independence, which at root demands space and support for a person to think, plan, and operate. Further, as we explained in Chapter 2, whether agents are personally autonomous turns on the extent to which they are capable of incorporating their values into important facets of their lives. Respecting an agents' autonomy requires not denying them what they need to incorporate their values into important facets of their lives. It is a failure of respect to prevent agents from exercising their autonomy, and it is wrongful to do so without sufficiently good reason. Incorporating one's values into important facets of one's life requires that one have access to relevant information. That is, autonomy requires having information important to one's life, and respecting autonomy requires not denying agents that information (and at times making it available). Algorithmic decision systems are often built in a way that prevents people from understanding their operations.[1] This may, at least under certain circumstances, preclude persons' access to information to which they have a right.[2]

That is the broad contour of our argument. Our task in the rest of the chapter is to fill that argument in. We begin by describing two new cases, each involving background checks, and we analyze those cases using the Reasonable Endorsement Test we developed in Chapter 3. We then explain important facets of autonomy that are missing from the analysis. To address that gap, we distinguish several different modes of agency, including *practical* and *cognitive* agency. We argue that individuals have rights to information about algorithmic systems in virtue of their practical and cognitive agency. Next, we draw on some scholarship surrounding a so-called right to explanation in the European Union's General Data Protection Regulation and how those relate to our understanding of cognitive and practical agency. Finally, we apply our criteria to our polestar cases.

To be clear, we are not arguing that individuals have a right to all information that is important in understanding their lives, incorporating their values into important decisions, and exercising agency. Rather, we argue that they have some kind of defeasible claim to such information. Our task here is to explain the basis for that claim, the conditions under which it creates obligations on others to respect, and the types of information the moral claims underwrite. A recent report on ethics in AI systems states, "Emphasis on algorithmic transparency assumes that some kind of 'explainability' is important to all kinds of people, but there has been very little attempt to build up evidence on which kinds of explanations are desirable to which people in which contexts."[3] We hope to contribute to this issue with an argument about what information is warranted.

4.1 THE MISFORTUNES OF CATHERINE TAYLOR AND CARMEN ARROYO

Let's begin by considering two new cases.

---

[1] Frank Pasquale (2016) argues that lack of transparency is one of the defining features and key concerns of technological "black boxes" that exert control over large swathes of contemporary life. Such obscurity can derive from many sources, including technological complexity, legal protections via intellectual property, and deliberate obfuscation. For our purposes the source of obscurity is initially less important than what autonomy demands. The source will become important when evaluating what duties people have to provide information as a matter of respecting others' autonomy.

[2] David Grant, Jeff Behrends, and John Basl argue that understanding what we owe to subjects of automated (or "black boxed") decision systems should not begin with questions of transparency and opacity. Rather, we should begin with an understanding of the morally relevant features of decision subjects, how decision-makers relate themselves to decision subjects, and a standard of "due consideration" to decision subjects. Grant et al., "What We Owe to Decision Subjects: Beyond Transparency and Explanation in Automated Decision-Making." We agree. Our account of practical and cognitive agency is a way of spelling out some of those morally salient features and relationships between decision-makers and subjects.

[3] Whittlestone et al., "Ethical and Societal Implications of Algorithms, Data, and Artificial Intelligence: A Roadmap for Research," 12.

Arkansas resident Catherine Taylor was denied a job at the Red Cross. Her rejection letter came with a nasty surprise. Her criminal background report included a criminal charge for intent to manufacture and sell methamphetamines.[4] But Taylor had no criminal history. The system had confused her with *Illinois* resident Catherine Taylor, who had been charged with intent to manufacture and sell methamphetamines.[5]

Arkansas Catherine Taylor wound up with a false criminal charge on her report because ChoicePoint (now a part of LexisNexis), the company providing the report, relied on bulk data to produce an "instant" result when checking her background.[6] This is a common practice. Background screening companies such as ChoicePoint generate reports through automated processes that run searches through large databases of aggregated data, with minimal (if any) manual overview or quality control. ChoicePoint actually had enough accurate information – such as Taylor's address, Social Security number, and credit report – to avoid tarnishing her reputation with mistakes.[7] Unfortunately for Taylor, the product ChoicePoint used in her case simply was not designed to access that information.[8]

ChoicePoint compounded the failure by refusing to rectify its mistake. The company said it could not alter the sources from which it draws data. So if another business requested an "instant" report on Arkansas Catherine Taylor, the report would include information on Illinois Catherine Taylor.[9]

This is not the only occasion on which Catherine Taylor (of Arkansas) would suffer this kind of error. Soon after learning about the ChoicePoint mix-up, she found at least ten other companies who were providing inaccurate reports about her. One of those companies, Tenant Tracker, conducted a criminal background check for Taylor's application for federal housing assistance that was even worse than ChoicePoint's check. Tenant Tracker included the charges against Illinois Catherine Taylor and *also* included a separate set of charges against a person with a different name, Chantel Taylor (of Florida).[10]

Taylor's case is not special. Another background screening case involving a slightly different technology shows similar problems. It is common for background screeners to offer products that go beyond providing raw information on a subject and produce an algorithmically generated judgment in the form of a score or some other kind of recommendation. "CrimSAFE," which was developed by CoreLogic Rental Property Solutions, LLC (CoreLogic), is one such product.[11] CrimSAFE is

4   O'Neil, *Weapons of Math Destruction: How Big Data Increases Inequality and Threatens Democracy.*
5   Yu and Dietrich, "Broken Records: How Errors by Criminal Background Checking Companies Harm Workers and Businesses."
6   Yu and Dietrich.
7   Yu and Dietrich.
8   Yu and Dietrich, citing Deposition of Teresa Preg at 63–64.
9   Yu and Dietrich.
10 O'Neil, *Weapons of Math Destruction: How Big Data Increases Inequality and Threatens Democracy.*
11 Nelson, "Broken Records Redux: How Errors by Criminal Background Check Companies Continue to Harm Consumers Seeking Jobs and Housing."

used to screen tenants. CoreLogic markets it as an "automated tool" that "processes and interprets criminal records and notifies leasing staff when criminal records are found that do not meet the criteria you establish for your community."[12]

When a landlord or property manager uses CrimSAFE to screen a tenant, CoreLogic delivers a report that indicates whether CrimSAFE has turned up any disqualifying records.[13] But the report does not indicate what those allegedly disqualifying records are or any information about them (such as their dates, natures, or outcomes). To reiterate, the report only states *whether* disqualifying records have been found, not *what* they are. CoreLogic provides neither the purchaser nor the subject of the report any of the underlying details.[14]

Let us now look at a particular case involving CrimSAFE. In July 2015, Carmen Arroyo's son Mikhail suffered an accident that left him unable to speak, walk, or care for himself.[15] Carmen was Mikhail's primary caregiver, and she wanted to have Mikhail move in with her when he was discharged from treatment. For Mikhail to move into his mother's apartment, he had to be screened by her complex, and so the complex manager had CoreLogic screen Mikhail using CrimSAFE.[16]

CoreLogic returned a report to the apartment complex manager indicating that Mikhail was not fit for tenancy, based on his criminal record.[17] The report did not specify the date, nature, or outcome of any criminal charges on Mikhail's record. Further, Mikhail had never been convicted of a crime. Despite being unaware of the date, nature, or outcome of the alleged criminal conduct – and without taking into consideration the question of whether Mikhail was at that point even capable of committing the crimes he had been accused of – the manager adopted CoreLogic's conclusion and denied Mikhail tenancy.[18] Hence, Carmen Arroyo was unable to move her severely injured son into her apartment where she could provide the care he needed.

Taylor and the Arroyos have suffered serious harms. And knowing the causes of their misfortunes is of little help in reversing those misfortunes. Decisions based on faulty criminal background reports are rarely overturned after those reports are identified as faulty.[19] As the National Consumer Law Center puts it, "[Y]ou can't unring the bell."[20]

Taylor learned of the problems with her background as her tribulations unfolded. Carmen Arroyo learned of the problem only after being denied the key thing she needed to support her son, though she did eventually learn the reasons for Mikhail

---

[12]   Nelson. See also *Connecticut Fair Hous. Ctr. v. Corelogic Rental Prop. Sols., LLC*, 369 F. Supp. 3d at 367–368.
[13]   Nelson, "Broken Records Redux: How Errors by Criminal Background Check Companies Continue to Harm Consumers Seeking Jobs and Housing."
[14]   Nelson.
[15]   Nelson.
[16]   Nelson.
[17]   Nelson.
[18]   Nelson.
[19]   Yu and Dietrich, "Broken Records: How Errors by Criminal Background Checking Companies Harm Workers and Businesses."
[20]   Yu and Dietrich.

being denied tenancy. Many who are denied housing or employment through automated screening do not ever learn why.[21]

One reason people do not find out is that under US law, consumer reporting agencies (companies that provide reports on consumers, such as background checks) do not have to tell the subjects of background checks that they are being screened. The relevant statute in this context is the Fair Credit Reporting Act (FCRA), which requires either notification *or* the maintenance of strict procedures to ensure that the information is complete and up to date.[22] This leaves reporting agencies the legal option of leaving the subjects of background searches out of the loop.

Further, many companies that provide background checks maintain that they are not consumer reporting agencies at all. So they maintain that the FCRA does not apply to them. As a result, they neither notify subjects of background checks nor maintain the strict procedures necessary to ensure the information in their systems is complete and up to date. One of the companies responsible for disseminating false information about Catherine Taylor, PublicData.com, simply denies that it is a consumer reporting agency.[23] When Taylor notified PublicData.com of the errors it had made about her, they were unwilling to do anything to correct those errors.[24] This was a matter of company policy, which is explicit that it "will NOT modify records in any database upon notification of inaccuracies."[25]

FCRA also requires employers using background checks to disclose that they will be doing background checks and to notify a candidate if adverse action may be taken in response to a background check.[26] However, employers often do not comply with notice requirements.[27]

4.1.1 *Taylor, Arroyo, and the Reasonable Endorsement Test*

One way to understand Taylor's and the Arroyos' situations is in the terms we spelled out in Chapter 3, namely whether the background reporting systems are ones that people subject to them can reasonably endorse. Both Taylor and Arroyo have

---

[21] For further discussion of background check algorithms and lack of regulation and oversight, see Kirchner and Goldstein, "Access Denied."

[22] 91st United States Congress, An Act to amend the Federal Deposit Insurance Act to require insured banks to maintain certain records, to require that certain transactions in US currency be reported to the Department of the Treasury, and for other purposes; Yu and Dietrich, "Broken Records: How Errors by Criminal Background Checking Companies Harm Workers and Businesses."

[23] Yu and Dietrich, "Broken Records: How Errors by Criminal Background Checking Companies Harm Workers and Businesses."

[24] Yu and Dietrich.

[25] Yu and Dietrich.

[26] 91st United States Congress, An Act to amend the Federal Deposit Insurance Act to require insured banks to maintain certain records, to require that certain transactions in US currency be reported to the Department of the Treasury, and for other purposes.

[27] Yu and Dietrich, "Broken Records: How Errors by Criminal Background Checking Companies Harm Workers and Businesses."

experienced considerable material burdens based on algorithmically aided decision systems. Both were held to account by systems that are based on factors for which Taylor and Arroyo are not responsible, and the stakes in each case are high. Hence, one could make the case that the reporting systems are ones that individuals subject to them cannot reasonably endorse as comporting with their material interests. Such an analysis, while compelling, would not be complete.

Something has gone wrong in the Taylor and Arroyo cases beyond the fact that they were materially harmed. This separate consideration is an informational wrong. Taylor and Arroyo did not know (at least initially) what information in their files led to their background check results. Carmen Arroyo did not discover the basis for Mikhail's check until it was too late to do anything meaningful about it. Taylor lost opportunities before she discovered the reason. Further, in Taylor's case, several companies providing the misinformation would not fix their files upon learning that they had made a mistake. Finally, both Taylor and Arroyo were left in the dark as to how exactly the results came out the way they did; they were not afforded an understanding of the systems that cost them the opportunities they had sought.

Arroyo has an additional, distinctive complaint. When her son's application was rejected, the apartment complex did not know the details of the disqualifying conduct because CoreLogic did not supply them. This means that Arroyo was not given enough information about Mikhail's rejection to even contest the claim. Compare Arroyo's case with Taylor's. Taylor at least knew that her file had contained a false drug charge. Knowing what she had been accused of informed her that she had to prove what she had not done. Arroyo lacked even that.

We have mentioned that there is at least some regulation that attempts to address these sorts of issues and that there is plausibly a question as to whether CoreLogic complies with its legal obligations under FCRA (as stated earlier, companies do not always follow the notification requirement). Could full compliance with FCRA bring about practices that Taylor and Arroyo could reasonably endorse? Again, we think not. For one, FCRA does not specify when subjects are owed notification.[28] So the notification requirement can be met without actually affording data subjects the underlying thing that really matters: time to effectively respond to any false or misleading information in their files and an understanding of where they stand with respect to decisions made about them. These are the claims we address in the following section.

4.2 TWO ARGUMENTS FOR INFORMATIONAL RIGHTS

Surely the Taylor and Arroyo cases grate on our intuitions, both because of the harms resulting from their background checks and because of the fact that each was in the dark about those checks. Such intuitions, however, can only take us so far. We

---

[28] Yu and Dietrich.

need an argument to explain the wrongs adequately. Our argument is that persons' autonomy interests have a substantial informational component that is distinct from the material components we argued for in Chapter 3. Specifically, respecting the autonomy of persons subject to algorithmic decision systems requires ensuring that they have a degree of cognitive access to information about those systems.

Agency refers to action and the relationship between a person (or other entity) and actions that are in some sense attributable to that person. That relationship may be merely causal (as when a person hands over their wallet at gunpoint), it may be freely willed, it may be deliberately planned, or it may be something else. Hence, agency is broader than autonomy, for a person may be an agent but neither psychologically nor personally autonomous. However, agency is morally important in that persons have claims to exercise agency (and to have room to exercise agency) in light of their (capacity) autonomy. On the relationship between autonomy and agency, Oshana writes: "An autonomous person is an agent – one who directs or determines the course of her own life and who is positioned to assume the costs and the benefits of her choices."[29] We return to the relationship between agency and autonomy, and the relation of both to conceptions of freedom, in Chapters 5 and 6.

To make our case, we first need to distinguish two aspects of agency. At base, agency is the capacity (or effective exercise of the capacity) to act. And agents are beings with such capacity.[30] There is substantial philosophical controversy surrounding conceptions and metaphysics of agency (e.g., whether it is simply a causal relation between an actor and event, whether agency requires intentionality, and the degree to which nonhumans may be agents). We can leave many of those to the side so that we can focus on agency with respect to action and mental states.

The most familiar facet of agency is the ability to act physically in a relatively straightforward way, for example, taking a walk, preparing a meal, or writing an email. A more complex exercise of agency involves taking actions that institute a plan or that realize one's values (which is to say, exercise agency in such a way that doing so successfully instantiates one's psychological autonomy). Call this "practical agency." Exercising practical agency so that it is consistent with one's preferences and values requires a great deal of information and understanding. So, for example, if it is important to a person to build a successful career, then it is important for them to understand how their profession and organization function, how to get to work, how to actually perform tasks assigned, and so forth. And if that person's supervisor fails to make available information that is relevant to their job performance, the supervisor fails to respect the person's practical agency because doing so creates a barrier to the employee incorporating their values into an important facet of their life. Notice that this understanding of practical agency

---

[29]   Oshana, *Personal Autonomy in Society*, vii.
[30]   Sven Nyholm puts it: "Agency is a multidimensional concept that refers to the capacities and activities most centrally related to performing actions, making decisions, and taking responsibility for what we do." Nyholm, *Humans and Robots*, 31.

shares similar foundations to the substantive independence requirement of personal autonomy outlined in Chapter 2. Being denied important information about the practicalities of planning and living one's life undermines the degree to which one has substantive independence from others.

The importance of information to exercising agency does not solely depend on agents' abilities to use information to guide actions. A second aspect of agency is the ability to *understand* important facets of one's life. Call this "cognitive agency." The distinction between practical agency and cognitive agency tracks Pamela Hieronymi's view that ordinary intentional agency, in which we exercise control over actions – deciding to take a walk or deciding to prepare a meal – is distinct from "mental agency" (although we use "cognitive agency," the notion is the same). Mental agency, Hieronymi explains, is the capacity to exercise *evaluative* control over our mental states (e.g., our attitudes, beliefs, desires, and reactive responses). The difference between ordinary intentional agency and mental agency is the difference between an actor deciding "whether to do" (i.e., whether to take some action in the world beyond oneself) and the actor deciding "whether to believe." Hieronymi's view is that agents indeed exercise control – to some degree and within important limits – over how they respond mentally to their circumstances. The scope of one's evaluative control over one's mental states and the extent to which one can exercise it effectively are less important to our project than recognizing the domain of cognitive agency.[31]

Cognitive agency grounds moral claims in much the same way as practical agency. Respecting persons as autonomous requires that they be able to incorporate their sense of value into decisions about conducting their lives as a matter of practical agency. Similarly, respecting persons as autonomous requires that they be able to incorporate their sense of value into how they understand the world and their place in it. As Thomas Hill, Jr., has argued, deception is an affront to autonomy regardless of whether that deception changes how one acts because it prevents persons from properly interpreting the world; even a benevolent lie that spares another's feelings can be an affront because it thwarts that person's ability to understand their situation.[32] We can extend Hill's argument beyond active deception. Denying agents information relevant to important facets of their lives can circumvent their ability to understand their situation just as much as deceit.[33] In other words, deceit circumvents persons' epistemic competence and may render their desires and beliefs inauthentic.

One might question here whether practical and cognitive agency are distinctive issues for algorithmic systems. Strictly speaking, the answer is no, because – as we explained in Chapter 1 – many of the arguments we advance in this book are

---

[31] For a similar division of aspects of our agency and discussion, see Smith, "A Constitutivist Theory of Reasons: Its Promise and Parts."

[32] Hill, Jr., "Autonomy and Benevolent Lies."

[33] Rubel, "Privacy and the USA Patriot Act."

applicable to a wide range of social and technical systems. However, there are several reasons to think that practical and cognitive agency raise issues worth analyzing in the context of algorithmic systems. For one, humans are well adapted to understanding, regulating, and interacting with other humans and human systems, but the same is not true of artificial systems. Sven Nyholm has recently argued that there are a number of important moral issues that arise in the context of human–robot interactions precisely because humans tend to attribute human-like features to robots, when in fact humans have a poor grasp of what robots are like.[34] The same can be said for algorithmic systems. Related is that the informational component of algorithmic systems may be more pronounced than it is for bureaucratic or other primarily human decisions. We may understand the limited, often arbitrary nature of human decisions. But infirmities of algorithmic systems may be harder for us to reckon, and we may lack the kinds of heuristics we can employ to understand human decision-making.

The view so far is that information is important for practical and cognitive agency, and that claims to such information are grounded in autonomy. Surely, however, it isn't the case that respecting autonomy requires providing *any* sort of information that happens to advance practical and cognitive agency. After all, some information may be difficult to provide, may be only modestly useful in fostering agency, or may undermine other kinds of interests. Moreover, some information may be important for exercising practical and cognitive agency, but no one has an obligation to provide it. If one wants to feel better by cooking healthier meals, information about ingredients, recipes, and techniques is important in exercising practical agency over their eating habits. However, it is not clear that anyone thwarts another person's agency by failing to provide that information. What we need, then, is a set of criteria for determining if and when informational interests are substantial enough that persons have claims to that information on the grounds of practical or cognitive agency.

4.2.1 *Argument 1: Practical Agency*

The first set of criteria for determining whether persons have claims to information about automated decision systems echoes the criteria we advanced in Chapter 3. Specifically, whether an individual has a claim to information about some algorithmic decision system that affects their life will be function of that system's reliability, the degree to which it tracks actions for which they are responsible, and the stakes of the decision.

Assume for a moment that Taylor's problems happen in the context of a reporting system that people cannot reasonably reject on grounds of reliability, responsibility, and stakes. Taylor nonetheless has a claim based on *practical agency*. To effectively cope with the loss of her opportunities for employment and credit, she needs to

---

[34] Nyholm, *Humans and Robots*, 15–18.

understand the source of her negative reports. To that extent, Taylor's claims to information based on practical agency resemble those of anyone who is subject to credit reports and background checks. And, of course, Taylor did indeed have access to very general information about the nature of background checks and credit reporting. That might have been sufficient to understand that her background check was a factor in her lost opportunity.

We can capture this sense of Taylor's claims with what we will call the Principle of Informed Practical Agency.

> **Principle of Informed Practical Agency (PIPA):** One has a defeasible claim to information about decision systems affecting one's life where (a) that information advances practical agency, (b) it advances practical agency because one's practical agency has been restricted by the operations of that system, (c) the effects of the decision system bear heavily on significant facets of one's life, and (d) information about the decision system allows one to correct *or* mitigate its effects.

Surely this principle holds, but it cannot capture the degree to which Taylor's practical agency was thwarted by ChoicePoint and other reporting agencies. Rather, a key limitation on Taylor's practical agency is the fact that the reporting agencies systemically included misinformation in her reports. In other words, Taylor's claims to information are particularly weighty because the background checks at once purport to be grounded in information for which she is responsible (including criminal conduct) *and* the reports were systemically wrong. Hence, to capture the strength of Taylor's claims, we can add the following:

> **Strong Principle of Informed Practical Agency:** A person's claim to information based on the PIPA is stronger in case (e) the system purports to be based on factors for which a person is responsible and (f) the system has errors (even if not so frequent that they, on their own, make it unendorseable).

Knowing that the background checking system conflates the identities of people with similar names, knowing that her own record includes information pertaining to other people with criminal records, and knowing that the system relies on other background checking companies' databases and thus repopulates her profile with mistaken information can provide Taylor with tools to address those mistakes. That is, she can better address the wrongs that have been visited upon her by having information about the system that makes those wrongs possible. To be clear, a greater flow of information to Taylor does not make the mistakes and harms to her any less wrongful. Even if it is true that a system is otherwise justifiable, respecting autonomy demands support for practical agency so that people may address the infirmities of that system.

What is key for understanding claims based on practical agency is the distinction we make in Chapter 2 between local autonomy (the ability to make decisions about relatively narrow facets of one's life according to one's values and preferences) and global autonomy (the ability to structure larger facets of one's life according to one's values and preferences). In many contexts, respect for autonomy is local. Informed consent for undergoing a medical procedure, participating as a subject in research, agreeing to licensing agreements, and the like have to do with whether a person can act in a narrow set of circumstances. Our principles of practical agency, in contrast, concern aspects of autonomy that are comparatively global. One rarely (if ever) provides meaningful consent to having one's data collected, shared, and analyzed for the purposes of background checks and hence enjoys only a little local autonomy over that process.[35]

Individuals have little (if any) power to avoid credit and background checks and hence do not have global autonomy with respect to how they are treated. However, understanding how their information is used, whether there is incorrect information incorporated into background checks, and how that incorrect information precludes them from opportunities may be important (as in Taylor's case) in order to prevent lack of local autonomy from becoming relatively more global. That is, mitigating the effects of algorithmic systems may allow one to claw back a degree of global autonomy. And that ability to potentially exercise more global autonomy underwrites a moral claim to information.

The two principles of informed practical agency only tell us so much. They cannot, for example, tell us precisely what information one needs. In Taylor's case, practical agency requires understanding something about how the algorithmic systems deployed by ChoicePoint actually function, who uses them for what purposes, and how they absorb information (including false information) from a range of sources over which they exercise no control and minimal (if any) oversight. But other decision systems and other circumstances might require different kinds of information. The principles also cannot tell us exactly *who* needs to be afforded information. While the claim to information in this case is Taylor's, it may be that her advocate, representative, fiduciary, or someone else should be the one who actually receives or accesses the relevant information. Taylor, for instance, might have a claim that her employer learn about the infirmities in ChoicePoint and Tenant Tracker's algorithmic systems. The principles cannot tell us the conditions under which persons' claims may be overridden.

The principles discussed so far only address the epistemic side of practical agency. But Taylor is owed more than just information. We can see this by considering one of the most deeply troubling facets of her case: the reluctance that the data controllers who are involved have toward fixing her mistaken data. One effect of their reluctance is that it undercuts her ability to realize her values, something to which she has a legitimate claim. To capture this, we need – in addition to the principles of informed agency – a principle that lays bare agents' claim to control.

Principle of Informational Control (PIC): One has a defeasible claim to make corrections to false information fed into decision systems affecting one's life where

---

[35]   Solove, "Privacy Self-Management and the Consent Dilemma."

(a) one's practical agency has been restricted by the operations of that system, (b) the effects of the decision system bear heavily on significant facets of a person's life, and (c) correcting information about the decision system allows one to correct *or* mitigate its effects.

As before, we need a second principle specifying certain cases where this claim is stronger.

> **Strong Principle of Informational Control:** A person's claim to correct information based on the PIC is stronger in case the system purports to be based on factors for which a person is responsible.

These principles demand of the systems used in the Taylor's case that she not only is able to learn what information a system is based on, but that she is able to contest that information when it is inaccurate. The claim she has in this case is (just like the principles of informed practical agency) grounded in her agency, that is, her claim to decide what is valuable for herself and pursue those values so long as they are compatible with respect for the agency and autonomy of others.

Now, the principles of informed practical agency and informational control cannot tell us what a person's informational claims are in cases where they are unable to exercise practical agency. We consider that next.

4.2.2 *Argument 2: Cognitive Agency*

Cognitive agency can also ground a claim to information. Consider a difference between the Taylor and Arroyo cases. Or, more specifically, a difference between Taylor's case once she had experienced several iterations of problems with her background checks and Carmen Arroyo's case after she had been denied housing with her son. Taylor at some point became aware of a system that treats her poorly and for which she bears no responsibility. Arroyo, in contrast, was precluded from moving her son into her apartment for reasons she was unable to ascertain, the basis for the decision was an error, and the result was odious. Denying tenancy to Arroyo's son Mikhail is surely an injustice. But that wrong is compounded by its obscurity, which precluded Arroyo from interpreting it properly. That obscurity violates what we call the principle of informed cognitive agency.

> **Principle of Informed Cognitive Agency (PICA):** One has a defeasible claim to information about decision systems affecting significant facets of a person's life (i.e., where the stakes are high).

As before – and for familiar reasons – we will add a second, stronger principle.

> **Strong Principle of Informed Cognitive Agency:** A person's claim to information based on the PICA is stronger in case the system purports to be based on factors for which a person is responsible.

Arroyo is an agent capable of deciding for herself how to interpret the decision, and she deserves the opportunity to do so. Her ability to understand her situation is integral in her exercising cognitive agency, but the facts that are crucial for her understanding are that her ability to care for her son is a function of the vagaries of a background check system.

Cognitive agency is implicated in Arroyo's case in part because her predicament is based on a system that bears on an important facet of her life (being able to secure a place to live and care for one's child) and purports to be based on actions for which she is responsible (moving her son, who had been subject to criminal charges, into her apartment). The system, meanwhile, is such that it treats old charges as dispositive even though they were withdrawn and as remaining dispositive regardless of whether the person is at present in any position to commit such a crime at all. The reason such facts about the background check system are important is not because they will allow Arroyo to act more effectively to mitigate its effects. She was unable to act effectively when she was precluded from moving her son into her apartment. Rather, those facts are important for Arroyo to be able to act as a cognitive agent by exercising evaluative control over what to believe and how to interpret the incident.

Notice that the criteria for a claim to information based on cognitive agency appears less stringent than for practical agency. However, it does not follow that cognitive agency demands more information. Rather, cognitive agency demands *different kinds* of information. Because practical agency requires information sufficient to effectively act, it may require technical or operational information. Cognitive agency, in contrast, requires only enough information to exercise evaluative control. In the context of background checks, this might require only that one be able to learn that there is an algorithmic system underlying one's score, that the system has important limitations, that it is relatively unregulated (as, say, compared to FICO credit score reporting), and the factors that are salient in determining outcomes.[36]

Of course, that leaves us with the question of what information is necessary to exercise evaluative control. Our answer is whatever information is most morally salient, and the claim to information increases as the moral salience of information increases. So, in the case of Arroyo's background check, morally salient information includes the fact of an automated system conducting the check and the fact that her son's current condition did not enter the assessment. It is true that there might be other morally salient information. For example, we can imagine a case where the future business plans of CoreLogic are peripherally morally salient to a case; however, a claim to that information is comparatively weaker and hence more easily counterbalanced by claims CoreLogic has to privacy in its plans.

---

[36] See also the discussion of counterfactual explanations in Section 4.4.2.

4.2.3 *Objections and Democratic Agency*

There are several objections to the view we have set out so far that are important to address here. The first is that it proves too much. There are myriad and expanding ways that algorithmic systems affect our lives, and information about those systems bears upon our practical and cognitive agency in innumerable ways. Hence, the potential scope for individuals' claims to information is vast.

It is certainly true that the principles of informed practical agency and of informed cognitive agency are expansive. However, the principles have limitations that prevent them from justifying just any old claim to information. To begin, the principles of practical agency require that an algorithmic system restrict an individual's practical agency. How to determine what counts as a restriction, of course, is an interpretative difficulty. For example, does an algorithmic system that calculates one's insurance premiums restrict one's practical agency? What about a system that sets the prices one is quoted for airline tickets? Nonetheless, even on a capacious interpretation, it won't be just *any* algorithmic system that affects one's practical agency. Another significant hurdle is that the algorithmic system must affect significant facets of a person's life. Perhaps insurance rates and airline prices clear that hurdle, but it is close. Other systems, such as what political ads one is served in election season, what music is recommended on Spotify, or which route Google maps suggests to your destination, do not impose restrictions on one's practical agency.[37] The requirement that information allows a person to correct or mitigate the effects of an algorithmic system, therefore, is a substantial hurdle for the information to clear. Claims to information that have no such effect would fall under cognitive agency (and as we explain later, information that respects cognitive agency is less onerous to provide).

A second, related, objection is that many people – probably most people – will not wish to use information to exercise practical or cognitive agency. It is cheap, so to speak, to posit a claim to information, but it is pricey for those who deploy algorithmic systems, and the actual payoff is limited. This criticism is true so far as it goes, but it is compatible with the principles we've offered. For one, the fact (if it is) that many people will not exercise practical agency does not say much in itself about the autonomy interests one might have in a piece of information. This is much the same as in the case of medical procedures: Few people opt out of care, but information about care remains necessary to respecting their autonomy interests. Moreover, the objection speaks mostly to the *strength* of individuals' claims. All else equal, the higher the stakes involved, and the more information can advance practical agency,

---

[37] There is a related question about the baseline against which some action counts as a restriction. A direction-suggesting algorithm (e.g., Google Maps) in most cases increases one's practical agency by allowing one to find one's way quickly and easily. In the rare case that such a system sends one on a suboptimal route, we could interpret that as a restriction of practical agency against a baseline of an overall expansion of practical agency. The best understanding of the principles of practical agency, though, is against a baseline of no algorithmic system.

the stronger the claims. And the more unwieldy it is for entities using algorithmic systems to provide information, the greater are countervailing considerations.

A third objection is that the arguments prove too *little*. There is presumably a lot of information to which people have some sort of claim, but which does not advance individuals' practical or cognitive agency. To introduce this objection, let's start with a claim to information based on cognitive agency. Imagine a person (call him DJ) born into enormous advantage: wealth, social status, educational opportunities, political influence, and so forth. Suppose, however, that these advantages derive almost entirely from a range of execrable practices by DJ's family and associates: child labor, knowingly inducing addiction to substances that harm individuals and hollow out communities, environmental degradation, and so forth. DJ's parents, we might imagine, shield him from the sources of his advantage as he grows up, and when he reaches adulthood, he does not inherit any wealth (though of course he retains all the social, educational, and political benefits of his privileged upbringing). The degree to which his ignorance limits his practical agency is not clear, given his advantages.[38] However, on the view we outline in the previous section, DJ's parents certainly limit his cognitive agency by continuing to shield him from the sources of his advantage; he is precluded from understanding important facts about his life, as well as the chance to interpret his circumstances in light of those facts.

DJ is not the only person whose cognitive agency is a function of understanding the source of enormous wealth and advantage. Anyone who has an interest in their society's social, political, financial, and educational circumstances has some claim to understand how DJ's family's and associates' actions bear upon those circumstances. And that is true regardless of whether they are in any position to change things. In other words, it is the fact that DJ's family's actions have an important effect on the world that grounds others' claims to information, not strictly how those actions affect each individual.[39] But it is difficult to see how the importance of that information is a function of either practical or cognitive agency.

With that in mind, let's return to algorithmic systems. In path-breaking work, Latanya Sweeney examined Google's AdSense algorithm, which served different advertisements, and different *types* of advertisements, based on names of search subjects.[40] Sweeney's project began with the observation that some advertisements appearing on pages of Google search results for individuals' names suggested that the individuals had arrest records. The project revealed that the ads suggesting arrest records were more or less likely to appear based on whether a name used in the search was associated with a racial group. That is, advertisements suggesting arrest

---

[38]   To the extent that DJ wishes to steer his course on the basis of his family and social background and reconcile that with his values and beliefs, shielding him may indeed limit his practical agency.

[39]   There might be plausible rationales for continued secrecy, for example, privacy rights. But those are countervailing considerations to individuals' autonomy interests – in this case grounded in cognitive agency.

[40]   Sweeney, "Discrimination in Online Ad Delivery."

records appeared to show up more often in Google ads served for searches that included names associated with Black people than in ads served for searches that included names associated with White people. This result was independent of whether the searched names actually had arrest records.[41] While Sweeney did not have access to the precise mechanism by which the AdSense algorithm learned to serve on the basis of race, as she explains, a machine learning system could achieve this result over time simply by some number of people clicking on ads suggesting arrest records that show up when they use Google to search for Black-identifying names.[42]

But what does this have to do with agency and information? After all, as Sweeney points out, the ads themselves may be well attuned to their audiences, and it might be that search engines have a responsibility to ensure that their targeted advertising does not reflect race simply on the basis of harm prevention. But our argument here is different. It is that people have claims to information about some kinds of algorithmic systems even where their individual stake is relatively small, even where the system is reliable, and even where the system makes no assumptions about responsibility. So while people who are White have relatively little *personal* stake in the issue of search engine advertising serving ads that suggest arrest records disproportionately to searches using Black-identifying names, they have an interest based on agency nonetheless. Specifically, they have an interest in exercising agency over areas of democratic concern.

For the moment we will call this *democratic agency* and define it as access to information that is important for persons to perform the legitimating function that is necessary to underwrite democratic authority. We will take up this facet of agency and autonomy in more detail in Chapter 8. The gist of the idea is this. Whether a democratic state, set of policies, actions, regulatory regimes, and so forth are justifiable (or *legitimate*) is an important part in the function of the autonomy of its citizens. Exercising the autonomy necessary to serve this legitimating function requires certain kinds of information. Google of course is not a state actor, but it serves an outsized role in modern life, and understanding how that interacts with basic rights (including treatment of people based on race) is important for people to understand.

---

[41] Sweeney.

[42] Results from algorithmic systems that differ on the basis of race and ethnicity are rampant. Examples include predominantly sexualized images of women and girls returned for searches including "Black," "Latina," and "Asian," but not "White," searches for high-status positions returning images predominantly of White people (e.g., "CEO"), facial recognition and image enhancement technologies that are more accurate for images of White people than Black people, health risk assessment machine learning tools that underestimate Black patients' eligibility for care interventions, and more. Garvie and Frankle, "Facial-Recognition Software Might Have a Racial Bias Problem"; Noble, *Algorithms of Oppression*; Obermeyer et al., "Dissecting Racial Bias in an Algorithm Used to Manage the Health of Populations." While organizations often aim to rectify these disparities, those responses are often reactive. Moreover, knowledge of those processes is important to democratic agency and legitimation, the topic of Chapter 8.

Having examined moral claims to information about algorithmic systems based on cognitive and practical agency, it will be useful to consider some of the scholarship on *legal* rights to information regarding algorithmic systems. Specifically, there is considerable scholarly discussion regarding informational rights in the context of the European Union's General Data Protection Regulation (GDPR).[43] Much of that discussion concerns whether the GDPR contains a "right to explanation," and if so, what that right entails. There is, in contrast, much less scholarly attention devoted to what moral claims (if any) underwrite such a right. The claims to cognitive and practical agency that we have established can do that justificatory work. But before we get to that, we want to draw on some of the right to explanation scholarship for some important context and to make a few key distinctions.

The General Data Protection Regulation (GDPR) is the primary data protection and privacy regulation in European Union law. For our purposes, we wish to discuss four specific rights related to decision systems: *the right of access* (the right to access the information in one's file), *the right to rectification* (the right to correct misinformation in one's file), *the right to explanation* (the right to have automated decisions made about oneself explained), and *the right to object* (the right not to be subject to a significant decision based solely on automated processing).

4.3.1 *The Right of Access and the Right to Rectification*

Article 15 of the GDPR outlines the *right of access*, which is the (legal) right of data subjects who are citizens of the EU to obtain from data controllers confirmation as to whether or not their personal data are being processed, confirmation that personal data shared with third parties is safeguarded, and to obtain a copy of personal data undergoing processing.[44] Article 16 outlines the *right to rectification*, which is "the [legal] right to obtain from the controller without undue delay the rectification of inaccurate personal data concerning him or her."[45] These legal rights can be underwritten by the same ideas that support the principles of practical and cognitive agency and the principles of informational control, and we can use the principles to underwrite them.

Begin with rectification. Where one's data is being used to make decisions affecting significant facets of one's life – such that the system restricts one's agency – the principle of informational control tells us that there is a defeasible claim to correcting that information. Insofar as our data is being used to make decisions about

43 European Union, Regulation (EU) 2016/679 of the European Parliament and of the Council of April 27, 2016, on the protection of natural persons with regard to the processing of personal data and on the free movement of such data, and repealing Directive 95/46/EC (General Data Protection Regulation).

44 GDPR, art. 15.

45 GDPR, art. 16.

us that will affect us, the right to rectification stands as a law that enjoys justification from this principle.

With these ideas in place, we can also offer a justification for the right of access. To know whether a controller has incorrect information about us or information that we do not want them to have or share, we need to know what information they in fact have about us. And so, if the right to rectification is to have value, we need a right of access. We can further support the right of access by reflection of the principles of practical and cognitive agency: Often we will need to know what information is being collected in order to improve our prospects or to simply make sense of decisions being made about us.

4.3.2 *The Right to Explanation*

Consider next the right to have significant automated decisions explained. The Arroyo case brings out the importance of this right. To respond to their predicament, Carmen and Mikhail need to understand it. We begin with a general discussion of the right.

Sandra Wachter, Brent Mittelstadt, and Luciano Floridi introduce two helpful distinctions for thinking about the right to explanation.[46] The first of these distinctions disambiguates *what* is being explained. A *system-functional* explanation explains "the logic, significance, envisaged consequences and general functionality of an automated decision-making system."[47] In contrast, a *specific* decision explains "the rationale, reasons, and individual circumstances of a specific automated decision."[48] Note that if a system is deterministic a complete description of system functionality might entail an explanation of a specific decision. So, in at least some cases, the distinction between the two kinds of explanation is not exclusive.[49]

The second distinction disambiguates *when* the explanation is being given. An *ex ante* explanation occurs prior to when a decision has been made. An *ex post* explanation occurs *after* the decision has been made. Wachter et al. claim that ex ante explanations of specific decisions are not possible; a decision must be made before it is explained. As Andrew Selbst and Julia Powles point out, in the special case of a complete system-level explanation of a deterministic system, decisions are predictable and thus, ex ante explanations of those decisions are at least sometimes possible.[50]

Rather than stake a claim in this dispute, we will take a pragmatic approach. We can say all we need to say about the right to explanation by discussing the three

---

[46] Wachter, Mittelstadt, and Floridi, "Why a Right to Explanation of Automated Decision-Making Does Not Exist in the General Data Protection Regulation."
[47] Wachter, Mittelstadt, and Floridi, 11.
[48] Wachter, Mittelstadt, and Floridi.
[49] Selbst and Powles, "Meaningful Information and the Right to Explanation."
[50] Selbst and Powles.

categories that Wachter et al. admit of (i.e., ex ante system functional, ex post system functional, and ex post specific). If a subject has a right to an ex ante explanation of a specific decision, the arguments for such explanations will follow naturally from our arguments for specific explanations; the only issue that the right will turn on is whether such explanations are possible – an issue that we are not taking a stand on here. We think that, morally, the right to explanation could encompass any of the possibilities Wachter et al. outline. So we will understand the right to explanation as the right to explanations about ex post specific decisions, ex ante system function, or ex post system function.

Let us then work through some ideas about what our account says about the right to explanation.

Ex ante system-functional explanations: Subjects of decisions that have not yet been made often have good reason to know how decisions of that sort will be made in the future. The principles of practical agency delineate some of these conditions.

One way to see this is to return to Catherine Taylor. She now knows that because of her common name, systems that perform quick, automated searches are prone to making mistakes about her. Based on this, she has an interest in knowing how a given system might produce a report on her. If she knows a system is one that might produce a false report about her, she can save herself – and the purchaser of the report – quite a bit of trouble, either by insisting to ChoicePoint that more careful methods are used or by preempting the erroneous results by providing an independent, high-quality counter-report of her own.

Ex post system-functional explanations: Subjects of decisions that have been made often have good reason to know how those decisions of that sort were made. These claims can be grounded in practical or cognitive agency.

Consider Taylor again. If Taylor is denied a job and she learns that an automated background check was involved, she has reason to suspect that the automated check might have erroneously cost her the opportunity. For her, simply knowing the most general contours of how a system works is powerful information. This alone may be enough to allow her to get her application reviewed again, and she could not reasonably endorse a system where she is denied this minimal amount of information. But even if she cannot accomplish this – that is, even if the principle of informed practical agency is not activated because her situation is hopeless – she still has a claim, via the principle of informed cognitive agency, to gain an understanding of her situation.

Specific explanations: Finally, subjects of decisions often have good reason to know how those specific decisions were made. These claims can be grounded in practical agency.

Recall Arroyo's denial of housing. Something is wrong with Arroyo's report, yet his mother does not (and cannot) know what it is. This leaves her especially vulnerable in defending her son, since she does not know what to defend him against. As the principle of informed practical agency demands, subjects of decisions that have been made should at least know enough about those decisions to respond to them if they have been made in error.

We want to pause briefly to discuss a recent proposal pertaining to *how* specific explanations might be given, namely via *counterfactual explanations*, which have been detailed extensively in a recent article by Wachter et al. An example of a counterfactual explanation, applied to the Arroyo case, is as follows

> "You have been denied tenancy because you have one criminal charge in your history. Were you to have had zero charges, you would have been granted tenancy."

Generalizing a bit, counterfactual explanations are explanations of the form "W occurred because X; Were Y to have been the case (instead of X), Z would have occurred (instead of W)," where W and Z are decisions and X and Y are two "close" states of affairs, identifying a small – perhaps the smallest – change that would have yielded Z as opposed to W.

Counterfactual explanations have several virtues qua specific explanations. For one, they are easy to understand.[51] They are efficient in communicating the important information users need to know to make sense of and respond to decisions that bear on them. Thus, such explanations are often sufficient for giving subjects what they are informationally owed. Another virtue is that they are relatively easy to compute, and so producing them at scale is not onerous: Algorithms can be written for identifying the smallest change that would have made a difference with respect to the decision.[52] Further, they communicate needed information without compromising the algorithms that underlie the decisions they explain; they offer explanations, as Wachter et al. put it, "without opening the black box."[53]

Counterfactual explanations can serve as a useful tool for delivering what is demanded by the cognitive and practical agency of data subjects without running roughshod over the interests of their data controllers. Of course, such explanations will not *always* meet these demands; they will only work in contexts where specific explanations are called for. And even then, they might not *always* offer everything an agent needs; for instance, one could imagine counterfactual explanations that are too theory laden to be useful or that are only informative against knowledge of myriad background conditions. Nevertheless, this style of explanation *can* be a very useful tool in meeting agents' needs. Thus, they serve as a good example of a realistic tool for giving data subjects what they are informationally owed.

Let's take stock of what our account has to say about the right to an explanation. We take it that the right to explanation is a defeasible right to meaningful ex post, ex ante, system-level, and specific explanations of significant, automated decisions. Using our cases and principles, we have demonstrated how our account can

---

[51]   Wachter, Mittelstadt, and Russell, "Counterfactual Explanations without Opening the Black Box: Automated Decisions and the GDPR."

[52]   Wachter, Mittelstadt, and Russell, 15–16.

[53]   Wachter, Mittelstadt, and Russell.

underwrite a claim: As autonomous beings, we need to understand significant events in our lives in order to navigate the world so as to pursue our values; as autonomous beings, we have a duty to support each other's autonomy; so, if we are in control of information pertaining to significant decisions affecting someone's life, we often owe it to them to make that information available.

4.3.3 *The Right to Object*

In addition to rights of access and rights to rectification and explanation, the GDPR outlines the *right to object*, "the right not to be subject to a [significant] decision based solely on automated processing."[54] As stated earlier, our interest is in understanding whether there is a moral right to object. However, examining a version of a legal right can help us make sense of moral claims. There are two key features of the right to object as it is stated in the GDPR.

Note first that the right is vague. Specifically, the "based solely" condition, as well as the notion of significance, admits of vagueness. As Kaminski notes,

> One could interpret "based solely" to mean that any human involvement, even rubber-stamping, takes an algorithmic decision out of Article 22's scope; or one could take a broader reading to cover all algorithmically-based decisions that occur without meaningful human involvement. Similarly, one could take a narrow reading of "[. . .] significant" effects to leave out, for example, behavioral advertising and price discrimination; or one could take a broader reading and include behavioral inferences and their use.[55]

We will not focus too heavily on issues of vagueness here. However, it is important to note that the limiting condition of the right – as well as some of its content – is vague.

Second, the right to object is ambiguous.[56] It could be understood broadly: as a broad prohibition on decisions that are based solely on automated processing. The same right could also be understood narrowly: as an individual right that data subjects can summon for the purposes of rejecting a particular algorithmic decision.[57] Here, we won't be interested in adjudicating which way to read Article 22 of the GDPR, because we regard both readings as supported by the same considerations that we cite in favor of the right to explanation.

Human oversight of an automated decision system requires that the system be functionally intelligible to at least some humans (perhaps upon acquiring the relevant expertise). So, in a world where the broad reading is observed, each significant automated decision is intelligible to some human overseers. What this means, in

---

[54] GDPR, art. 22.
[55] Kaminski, "The Right to Explanation, Explained."
[56] Kaminski; Mendoza and Bygrave, "The Right Not to Be Subject to Automated Decisions Based on Profiling."
[57] The terminology of broadness and narrowness is from Kaminski, "The Right to Explanation, Explained."

turn, is that the reasons for its decisions could be meaningfully explained to data subjects (or at the very least to their surrogates). The significance of this, from our point of view, is that it would help to secure the right to explanation, as it would require systems to be designed so that they are intelligible to humans. Further, in cases where a data subject cannot request an explanation, it serves to assure them that significant automated decisions made about them make sense. Similarly, in a world where the narrow right is observed, systems are designed to be intelligible so that, *were* their decisions meaningfully checked by a human decision maker, they *would* make sense. This, of course, means that they are designed so that they do make sense to humans (even if those humans are experts). Moreover, like the broad reading, it also affords data subjects the opportunity to have decisions checked when they themselves cannot check them (perhaps for reasons of trade secrecy). However, the narrow right might sound more plausible than the broad right because it means fewer human decision makers would have to be employed to satisfy it, allowing systems to operate more efficiently.

Now, unlike the previously mentioned rights, the right to object – particularly in its broad formulation – might sound onerous. However, abiding the rights to access, rectification, and explanation already requires that data controllers provide data subjects meaningful human oversight of decisions made about them, so perhaps the broad right isn't as implausible as it may first seem. Further, the broad right has the advantage that it makes the exercise of the right to object less costly to those individuals who would otherwise have to explicitly exercise it. We can imagine data subjects worrying that they will face prejudice for exercising the right; for instance, a job applicant might worry that if she exercised the right, the potential employer will think that she is going to cause trouble.

What does the right to object add, then? Importantly, there are systems where inferences must be kept secret – either to prevent subjects from gaming it or because the system is simply too complicated – in these circumstances, the right to object plays the important role of ensuring that surrogates of data subjects understand whether high-stakes decisions made about those subjects make sense.

4.4 POLESTAR CASES

We can finally return to the cases that provide our through line for the book.

4.4.1 *Loomis*

One of Loomis's primary complaints in his appeal is that COMPAS is proprietary and hence not transparent. Specifically, he argued that this violated his right to have his sentence based on accurate information. He bases the argument in part on *Gardner v. Florida.*[58] In *Gardner*, a trial court failed to disclose a presentence

---

[58] *Gardner v. Florida*, 430 U.S. 349 (1977).

investigation report that formed part of the basis for a death sentence. The U.S. Supreme Court determined that the failure to disclose the report meant that there was key information underwriting the sentence which the defendant "had no opportunity to deny or explain." Loomis argued that the same is true of the report in his case. Because the COMPAS assessment is proprietary[59] and because there had not been a validation study of COMPAS's accuracy in the state of Wisconsin (other states had conducted validation studies of the same system), Loomis argued that he was denied the opportunity to refute or explain his results.

The Wisconsin Supreme Court disagreed. It noted that Northpointe's *Practitioner's Guide to COMPAS Core* explained the information used to generate scores, and that most of the information is either static (e.g., criminal history) or in Loomis's control (e.g., questionnaire responses). Hence, the court reasoned, Loomis had sufficient information and the ability to assess the information forming the basis for the report, despite the algorithm itself being proprietary.[60] As for Loomis's arguments that COMPAS was not validated in Wisconsin and that other studies criticize similar assessment tools, the court reasoned that cautionary notice was sufficient. Rather than prohibiting use of COMPAS outright, the court determined that presentence investigation reports using COMPAS should include some warnings about its limitations.

According to the principles of practical agency, Loomis has a defeasible claim to information about COMPAS if (a) information about COMPAS advances his practical agency, (b) COMPAS has restricted his practical agency, (c) COMPAS's effects bear heavily on significant aspects of Loomis's life, and (d) information about COMPAS allows Loomis to correct or mitigate the effects of COMPAS. If there is such a claim, it is strengthened (e) if COMPAS purports to be based on factors for which Loomis is responsible and (f) if COMPAS has errors.

It is certainly plausible that COMPAS limits Loomis's practical agency insofar as it had some role in his sentence. Loomis faced a number of decisions about what to do in response to his sentence. One is whether he should appeal and on what grounds. Another is whether he should try to generate public support for curtailing the use of COMPAS. For Loomis, settling these questions about what to do depends on knowing how COMPAS generated his risk score. And there is much he doesn't know. He doesn't know whether the information fed into COMPAS was accurate. He doesn't know whether, and in what sense, COMPAS is fair. And he doesn't know whether the algorithm was properly applied to his case. That lack of information curtails his practical agency. The length of his criminal sentence certainly involved a significant facet of his life, and it is at least plausible that greater information would allow him to mitigate COMPAS's effects. The strength of his claims increases in

---

[59] *Wisconsin v. Loomis*, 881 N.W.2d paragraph 51.
[60] *Wisconsin v. Loomis*, 881 N.W.2d paragraphs 54–56.

light of the fact that it is best understood as being based on factors for which he is responsible, viz., his propensity to reoffend.

So Loomis has a prima facie and defeasible claim to information about COMPAS. But that leaves open just what kind of information he has a claim to, what that claim entails, and whether there are countervailing considerations that supersede Loomis's claim. It would seem that Loomis needs to know that the data fed into COMPAS was accurate, evidence that COMPAS is in fact valid for his case, and, finally, some kind of explanation – perhaps in the form of a counterfactual explanation – that makes clear why he received the score that he did. Such information would advance Loomis's practical agency, either by giving him the information needed to put together an appeal *or* by demonstrating to his satisfaction that his COMPAS score was valid, allowing him to focus his efforts elsewhere.

Independent of the concerns based on practical agency, Loomis has a claim to information based on cognitive agency. Both factors in the principle of informed cognitive agency are present. COMPAS purports to be based on factors for which Loomis is responsible, and the stakes are high. Being imprisoned is among the most momentous things that may happen to a person and understanding the basis of a prison sentence is essential to one's agency. That extends beyond the factors that matter in determining one's sentence to include whether the process by which one is sentenced is fair. And as we have argued, agents have a claim to understand important facets of their situations. Hence, Loomis has a claim based on cognitive agency to better understand the grounds for his imprisonment.

While Loomis plausibly has claims to information based on both practical and cognitive agency, there are differences in what those claims entail. While practical agency will only underwrite information that can be used in advancing Loomis's case – and hence, mostly supports information for Loomis's legal representation – cognitive agency underwrites the provision of certain pieces of information to Loomis himself. It would involve providing him information about the fact that a proprietary algorithm is involved in the system, information about how well the system predicts reoffense, and information about the specific factors that led to Loomis's sentence. There is no reason to think that it would advance Loomis's cognitive agency to provide him with specific information about how COMPAS functions.

Moreover, the court did, in fact, respect Loomis's cognitive agency. The Wisconsin Supreme Court upheld the circuit court's decision in substantial part because the circuit court articulated its own reasons for sentencing Loomis as it did. In other words, it provided an account sufficient for Loomis to exercise evaluative control with respect to his reactive attitudes toward the decision and sentence.

4.4.2 *Wagner and Houston Schools*

The principles of informed practical agency and informed cognitive agency also aid our understanding of the K-12 teacher cases, especially *Houston Schools*. Recall that

Houston Schools uses a VAM called EVAAS, which produces each individual teacher's score by referencing data about all teachers.[61] This practice makes EVAAS's scores highly interdependent. Recall also that Houston Schools was frank in admitting that it would not change faulty information because it would require a costly reanalysis for the whole school district and the potential to change all teachers' scores. This was all despite warnings (as we note in Chapters 1 and 3) that value-added models have substantial standard errors.[62] So EVAAS's scores are extremely fragile, produced without independent oversight, and cannot be corroborated by teachers (or the district or, recall, an expert who was unable to replicate them).

It seems clear enough that information about EVAAS is vital for teachers to exercise practical agency. Certainly, it is relevant to several significant aspects of teachers' lives. For teachers who were fired or did not have their contracts renewed based on low performance, gaining an understanding of the system advances their practical agency in a couple of ways. It gives them (and their union leaders and lawyers) the bases of either an appeal (whether in court or to the public) of the firings or an appeal of the system altogether. It also gives teachers who are finding employment in other schools some context that could help them convince administrators that their departure from the Houston Independent School District (HISD) was not evidence of poor teaching. That is, affected teachers have a (defeasible) claim to information about EVAAS's functioning, because it could allow them to correct or mitigate the system's effects. Their claim is strengthened because EVAAS purports to be based on factors for which the teachers are responsible (viz., their work in the classroom), and yet (as HISD admits) EVAAS has errors. These claims also underwrite teachers' claims to informational control, specifically their claim to have any inaccuracies reflected in their scores corrected.

The fact that EVAAS affects such important parts of teachers' lives and purports to be based on factors for which they are responsible also gives them a claim to information based on cognitive agency. As in the COMPAS case, the *type* of information necessary for teachers to exercise evaluative control – that is, to assess their treatment at the hands of their school system – may be different from the information necessary for them to exercise practical agency. Cognitive agency may only require higher-level information about how EVAAS works, a frank assessment of its flaws, and a candid accounting of Houston Schools' unwillingness to incur the cost of correcting errors rather than the more detailed information necessary for teachers to correct errors. To put a bookend on the importance of cognitive agency, we will return to an exemplary teacher's public reaction to the VAM used by DC Schools: "I am baffled how I teach every day with talent, commitment, and vigor to

[61]   *Houston Fed of Teachers, Local 2415 v. Houston Ind Sch Dist*, 251 F. Supp. 3d.
[62]   American Statistical Association, "ASA Statement on Using Value-Added Models for Educational Assessment: Executive Summary," 7; Morganstein and Wasserstein, "ASA Statement on Value-Added Models."

surpass the standards set for me, yet this is not reflected in my final IMPACT score."[63] This would seem to be an appeal to exercise evaluative control.

4.5 CONCLUSION

In Chapter 2, we argued that autonomy ranges beyond the ability to make choices. Properly understood, self-governance includes competence and authenticity and sub-stantive independence, and it demands acting in accord with others. Chapter 3 exam-ined the requirements for respecting persons' autonomy related to their material conditions. In the present chapter, we explain the informational requirements of auton-omy. Specifically, we argued that autonomy demands respect for both practical and cognitive agency. We articulated several principles of practical and cognitive agency and argued that those principles could underwrite key provisions in the GDPR. Finally, we explained that those principles entail that the subjects of our polestar cases deserve substantial information regarding the algorithmic systems to which they are subject.

Recall, though, that the organizing thesis of the book is that understanding the moral salience of algorithmic systems requires understanding how such systems relate to autonomy. That involves more than respecting the autonomy of persons who are, at the moment, autonomous. It also involves securing the conditions under which they can actually exercise autonomy. That's the issue we turn to in next two chapters.

---

[63] Strauss, "D.C. Teacher Tells Chancellor Why IMPACT Evaluation Is Unfair."

PART III

Ensuring the Conditions of Agency

5

Freedom, Agency, and Information Technology

So far, we have given some arguments about what we owe to each other, and we have supported these arguments in part by relating them to some of the ways algorithmic systems and technologies can conflict with our autonomy. One of our key tasks has been to examine the various complaints and criticisms of algorithms and other information technologies in terms of *wrongs* rather than harms. To this end, we have argued that these systems can create circumstances people cannot reasonably endorse and they can preclude people from information they are owed.

In Chapter 4, we discussed two forms of agency that go beyond the mere manifestation of intentional action and its natural causes.[1] One sort is practical agency, which involves making decisions, formulating plans, and executing strategies. The other is cognitive agency, which involves exercising evaluative control over our mental attitudes, in the form of personal consideration of our beliefs and values.[2] Autonomy, meanwhile, involves something above mere agency: self-government. Our view is that autonomy requires both procedural independence (requiring that an agent be competent and that their beliefs, preferences, desires, and values be authentic) and substantive independence (requiring that an agent be supported by their social and relational circumstances).

Agency is a broader concept than autonomy, in the sense that it is possible for one to act, decide, or plan without those actions or attitudes exemplifying the relevant sorts of self-government. However, we will not take a strong position here on the metaphysical conditions distinguishing autonomy from agency, because our focus is on both cases of diminished agency and diminished autonomy. Our argument in this chapter is that both sorts of case result in a shortfall of freedom, properly understood.

We argue in Section 5.1 that freedom has two fundamental conditions: that persons be undominated by others and that they have an adequate degree of autonomy and agency. However, we will argue in Section 5.2 that algorithmic systems can threaten

---

[1] The standard theory of agency holds that the agency involves intentional action and its causes. For the classic versions of this sort of account, see Davidson, *Essays on Actions and Events*; Goldman, *Theory of Human Action*; Bratman, *Intention, Plans, and Practical Reason*.
[2] See also Hieronymi, "Two Kinds of Agency."

both the domination-based and the agency-based requirements, either by facilitating domination or by exploiting weaknesses in human agency. We will explicate these types of threats as three sorts of challenges to freedom. The first we discuss are "affective challenges," which involve the role of affective, nonconscious processes (such as fear, anger, and addiction) in human behavior and decision-making. These processes, we argue, interfere with our procedural independence, thereby threatening persons' freedom by undermining autonomy. The second type of challenge is what we call "deliberative challenges." These involve strategic exploitation of the fact that human cognition and decision-making are limited. These challenges also relate to our procedural independence, but they do not so much interfere with it as they exploit its natural limits. A third sort of challenge, which we describe as "social challenges," involves toxic social and relational environments. These threaten our substantive independence and thus, our freedom. In Section 5.3, we sketch a policy agenda aimed at combating these challenges and promoting the conditions of freedom.

We have two main goals in this chapter. One is to extend our analysis to the affective, deliberative, and social challenges that algorithmic systems pose. The other is to relate our overall project to the notion of freedom. Our understandings of freedom and autonomy are closely linked, and it would be possible to consider affective, deliberative, and social challenges of algorithmic systems solely in light of autonomy. However, such an analysis would fail to connect algorithmic systems to a good that is on many views basic. Exploring these issues from the vantage point of freedom allows us to make that connection. In Chapter 6 we will draw on this conception in our discussion of epistemic paternalism.

5.1 FREEDOM AS UNDOMINATED SELF-GOVERNMENT

5.1.1 *The Forms of Freedom*

The concept of freedom is often discussed in terms of one's "negative" freedom; that is, in terms of noninterference, nonaggression, noncoercion, or in general, the absence of external constraints on one's ability to act.[3] A person enjoys negative freedom when they are not being actively interfered with or coerced. Negative freedom is often considered primary, for a couple of reasons. One is that limitations on negative freedom are intuitively obvious; if one is prohibited by law or physically prevented from taking an action, their freedom has been restricted. Another reason is that some shortfalls in negative freedom are especially restrictive, which makes negative freedom appear to be the most important form of freedom. For instance, if one has been kidnapped or forced at gunpoint to hand over one's possessions, one's current political freedoms are of secondary concern.

---

[3] On noninterference, see Berlin, "Two Concepts of Liberty"; Butt, *Rectifying International Injustice: Principles of Compensation and Restitution between Nations*; Rothbard, *For a New Liberty: The Libertarian Manifesto*; Hayek, *The Constitution of Liberty*.

Yet, looking beyond the obvious importance of negative freedom to human life, the value of noninterference does not swamp the value of all other forms of freedom one could value. Freedom must be understood as in two ways extending beyond the mere absence of interference. To see why, consider two cases. First, consider the case of a woman living under an oppressive political regime in which she is permitted to vote only with her husband's permission. Supposing that her husband does, in fact, allow her to vote, she would have negative freedom. After all, no one has coerced her, interfered with her, or physically prevented her from voting. But her husband could have chosen otherwise and could have interfered. Depending on someone else's approval to vote is a deeper sort of unfreedom underneath her thin, negative freedom to vote. Second, consider the case of a person who is not dependent on the approval of someone else to vote, but who *does* require a wheelchair for mobility. If there are stairs that they must navigate to access their polling place, and there are no ramps or alternative means of casting a ballot, they are not free to vote, their ample negative freedom (insofar as no one coerces, prohibits, or physically blocks access to voting) aside. They are unfree because they cannot effectively do what they wish to do, namely vote.[4]

One conception of freedom that extends beyond negative freedom, corresponding to the case of the first woman, is called "republican freedom." Beyond mere noninterference, republican freedom requires non-domination, which is to say, the absence of arbitrary power or domination. On this conception, even the possibility of interference counts as unfreedom. Noninterference that occurs at the whim of a benevolent ruler does not count as genuine freedom. For republican freedom, it is not enough that there is no interference. Rather, as Philip Pettit puts it, interference must be "robustly" absent, meaning that interference is "absent over variations in how far others are hostile or friendly."[5] For the first woman to be free, her husband's benevolence cannot play a role in her ability to vote; she must be able to do it without needing his permission.

The republican theory of freedom does not emphasize that the fullest sort of freedom requires having not just choices, but autonomous choices. Pettit, for instance, argues that his account "does not require that resources [...] must be present over variations in your personal skills, the natural environment, or the structure of society," because "[i]n order to choose freely between the options in a certain choice, it is enough that you actually have such assets available."[6] The republican theory holds people to account for the choices they make, no matter why they made them or what challenges they faced leading up to the choice. Yet, if the

---

[4] One might object here that having stairs, while lacking ramp access or alternative means of voting, is indeed a way in which one is physically prevented from voting. That is true, and the line between negative freedom (lack of external constraints on one's actions) and positive freedom (the ability to carry out one's intentions) is blurry. See Cohen, "Freedom and Money."

[5] Pettit, *Just Freedom*, 50.

[6] Pettit, 50.

affective and deliberative challenges to human agency are real, it must be in part through their influence on our choices. To fully understand our freedom, we must take into consideration not just our choices, but how those choices get made.

Another conception of freedom that is distinct from negative freedom, corresponding to the case of the second voter, is "positive freedom." It involves not only the absence of external constraints, but the ability to effectively carry out one's interests. While negative freedom is defined in terms of (and, to some extent, presupposes) the capacity for autonomy,[7] positive freedom requires the ongoing exercise of self-government. Republican freedom, moreover, cannot by itself guarantee positive freedom. This is because the republican account is primarily oriented toward the alleviation of subjugation, or "defenseless susceptibility to interference,"[8] rather than to the positive development of persons' talents and capacities. But this glosses over the fact that one might be undominated by all others but nonetheless have interests that one cannot pursue because they lack the capacities to effectuate their desires or realize their interests. For the second voter to be free, they must not only be undominated by all others, their polling station must also have the relevant accessibilities, allowing them to actually vote rather than merely have the (empty) right to do so.

"Unfreedom" in the positive sense can be tricky to diagnose or discern, in part because it can become fully internalized. Consider, for instance, a third person who has been raised in an insular religious community. Suppose that in this community, people adhere to a narrow set of religious precepts, their access to information is restricted by their religious leaders, and their social roles are defined in terms of highly gendered categories. By the time the person reaches adulthood, they are likely to have internalized their community's standards about the nature of personhood and about what counts as an adequate range of options. Unlike the first woman, this person is not externally constrained, in the sense that someone could prevent them from acting according to their desires, and unlike the second person, their choices have not been undermined or frustrated by inaccessibility. Indeed, they may even possess all the material resources necessary to exit the community. Yet there is an important sense in which they lack freedom, owing to how their space of possibility has been circumscribed; their agency itself has been short-circuited in a way that they cannot repair or (possibly) even recognize. To be clear, this is a generic, hypothetical example. Gesturing at this kind of example does not justify any inference about the authenticity or "false consciousness" in any real cases. Rather, it is an example to show that freedom is not reducible to persons' abilities to act on their preferences, as preferences can be formed in response to oppressive conditions, which are themselves antithetical to freedom.

It's worth pausing to explain this a bit more. We have distinguished negative freedom (freedom from external constraints) and positive freedom (ability to

---

[7] Raz, *The Morality of Freedom*; Feinberg, "Autonomy."
[8] Pettit, "Freedom as Antipower," 577.

effectively carry out one's interests). One might argue that these apparently distinct facets of freedom are reducible to a single conception. Gerald MacCallum, for example, argues that we can reconcile negative and positive freedom under a single, tripartite conception of freedom: between (1) a person, (2) their goals (their "doings" or "becomings"), and (3) the relevant constraints.[9] From this perspective, understanding freedom as primarily being about external constraints or as primarily being about individuals' effective capacity to act is a mistake. Rather, what matters is a person, some action they wish to take or way they would like to live, and whether there are constraints on the person's ability to take the action or to live the way they would like. Hence, a person driven by an addiction might be free of external constraints, but unfree insofar as their addiction prevents them from acting or living in a way that comports with their higher-order desires.

But even a conception that collapses positive and negative freedom cannot adequately explain our third case. The problem there is that despite the fact that there are no external constraints and despite the fact that the person is able to act upon their values, it is odd to say that they are free tout court. Being raised in oppressive circumstances may preclude them from developing reasonable sets of values and preferences. The limitations of freedom in this case are, as Christman puts it, to their "quality of agency." That is, a person who has had unreasonable constraints on their ability to develop their own sense of value has diminished "effectiveness as an agent."[10] More is needed to secure their effectiveness as an agent than the mere absence of external constraints and ability to act upon their preferences. Quality of agency requires that their beliefs and desires be both authentic and competently acquired for an adequate range of options. It also requires social and political structures that support those beliefs and desires and that one has sufficient affordances to act on those beliefs and desires. This quality of agency view can explain how challenges to authenticity, such as in cases of severe addiction, limit freedom. For instance, we might imagine a person who is driven by addiction but who also has enough resources and opportunities to sustain their habits in perpetuity.[11] Such a person lacks freedom in the fullest sense because their addiction limits their efficacy as an agent.

Our view of freedom aims to capture both freedom as quality of agency (which itself encompasses both negative and positive freedom) and non-domination (which encompasses republican freedom). In this sense it is as ecumenical as our conception of autonomy from Chapter 2. Specifically, we recognize both non-domination and autonomy as vital facets of freedom.[12] An agent's freedom requires what we will call "ecological non-domination." It is ecological in the sense that one's freedom encompasses both facts

9   MacCallum, "Negative and Positive Freedom."
10 Christman, "Saving Positive Freedom," 80.
11 Eric Clapton, for instance, has estimated that during the worst periods of his addiction, he was spending $16,000 per week. See "A Life in Twelve Bars."
12 To some degree we are taking our cue from Anderson, *Private Government*, chapter 2.

about oneself (quality of one's agency) and their environment (absence of external constraints and non-domination). One is not free without both.

Notice that it is possible to enjoy some aspects of autonomy without full republican freedom (or even negative freedom). Consider, for instance, the "Russian oligarchs"; the group of wealthy Russian kleptocrats who rapidly acquired enormous wealth in the wake of post-Soviet privatization. They enjoy unfettered positive freedom, in that they have at their disposal the means to purchase world-class football clubs,[13] record-breaking superyachts,[14] and former royal estates.[15] Yet, at the same time, their enjoyment of noninterference is not all that robust: Their personal safety depends on remaining in good favor with the regime. Mikhail Khodorkovsky's oil company (Yukos) came to control a sizable fraction of Russia's oil supply. Yet when Khodorkovsky engaged in a power struggle with the government, he was imprisoned for nearly a decade over trumped-up fraud charges. Similarly, the chairman of the country's biggest telecom, Vladimir Yevtushenkov, was placed under house arrest by Russian authorities under suspicion of money laundering.[16] Indeed, to some extent even the president of Russia, Vladimir Putin,[17] faces this sort of precarity: Both his wealth and safety depend on retaining political power, and this in turn requires at least minimal cooperation with the oligarchs. For him, interference is absent, but perhaps not robustly absent. That is, it may not be absent over variations in the friendliness of others.

5.1.2 *The Value of Freedom*

It is still an open question as to the relation between freedom and morality. Why, in other words, is freedom good or morally significant (if it is)?

As in our discussion of autonomy earlier in this book, we can understand the value of freedom by considering its boundaries. We have already seen that autonomy is not good without qualification. For example, using one's autonomous capacities to undermine others' freedom is bad. Consider the oligarchs just mentioned: not only does their freedom permit them to capture a sizable proportion of the wealth and national product of Russia for their personal benefit; they also have a long history of using their freedom as a tool for promoting the domination and diminished quality of agency of others. With this sort of example in mind, John Danaher argues that freedom is an "axiological catalyst" – that it "makes good things better and bad things worse."[18] Yet even this seems too strong when we consider cases that raise the "paradox of choice."[19] This paradox is that although we often believe that

---

[13] BBC Staff, "Russian Businessman Buys Chelsea."
[14] Segal, "A Russian Oligarch's $500 Million Yacht Is in the Middle of Britain's Costliest Divorce."
[15] Cramb, "Scotland's Most Expensive Sporting Estate Bought by Russian Vodka Billionaire."
[16] *Guardian* staff, "Sistema Boss Arrested in Russia on Money-Laundering Charges."
[17] Aslund, *Russia's Crony Capitalism.*
[18] Danaher, "Freedom in the Age of Algocracy"; Kagan "The Additive Fallacy."
[19] Schwartz, *The Paradox of Choice.*

having more options is good, in fact having a large number, wide diversity, or substantial nuance in our choices leads to anxiety and stress rather than happiness or satisfaction. A greater range of choices is simply not always better, for either the chooser or those who depend on their choices.

These cases suggest that it will be impossible to coherently explain either freedom or autonomy as intrinsically good. Of course, we need not ignore the fact that freedom and autonomy are almost always good. An easier proposition to defend is cast in terms of unfreedom: shortfalls in freedom (that is, either shortfalls in self-government or instances of domination) are prima facie bad. This commitment is compatible with freedom being outweighed by any number of other values in any number of cases, such as when we take the freedom of oppressors to be outweighed by the value of human rights. There may be cases where the protections licensed by the assumed value of freedom are morally and politically outweighed by the public interest, such as public health mandates. The shift in emphasis from freedom to unfreedom is motivated by the fact that in practice, it is easier to discern what is objectionable (or not) about a given freedom deficit than to discern how freedom (conceived of as an intrinsic good) must be limited.

This account has substantive implications. It holds that freedom deficits are usually morally bad and that unfreedom can be thought to serve morally good purposes only in certain circumstances. Figuring out how to best promote human freedom, then, is not as simple as settling debates about which sorts of interference would be objectionable to rational actors. Unlike freedom, which can be defined in the abstract, unfreedom can only be defined in terms of the specific foibles of human agency, specific architecture of human environments, and specific implications of social choices. As we show in the next section, the effects that shortfalls in freedom can have on our freedom are well illustrated in terms of the challenges to freedom mentioned earlier.

5.2 THREE CHALLENGES TO FREEDOM: AFFECTIVE, DELIBERATIVE, AND SOCIAL

At the start of this chapter we introduced three challenges to freedom: the affective challenge, the deliberative challenge, and the social challenge. In this section we will examine each of these challenges by considering several different algorithmic systems. We will argue that, to the extent that these technologies can undermine either people's autonomy or their freedom from domination without good reason, they can objectionably undermine our freedom.

5.2.1 *Affective Challenges to Autonomy*

The first sort of challenge to freedom is that human behavior is driven by affective influences, such as fear, anger, resentment, or addiction, as opposed to purely being driven by rational attitudes. These affective states, we will argue, can undermine the authenticity of people's preferences and desires, threatening our freedom by threatening our autonomy.

People are so driven by affective states that it might seem difficult or impossible to clearly pinpoint any kernel of rational attitudes that lie underneath. Humans, it might seem, experience affective influences "all the way down," in the sense that our authentic attitudes cannot be distinguished from any other attitudes one might have in a principled way.[20] But in some cases, the influence can be so dramatic that it is hard to accept that the resulting behavior could be freely chosen or even independently motivated. The AAA Foundation for Traffic Safety has found, for instance, that around 4 percent of drivers each year have gotten out of their cars to angrily confront another driver, and 3 percent have purposefully run into another car for the same reason.[21] Anger is not the only source of authenticity-undermining affective influence: It is difficult to believe that a person could have an authentic desire or preference to go to an internet cafe and play a game for fifty straight hours before dying of exhaustion, yet this has happened on several occasions.[22]

As has been known since B. F. Skinner, people's susceptibility to operant conditioning can be used by third parties (such as casinos) to reinforce certain patterns of behavior over others. Many digital platforms employ conditioning strategies in the same sort of way, engendering affective states in their users that undermine the authenticity of their choices. The targets of optimization are different, of course; mobile developers optimize in terms of clicks, views, watch times, and so on, rather than lever pulls or revenue benchmarks. However, the underlying strategy – engendering some sort of artificial dependency – is the same.

As Nir Eyal points out, engendering artificial dependencies is a crucial element of the general strategy of keeping users "engaged." He outlines a four-step method for effectively "Skinner boxing" a digital platform.[23] The first step involves a trigger, which draws the user's attention to the app or platform. The quintessential modern trigger is, of course, the "push notification," which literally forces you to pay attention to it enough to dismiss it. The second step of Eyal's method involves getting users into acting on the trigger. The best way of getting users to do this is to get them to anticipate some sort of reward. The third step involves tying user behavior to these rewards but making the rewards variable, in the sense that they are sometimes highly rewarding but at other times mundane, in a way that is unpredictable. Dopamine surges whenever the brain has been conditioned to expect a reward, but without variability, the experience becomes unsatisfyingly predictable. The fourth step, finally, involves getting users to make some sort of investment in or commitment to the app, to maintain their engagement with it in the future.

[20] Thanks to Sarah Worley and Dana Nelkin for drawing our attention to this point.
[21] AAA Foundation for Traffic Safety, "Aggressive Driving | AAA Exchange."
[22] BBC Staff, "S Korean Dies after Games Session."
[23] Eyal, *Hooked: How to Build Habit-Forming Products*, 8–9.

The Duolingo platform offers an illustration of how Eyal's model can be employed. The app uses push notifications to draw the user's attention to the app, sometimes coupled with a guilt trip. When a user has stopped using Duolingo for a period, they will receive a notification depicting the very cute Duolingo mascot in tears, stating that "Language Bird is crying," that a failure to go back to learning a language will lead the mascot to "eat a poison loaf of bread," and that the next email to the user will be an e-vite to Language Bird's funeral.

Skill badges, which represent user achievements, are displayed at the end of rounds in a pleasingly unpredictable way. Finally, the platform has a number of mechanisms for investment: users' earned skills decay over time, requiring ongoing practice, and the platform itself also contains a microtransaction market for premium avatars, allowing users to invest in the app using real money.

In several ways, then, Duolingo uses its users' affective states to undermine their autonomy and, thus, limit their freedom. For the most part,[24] its freedom-impinging tactics do not raise anyone's hackles, because there is a background presumption in any discussion of it that language acquisition really *is* valuable for its users (thereby serving their global autonomy if not quite their local autonomy). The same tactics, however, are more troubling in the context of employment, where people can be compelled to act in dangerous ways to protect their basic livelihood. Consider the practices of the ride-hailing company Uber.

Uber has come under substantial criticism on the basis of how its algorithms have negatively affected its drivers.[25] The company uses these systems for a variety of purposes: to track passengers, to anticipate market demand, and (at one point) even to identify and deceive regulators, media, and law enforcement. As we discuss in Chapter 7,[26] the company employs several practices to keep its drivers working longer than they might otherwise. Here we will discuss two sorts of practice, arguing that one serves to undermine the freedom of drivers while the other is more morally benign.

Both sorts of practice can be linked to the strategy outlined by Eyal. The first involves Uber's user interface design choices. The driver app, for instance, is configured by default to remind drivers of their goals through push notifications, and it is also configured by default to queue another rider before the current rider has been delivered. Presumably, the motivation for Uber to employ this particular set of defaults rather than the alternative sets is that their chosen configuration is statistically more likely to induce drivers to accept more riders than the others. (In fact, it is likely that Uber has discerned the precise overall effect of this design choice through massive-scale A/B testing.)

Nevertheless, Uber's design choices do not necessarily undermine drivers' freedom in this case. It is plausible that drivers have their own reasons for such settings

[24] However, see Lee, "Duolingo Redesigned Its Owl to Guilt-Trip You Even Harder."
[25] Rosenblat, *Uberland*, 98–100.
[26] Rubel, Castro, and Pham, "Agency Laundering and Information Technologies."

being one way or the other. It is plausible that someone might want to work a shift determined by a particular monetary goal or period of time and, thus, to simply queue as many customers as fast as possible without having to continue manually making choices at each possible choice point. Uber would certainly not increase the freedom of users by doing away with the choice altogether. So long as Uber does not covertly reset the defaults, or design the interface in a predatory fashion, the company's UI design choices do not strike us as an issue of serious moral concern (or even, for that matter, an issue of freedom at all).

The second practice for keeping drivers working longer than they would other-wise, however, is less apparent to the drivers and much more troubling from the standpoint of autonomy. It involves such practices as "surge pricing," which is a cost-multiplier that raises the price of a ride (sometimes dramatically) in a location at a time when the demand for drivers is high or the supply of drivers is low. Some of the additional revenue from this cost markup is passed to the drivers, so the surge-pricing system gives drivers a financial incentive to work more than they would otherwise, because they will be able to make more money than they would have otherwise. The "surge-pricing" mechanism is a familiar device in modern retail – it's just a form of dynamic pricing – but essential to Uber's use of it is an element of uncertainty and variability that is not readily apparent to the drivers at first: when drivers accept a ride at a "surge priced" rate, they do not know whether the ultimate payment for the ride will be surge priced.[27]

The fact that these practices are opaque to drivers might lead one to question Uber's motives. Our concern here, though, is the drivers' autonomy. A recent report describes the phenomenon of "chasing the surge" at length.[28] Since 2016, Uber has employed the "boost" system, which grants automatic surge pricing to drivers who have completed a certain number of rides the previous week, in a tiered arrangement from "Bronze" to "Platinum." One driver described his relationship with Uber in the following way:

> I had some days off from work. So I was on the road. I mean, I just had coffee upon coffee, and I'm just on the road. So I ended up doing about, I thought it was over 100, but I did 94 rides . . . It was 94 rides in essentially 3 days . . . After you do 90 rides, I think it's 90 or 95, they bump you to platinum . . . And then basically you're always chasing platinum.[29]

The authors of the report note that "[t]he stress of these games, be it chasing a surge or platinum, was a refrain in 50% of our interviews in surveys."[30]

What is the moral upshot of the Uber case? According to our view of the value of freedom, the verdict is mixed. The nudges Uber employs in its user interface, which

[27] Rosenblat, *Uberland*, chapter 4.
[28] Wells and Cullen, "The Uber Workplace in Washington, D.C."
[29] Wells and Cullen, 47.
[30] Wells and Cullen, 47.

for the most part serve obvious functions for its users (and which are also relatively low stakes and transparent), are unproblematic as a class. From the perspective of alleviating the domination of its users or promoting their autonomy, it is not clear that Uber could have done better.

Uber's Skinner-boxing of its drivers to "chase platinum," in contrast, is considerably more troubling and gives rise to a freedom-based complaint. The authenticity condition of autonomy precludes users being in affectively compromised states; if people's actions lack authenticity – in the sense that those actions serve to alienate the person from their basic values – then those actions will not be autonomous. However, the boost aspect of the Uber surge-pricing system exists precisely to place users in such a state and, in so doing, urges them to "chase" overwork even at the expense of their health. The same freedom-impinging features that seem somewhat innocuous in the context of Duolingo and language acquisition become more troubling when a dangerous degree of overworking is a potential effect.

5.2.2 *Deliberative Challenges to Agency*

Exploiting our emotional vulnerabilities is not the only way to hack human agency. Even if we set aside the fact that human agency can be undermined by noncognitive affective states, human cognition itself is limited in ways that can be exploited to limit our quality of agency.

Our actual deliberative process is both *bounded* and *inaccurate*; the information we receive as reasoners is limited by our computational capacities and fitted to our choice environments, and our processing of the information we do get is subject to a variety of errors and biases.[31] Many of these biases – the availability bias, anchoring bias, conjunction fallacy, base-rate neglect, and so on – are well known.[32] To this end, in the next chapter we discuss problematic search suggestions and algorithmically curated news feeds, which allows people to expose themselves only to information that reinforces their existing beliefs. Here, we focus more on the boundedness of human agency.

Algorithmic systems, particularly digital platforms, introduce new sources of economic value – namely personal and consumer datasets at big data scale[33] – as well as new sources of risk – data breaches and other forms of exposure.[34] These systems can be so complex both for developers and for end users that it is impossible to live up to the Reasonable Endorsement Test in practice. To be sure, the choice environment of our digital daily lives does not live up to this moral standard: most people do not and

---

[31] Simon, *Models of Man: Social and Rational-Mathematical Essays on Rational Human Behavior in a Social Setting.*

[32] Kahneman, Knetsch, and Thaler, "Experimental Tests of the Endowment Effect and the Coase Theorem."

[33] Pham and Castro, "The Moral Limits of the Market: The Case of Consumer Scoring Data."

[34] Yaffe-Bellany, "Equifax Data-Breach Settlement"; Abrams, "Target to Pay $18.5 Million to 47 States in Security Breach Settlement."

could not always read all of the fine print to which they claim to consent and the idea of "common terms" has been stretched thin by massive swathes of boilerplate that are unreadable by humans in practice.[35] In practice, we face an avalanche of digital "pseudo-contracts" – contracts that are so convoluted that they assume impossible levels of human competence and thus fail to represent any actual "meeting of the minds" between the parties.[36]

Our constant subjection to these "contracts" violates our procedural independence, by exploiting the limits of our epistemic competence and thereby undermining our consent. One study, for instance, found that "only one or two of every 1,000 retail software shoppers" actually access the contract "and that most of those who do access it read no more than a small portion."[37] In 2014, Europol conducted an experiment in which they offered access to a Wi-Fi hotspot behind a contract that granted access only if the recipient signed a so-called Herod clause, in this case, to agree "to assign their first born child to us for the duration of eternity."[38] Six people still signed the contract. In 2015, a *Guardian* journalist resolved to read all the terms of conditions for all his services and wound up reading 146,000 words in a single week.[39]

Most modern web services now have end-user licensing agreements (EULAs), but Brainly, a peer-to-peer learning platform in which users can provide homework help to one another, offers an especially striking example of a pseudo-contract. The platform's end-user licensing agreement is expansive. First, the company is permitted to force users into arbitration. Second, it is permitted – despite its claim to protect users with a privacy policy – to license user content to third parties, distribute it through any media, or even sell personal data outright as part of bankruptcy, *even after its users have terminated their accounts*. Third, it is permitted to change the terms of service at any time without notice.

Each of the components of the Brainly pseudo-contract can be seen to exploit the undermined capacity of its users to reflect on their values, motivations, and decision-making in the digital environment. The company's ability to automatically force users into arbitration allows it to settle disputes with its users on legal terrain that is broadly unfavorable to them; its privacy policy serves as a smokescreen that obscures the extent to which it can freely trade or sell user data; its right to change its terms of service at any time prevents and discourages users from reading any one version of it and contributes to the overwhelming deluge of information users must cope with.

This pseudo-contract exploits its users' limited quality of agency. By holding them responsible for self-government in a context where this is humanly impossible, the contract exploits their lack of understanding of their circumstances for corporate

---

35   Benoliel and Becher, "The Duty to Read the Unreadable."
36   Kar and Radin, "Pseudo-Contract & Shared Meaning Analysis," 1140.
37   Bakos, Marotta-Wurgler, and Trossen, "Does Anyone Read the Fine Print?"
38   Fox-Brewster, "Londoners Give up Eldest Children in Public Wi-Fi Security Horror Show."
39   Hern, "I Read All the Small Print on the Internet and It Made Me Want to Die."

benefit. In many cases, the stakes are sufficiently low: the opacity of Brainly's EULA aside, it is difficult to argue that anyone has been harmed by having their content unknowingly open-sourced to the educationally minded public. Yet users have proven eager in the past to allow their likenesses to be sold by Instagram,[40] and (as we discuss in Chapter 8) they have more recently allowed their (and their friends') personality profiles to be mined by Cambridge Analytica, even if they later come to regret these choices. In the context of complex algorithmic systems, epistemic competence – and therefore, freedom – is impossible to achieve.

5.2.3 *Social Challenges to Freedom*

So far in this section, we have argued that one way that human agency can be undermined is if its processes come to be directed by affective states rather than by conscious deliberation, violating the authenticity condition. Another way agency can be undermined, we have argued, relates to the fact that our cognitive capacities themselves are bounded, violating the competence condition. In this subsection, we explore a third way that agency can be undermined: through the influence of the affective states and erroneous deliberative processes *of other people*, in the context of an epistemologically toxic social environment.

Consider, for instance, YouTube's recommendation algorithm, whose autoplay mechanism drives users toward echo chambers and other ideologically extreme and conspiratorial content. By YouTube's own analysis, almost three-quarters of viewing time spent on the site is driven by this recommendation system as opposed to their viewers' independent actions,[41] so the operation of this system is of overriding significance in determining what content people are exposed to. When left unsupervised by humans, it fosters an unsafe environment for children: it allows bad actors to expose them to distressing parody content, such as a fake Mickey Mouse cartoon depicting eye-gouging[42] or a fake Paw Patrol episode where one of the main characters attempts suicide.[43]

YouTube's recommendation system has also arguably been a source of violent self-radicalization. The reason has at least in part to do with YouTube's business model and with the evolution of its incentive structure. Originally, the YouTube recommendation algorithm had been designed simply to maximize the number of clicks,[44] but this proved to offer content creators an incentive to post "clickbait" videos, ones that entice users to initially click on the video but that do not necessarily hold their interest through the duration of the video. In light of this, YouTube

---

[40] Arthur, "Facebook Forces Instagram Users to Allow It to Sell Their Uploaded Photos." Instagram reversed this policy after public outcry.
[41] Neal Mohan, YouTube's Chief Product Officer, claimed this at the 2018 CES convention.
[42] Orphanides, "Children's YouTube Is Still Churning Out Blood, Suicide and Cannibalism."
[43] Maheshwari, "On YouTube Kids, Startling Videos Slip Past Filters."
[44] Roose, "The Making of a YouTube Radical."

changed its algorithm in 2012 to optimize more for *watch time* than for number of clicks so that "creators would be encouraged to make videos that users would finish, users would be more satisfied and YouTube would be able to show them more ads."[45] The change worked – watch time increased by 50 percent each year from 2012 to 2015 – but it also conferred an advantage to those content creators who produce naturally engaging videos: conspiracy theorists.

Guillaume Chaslot, a former Google engineer who left the company over issues with the development of the YouTube algorithm, wrote a piece of web software that examines which videos follow others via the recommendation system. When the *Guardian* examined the one thousand top-recommended videos, it found that YouTube had an 85 percent chance of recommending a pro-Trump video rather than a pro-Clinton video. The newspaper also interviewed several conspiracy theorists, whose videos normally receive only a few hundred views but whose traffic increased dramatically right before the 2016 election, and it found that most of these content creators got their traffic from the YouTube recommender system rather than from external links.[46] These videos, which almost always have titles like "WHOA! HILLARY THINKS CAMERA'S OFF ... SENDS SHOCK MESSAGE TO TRUMP" and "Irrefutable Proof: Hillary Clinton Has a Seizure Disorder!" are more engaging than they are factual. The natural result of this state of affairs is a social environment in which divisiveness and sensationalism are in themselves advantageous traits for content, quite apart from whether or not that content reflects misinformation or authoritarian aims.

Given the affective and deliberative challenges to agency that we have already discussed, we should not be surprised that sensational and conspiratorial content grounded in fear, anger, and resentment turns out to deliver greater engagement than the messy realities of legitimate news reporting. But it is worth noticing how toxic social environments can aggravate the other challenges to agency: When users who are already prone to fear-conditioning are fed an escalating diet of misinformed, radicalizing content, their autonomy is *socially* comprised. For such users, both the possibility of autonomy and the possibility of high-quality agency are ruled out from the start.

5.2.4 *Summarizing the Challenges to Freedom*

As we have seen in this section, drivers who have become caught up in the gamified ridesharing ecosystem, information consumers who have become overwhelmed by a deluge of labyrinthian pseudo-contracts, and conspiracy theorists who have become radicalized all have been made less free in a broadly similar way: either their autonomy has been undermined or their quality of agency has been

---

[45] Roose.
[46] Lewis, "Fiction Is Outperforming Reality."

diminished.[47] However, the traditional conceptions of freedom (negative, positive, republican) that we canvassed at the beginning of the chapter do not provide an adequate explanation for these shortfalls of freedom. That is because drivers, information consumers, and conspiracy theorists all seem to satisfy the traditional conceptions. They are not subject to external constraints, they are not subject to arbitrary exercises of power, and they often even have the capacity to make choices to realize their preferences. The challenges to freedom we have outlined here make clear that freedom requires autonomy, high-quality agency, and non-domination.

Taking these three challenges seriously motivates an important shift in how we think about freedom. Recall that our account of freedom is ecological non-domination, which includes quality of agency and republican freedom. That account captures the emotionally volatile, cognitively limited, and fundamentally social nature of human agency. It is also consistent with the fact that it remains possible to coherently act even under some degree of individual, psychological disunity, such as when one is internally conflicted about a course of action. Surely the authenticity of Uber drivers, the competence of overwhelmed service users, and online radicalization of conspiracy theorists are not all-or-nothing affairs. People in those circumstances are neither fully free nor acting purely on reflex. When we reconsider human agency in light of its distinctive challenges, any plausible account of freedom must cope with this complexity.

We are finally able to make more precise the sense in which these users of technology have been made unfree: their beliefs, preferences, constraints, and values have been formed in a way that conflicts with agency. Freedom requires, in addition to non-domination and effective choice, that one's beliefs, preferences, constraints, and values themselves have been formed without undue influence. It is only when people are both undominated *and* unstricken by such malformations that they can be said to be free in the fullest sense.

5.3 ECOLOGICAL NON-DOMINATION, POLICY, AND POLESTAR CASES

The next question to consider is this: what kinds of moral claims does ecological freedom ground? Both the new cases we have examined in this chapter and the cases we have examined in previous ones can offer some guidance.

Preserving our autonomy – and thus, our freedom – requires managing the possible sources of compromising affective states. However, at least in the United States, policymakers have discussed the issue only where the analogy between the digital and non-digital addiction is sufficiently robust.[48] Consider, for instance, "loot boxes," which are certain economic transactions within digital games that

---

[47] Rubel, "Privacy and Positive Intellectual Freedom," 399–401.
[48] See the Protecting Children from Abusive Games Act.

involve a randomized reward structure. These transactions bear a clear resemblance to traditional forms of gambling, such as slot machines and lotteries, including the fact that the model is primarily funded by a tiny proportion of "whales."[49] There is, therefore, reason to think that the "loot box" market is noxious and, thus, apt for public regulation.[50] One bill has been introduced to ban the use of loot boxes in games marketed to children, but as of 2020, there are effectively no regulations in place about them. In the European Union, in contrast, the practice has already been banned completely by the authorities in at least two member states (Belgium and the Netherlands).[51] Our account offers, on relatively minimal and ecumenical grounds, support for regulation that nudges users to be self-critical about their agency.

Preserving our quality of agency might also require designing law and policy in a way that is mindful of human cognitive limitations. Robin Kar and Margaret Radin, for instance, offer a heuristic for courts: They should imagine that all text exchanged during the formation of the contract "be converted into oral form" and then imagined to occur "in a face-to-face conversation between the relevant parties."[52] Courts then are not obliged to accept all boilerplate as meaningful from the start. Instead, they are enabled to scrutinize whether the text genuinely conforms to "the cooperative norms that govern language use to form a contract."[53]

Finally, we might consider ways of combating toxic online social environments, which serve as threats to all sorts of freedom, republican freedom included. Platforms have implemented some light-touch solutions on their own, at least for the most egregious problems. For instance, YouTube searches for content associated with the Islamic State, now attract banners promoting skepticism about their aims.[54] However, broader and more general solutions remain elusive. How can would-be political radicals be nudged toward content that promotes gentler aims and methods than violence, when the business models of the platforms hosting this content depend on the engagement produced by the more radical content? The depth of this problem suggests that the engagement-centric business model itself might need to be abandoned to see progress.[55]

---

[49] The name draws its source from casino slang and refers to those gamblers who are known to bet large amounts of money. And just as casinos compete for the largest high rollers, app developers depend heavily on those users who spend the most money: A recent Swrve survey showed that about 0.15 percent of mobile users contributed approximately half of all in-app purchases in "freemium" games.

[50] Satz, *Why Some Things Should Not Be for Sale: The Moral Limits of Markets*; Castro and Pham, "Is the Attention Economy Noxious?"

[51] Netherlands Gaming Authority, "Study into Loot Boxes: A Treasure or a Burden?"; Belgian Gaming Commission, "Loot Boxes in Three Video Games in Violation of Gambling Legislation."

[52] Kar and Radin, "Pseudo-Contract & Shared Meaning Analysis," 1167.

[53] Kar and Radin, 1167.

[54] Alfano, Carter, and Cheong, "Technological Seduction and Self-Radicalization," 25.

[55] Lanier, *Ten Arguments for Deleting Your Social Media Accounts Right Now*.

We can also reconsider some of the polestar cases in light of the techniques we have used to address the new cases. Do Eric Loomis or the teachers have a reason to think that their freedom was undermined?

For *Loomis*, the argument that his freedom was wrongly or unjustly curtailed is difficult to get off the ground. It is hard to argue that the use of COMPAS somehow undermined the authenticity of Loomis's desires, so his autonomy-based arguments would rest on claims about how the proprietary nature of the system exploited his diminished quality of agency. However, as the Wisconsin Supreme Court noted, most of the information used to generate his risk assessment report was either static or under his control, so agency-based concerns are also somewhat implausible. Now, he certainly had his freedom curtailed by the court, but it is hard to argue that he was somehow dominated by it in a way that defies sensible criminal justice; as the court confirmed, he likely received the same sentence he would have otherwise. So whatever autonomy- and agency-based affronts he was unreasonably subjected to, he did not face a morally objectionable affront to his freedom.

For the teachers from *Wagner* and *Houston*, the freedom-based argument is more persuasive. As we also discussed in Chapter 4, the EVAAS system produces results that are fragile (and, as they acknowledge, unreproducible) and it produces those results without any specific explanation of its method or independent oversight. And – unlike in *Loomis* – were the two teachers to have gained the necessary understanding of the system, they would have been able to act differently (and a lot more directly): They could have anticipated their problems and been prepared to impugn the results to future employers, or they could have mounted a comprehensible public campaign against the system. But they were denied such choices and therefore had no choice but to litigate the issue. To the extent that litigation against technology companies is prohibitively costly for individual litigants such as Teresa Wagner or Jennifer Braeuner (and, for that matter, Catherine Taylor and Carmen Arroyo), such sources of domination constitute objectionable affronts to freedom.

There are general lessons to be learned even for those who do not find themselves on the wrong side of such systems. Each of us has an individual obligation to accept that we are driven partly by affective states, boundedly competent, and highly influenced by others. We can be influenced to agree to transactions we might not otherwise, we are unlikely to be aware of the finer details of most of the contracts we sign, and we are especially susceptible to radical ideas – good or bad – when we encounter them from within the community in which they arose. We need not take these features of our nature to undermine the legitimacy of every agreement or transaction we make through these apps and platforms, but we must accept that these features undermine the legitimacy of some of those agreements and transactions.

5.4 WHY NOT MANIPULATION?

Manipulation is a common element of many of the cases we consider in this chapter and the next. The "blind-draw" loot boxes resemble lotteries and slot machines in all ways other than that they are digital rather than physical, luring their users to play through classic tricks of the advertising trade. Facebook's Click-Gap metric, which we discuss in the next chapter, offers the platform's developers the ability to invisibly curate individual News Feeds. Cambridge Analytica's targeting of Facebook users for the purposes of political advertising, too, involved influencing that was tailored to users' deep tendencies. Even in cases where there does not appear to be any direct manipulator, such as the case of the YouTube recommendation system, manipulation is still involved, in virtue of involving someone who seems to have been manipulated. Considering these cases, one might wonder whether our analysis of the ethics of algorithmic systems could be subsumed under the rubric of manipulation. And if not, then what *does* make manipulation objectionable as a practice?

Before answering questions relating our analysis to manipulation, we would do well to specify the concept itself, at least loosely. However, there is no consensus in the philosophical literature on what exactly constitutes manipulation, nor is there a consensus on how manipulation relates to autonomy and freedom. Moreover, there are problematic implications related to each possible conception. Some view manipulation in terms of threats to rationality. Raz, for instance, understands manipulation in terms of undercutting rational decision-making; as "pervert[ing] the way that a person reaches decisions, forms preferences or adopts goals."[56] Yet manipulators need not always threaten rationality; in some cases rational implications can themselves be used manipulatively.[57] Others, such as Anne Barnhill, Karen Yeung, and Daniel Susser, Beate Roessler, and Helen Nissenbaum, conceive of manipulation in terms of forms of deception or hiddenness that undermine people's self-interest and autonomy.[58] This, too, seems right, but many of our key cases, such as that of Catherine Taylor (Chapter 4), reflect vulnerabilities that do not include elements of deception, hiddenness, or trickery. At times, such as in the COMPAS, EVAAS, and CrimSafe cases, the practices we scrutinize shade closer to coercion than to deception. To this end, Joel Feinberg and Allen Wood understand manipulation as lying on a "spectrum of force" between compulsion and enticement.[59] But this analysis is also incomplete: It does not cover the cases of manipulation that seem to involve deception. So none of the analyses cover all of the cases that seem to fall under the concept of manipulation.

[56] Raz, *The Morality of Freedom*, 377–378.
[57] Gorin, "Do Manipulators Always Threaten Rationality?"
[58] Barnhill, "What Is Manipulation?"; Yeung, "'Hypernudge': Big Data as a Mode of Regulation by Design"; Susser, Roessler, and Nissenbaum, "Online Manipulation: Hidden Influences in a Digital World"; Lanzing, "'Strongly Recommended' Revisiting Decisional Privacy to Judge Hypernudging in Self-Tracking Technologies."
[59] Feinberg, *Harm to Self: The Moral Limits of the Criminal Law*, 3:189.

We do not ground our moral analysis in any specific conception of manipulation. Rather, we will only aim to highlight two salient points. First, a point about method: the moral permissibility of manipulation depends on how manipulation is construed. In considering the disputes mentioned earlier about how to identify manipulation, for instance, it might seem reasonable to adopt a broad or disjunctive conception, under which *either* deceptive or coercive practices count as manipulative. However, this leaves unresolved what unifies the concept of manipulation, that is, what all instances of the phenomenon have in common. Moreover, since entirely avoiding both deception and coercion seems impossible in practice, this broad sort of conception does not justify categorical condemnation of manipulation.

Our second point is that manipulation is probably best understood in a non-moralized way. Instead of viewing manipulation as constitutively wrong, we should view it as identified by "objective facts about a situation that give us good reasons for condemning or approving certain things."[60] Insofar as reasons can be good yet nonetheless be undercut or outweighed, this view about the nature of manipulation is compatible with a moral evaluation of it as prima facie or pro tanto wrong – that is, as "not always wrong" but "generally wrong."[61] So, just as we can accept the defeasible badness of unfreedom, in light of examples where paternalism serves the public interest, here we accept the defeasibility of the badness of manipulation in light of examples where manipulation serves those interests. These examples might be few and far between, but they remain important. As we argue in the next chapter, the managers and developers of some technological systems might have obligations to influence their users in ways that are non-persuasive, deceptive, or perhaps even coercive. In these cases, such as in the case of the Click-Gap metric (discussed in the next chapter), the obligation not to manipulate simply gives way.

In general, we think that the problems with algorithmic systems are closely related to, but not reducible to, the affronts to autonomy wrought by manipulation. To this end, Marjolein Lanzing discusses the manipulative aspects of information technologies in terms of affronts to informational and decisional privacy. Yet, for her, as for us, the fundamental lesson is about affronts to autonomy, not manipulation per se: she writes that "[s]ince informational and decisional privacy protect autonomy, autonomy is under threat."[62] From this broader perspective, it is not only clear why manipulation is morally problematic, it is clear why manipulation is wrong to the extent that it engenders or reflects an affront to autonomy.

---

[60]　Wood, "Coercion, Manipulation, Exploitation," 19–20.
[61]　Baron, "The Mens Rea and Moral Status of Manipulation," 108.
[62]　Lanzing, "'Strongly Recommended' Revisiting Decisional Privacy to Judge Hypernudging in Self-Tracking Technologies," 565.

5.5 CONCLUSION

Human agency and autonomy are, as we have seen, difficult to pin down. As we have argued, understanding these important ideas as they apply to actual people requires examining human behavior in depth. Here, we have conceptualized human agency in terms of three "natural challenges" to human agency, and we have argued that each of these challenges influences the nuances of a third important idea: freedom. Human freedom is fundamentally ecological: it is shaped by our capacity to act on our emotions, the limits of our cognition, and the centrality of our social relations to our decision-making.

6

Epistemic Paternalism and Social Media

In the previous chapters, we explored various ways in which algorithms can undermine our freedom or threaten our autonomy, paying particular attention to the context of the prison sentencing and employee management (specifically, teachers and Uber drivers). In this chapter, we turn to a different context – which we briefly touched on in the previous chapter – that of our current media environment, which is in large part shaped by algorithms. We discuss some distinctively epistemic problems that algorithms pose in that context and some paternalistic solutions they call for. Our paternalistic proposal to these problems is compatible with respect to freedom and autonomy; in fact, our freedom and autonomy demand them.

Let us begin with some reflections on our current media environment. In 1995, MIT media lab founder Nicholas Negroponte foresaw a phenomenon that we are now all familiar with: the replacement of traditional newspapers with virtual newspapers, custom-fitted to each reader's particular taste. In his speculations, he called the virtual newspaper "the Daily Me." Cass Sunstein elaborates on the idea of the Daily Me:

> Maybe your views are left of center, and you want to read stories fitting with what you think about climate change, equality, immigration, and the rights of labor unions. Or maybe you lean to the right, and you want to see conservative perspectives on those issues, or maybe on just one or two, and on how to cut taxes and regulation, or reduce immigration. Perhaps what matters most to you are your religious convictions, and you want to read and see material with a religious slant (your own). Perhaps you want to speak to and hear from your friends, who mostly think as you do, you might hope that all of you will share the same material. What matters is that with the Daily Me, everyone could enjoy an *architecture of control*. Each of us would be fully in charge of what we see and hear.[1]

As Negroponte anticipated, custom-fitted virtual news has become widespread and popular. This has been facilitated by the advent of "new media" – highly interactive digital technology for creating, sharing, and consuming information. New media is

---

[1] Sunstein, #*Republic: Divided Democracy in the Age of Social Media*, 1 (emphasis added).

now pervasive, with more Americans getting their news from social media (the predominant form of new media) than traditional print newspapers.[2]

In 1995, the Daily Me might have sounded like a strict improvement on traditional news. However, we now know that the architecture of control that it affords us has serious drawbacks. Consider an episode that briefly caught the nation's attention in the summer of 2019. About a month after the Mueller Report – the *Investigation into Russian Interference in the 2016 Presidential Election*[3] – was released, Justin Amash (who was a Republican member of the U.S. House of Representatives) gave a town hall to explain why he thought the report was grounds for impeaching the president. At the town hall, NBC interviewed a Michigan resident who stated that she was "surprised to hear there was anything negative in the Mueller Report *at all* about [the President]"[4] (Golshan 2019; emphasis added). At the time, it was hard to see how anyone could think this. Yet she thought the report had exonerated the president.

When the resident learned that the report contained negative revelations about the president, it was through serendipity. Amash was the only Republican representative calling for impeachment following the release of the report, and she happened to live in his district. Had it not been for this, she likely would have continued to believe that report had exonerated the president.

The Michigan resident is not a special case. Many people continue to believe that the Mueller Report explicitly concludes that the president and members of his campaign did nothing wrong. Moreover, the phenomenon of people being misinformed in similar ways is common. Along with the architecture of control afforded by customized news comes the danger of encapsulating ourselves in "epistemic bubbles," epistemic structures that leave relevant sources of information out and walling ourselves off in "echo chambers," epistemic structures that leave relevant sources of information out, and actively discredit those sources.[5] This is, in part, due to the automated way in which news feeds and other information-delivery systems (such as search results) are generated. Eli Pariser explains:

> The new generation of Internet filters look at the things you seem to like [...] and tries to extrapolate. They are prediction engines, constantly creating and refining a theory of who you are and what you'll do and want next. Together, these engines create a unique universe of information for each of us and [...] alters the way we encounter ideas and information.[6]

---

[2]   Shearer, "Social Media Outpaces Print Newspapers in the U.S. as a News Source."
[3]   U.S. Department of Justice, "Report on the Investigation into Russian Interference in the 2016 Presidential Election, Volume I ('Mueller Report')"; U.S. Department of Justice, "Report on the Investigation into Russian Interference in the 2016 Presidential Election, Volume II ('Mueller Report')."
[4]   Caldwell and Moe, "Republican Justin Amash Stands by Position to Start Impeachment Proceedings" (emphasis added).
[5]   Nguyen, "Echo Chambers and Epistemic Bubbles."
[6]   Pariser, *The Filter Bubble*, 9.

This is why cases like the Michigan resident are far from isolated: Many of us are in epistemic bubbles or echo chambers built through the cooperation of internet filters and ourselves.

Consider the user interface of YouTube, the world's largest social media platform.[7] The site's homepage opens to a menu loaded up with algorithmically generated options, curated to match each user's tastes. Immediately after watching any video on the homepage, users are met with algorithmically generated suggestions based on what they have just watched. The suggestions that appear on the home page and at the conclusion of videos are, of course, chosen to keep users on the site. So users who are inclined toward, say, left-of-center politics are more likely to receive suggestions for videos supporting that worldview. Given that two-thirds of Americans get news through social media – with one in five getting news from YouTube[8] – it is no wonder we can consume a lot of news but be mis- or under-informed about current affairs of monumental importance.

New media's design and popularity also facilitate the mass spread of misinformation. This is not only unfortunate but dangerous. Consider the recent surge in "vaccine hesitancy" – the reluctance or refusal to vaccinate – a phenomenon that the World Health Organization now considers one of the top ten threats to global health.[9] The surge of vaccine hesitancy seems to be inseparable from the success of new media, with Facebook, Twitter, and YouTube playing a large role in spreading misinformation about vaccines.[10] Now, decades after it had been declared "eliminated," measles has returned to the United States.[11] And in the recent COVID-19 pandemic, one early concern was that the low rates of seasonal flu vaccine would increase strain on health-care systems both by requiring more testing to differentiate COVID-19 and seasonal flu cases and by increasing strain on treatment resources.

This raises questions about the responsibility new media developers have to manage the architecture of control that its users currently enjoy. It also raises questions about the latitude that social media developers have in making alterations to their sites. On the one hand, it seems reasonable to think that developers should lead their users to consider a more diverse array of points of view, even if that is not in line with users' immediate wishes. On the other, there seems to be something objectionably paternalistic about this: Users should be able to (at least in some sense) decide their information diets for themselves.

We will argue that there is plenty of room for epistemic paternalism online. Moreover, because the internet information environment is epistemically noxious, such epistemically paternalistic policies should be a persistent part of the internet information environment. This chapter proceeds as follows. First, we discuss an

7   Kaiser and Rauchfleisch, "Unite the Right?"
8   Shearer and Matsa, "News Use across Social Media Platforms 2018."
9   World Health Organization, "Ten Health Issues WHO Will Tackle This Year."
10 Hussain et al., "The Anti-Vaccination Movement."
11 Joy, "What's Causing the 2019 Current Measles Outbreak?"

intervention that Facebook has run in hopes of demoting the spread of fake news on the site. We explain why the intervention is paternalistic and then, using the framework of this book, defend the intervention. We argue that while Facebook's intervention is defensible, it is limited. It is an intervention that may pop some epistemic bubbles but will likely be powerless against echo chambers. We then discuss heavier-handed interventions that might be effective enough to dismantle some echo chambers, and we argue that at least some heavier-handed epistemically paternalistic interventions are permissible.

6.1 DEMOTING FAKE NEWS

In April 2019, Facebook announced that it would use a new metric, Click-Gap, to determine where to rank posts in its users' News Feeds.[12] Click-Gap measures the gap between a website's traffic from Facebook and its traffic from the internet at large, and it demotes sites with large gaps. According to Facebook, the idea is that "a disproportionate number of outbound Facebook clicks [. . .] can be a sign that the domain is succeeding on News Feed in a way that doesn't reflect the authority they've built outside it."[3] Click-Gap attempts to identify and demote low-quality content, such as fake news, in News Feed to prevent it from going viral on the website.[14]

We will argue that Click-Gap is an instance of epistemic paternalism and that it is morally permissible. We begin by explaining why we take Click-Gap to be an instance of epistemic paternalism. We then argue that it is permissible, despite its being paternalistic. It may seem strange that in a book about the threat that algorithms can pose to autonomy that we would take this line. As we will soon argue, however, the epistemically noxious online information environment creates a need for action. And, whether such action is paternalistic or executed algorithmically does not matter *as such*. Instead, what matters is whether these actions are consistent with respect for persons, properly understood. We will demonstrate that Click-Gap – and a host of other potential interventions – occupies this exact space. Certain paternalistic interventions, like Click-Gap, do not undermine users' autonomy; they, in fact, support it.

Let's begin by discussing our understanding of paternalism, as it deviates from the standard philosophical understanding of the concept. A standard conception of paternalism is as follows:

Paternalism: P (for "paternalist") acts paternalistically toward S (for "subject") by φ'ing (where "φ" denotes an action) *iff* the following conditions are met:

---

[12] "News Feed is a personalized, ever-changing collection of photos, videos, links, and updates from the friends, family, businesses, and news sources you've connected to on Facebook." Facebook, "News Feed."
[13] Rosen and Lyons, "Remove, Reduce, Inform."
[14] Rosen and Lyons.

Interference: φ'ing interferes with the liberty or autonomy of S.

Non-Consent: P does so without the consent of S.

Improvement: P does so just because φ'ing will improve the welfare of S (where this includes preventing S's welfare from diminishing), or in some way promote the interests, values, or good of S.[15]

As we will soon argue, the interference condition is not met in the case of Click-Gap. Yet, as we have already noted, we take it that the intervention is an instance of paternalism. This is because we reject the interference condition.

Let us next explain why Click-Gap does not meet the interference condition. We take it that agents are *autonomous* when they enjoy procedural independence (i.e., when they are competent and their beliefs, preferences, desires, and values are authentic) and substantive independence (i.e., when their procedural independence is supported by their social and relational circumstances). We understand agents as *free* when they are undominated, autonomous, and sufficiently effective as agents. To show that Click-Gap does not meet the interference condition, then, we will show that the case does not, by the lights of these definitions, undermine freedom, autonomy, or quality of agency.

First consider autonomy. If Click-Gap is successful, it will influence the attitudes of Facebook users – some, for example, will adopt different views about vaccine safety than they otherwise would have. This influence is not enough, though, to undermine users' autonomy. The relevant question for the purposes of assessing their autonomy is whether the attitudes the users adopt will be authentic – which is to say that those attitudes are ones that they would endorse upon critical reflection as consistent with their beliefs and values over time – not simply whether they were influenced in some way or other. And Click-Gap influences users by shielding them from content that may seem more credible than it actually is because it rose to the top of News Feed by gaming the News Feed algorithm. Presumably, the attitudes formed in the absence of such manipulation and misinformation are the sort agents can authentically endorse. Click-Gap, then, will *prevent* users from forming inauthentic attitudes. This is owed to the fact that people (at least typically) will desire that their beliefs be justified and accurate.

Fair enough, one might say, but what about users who do not care about the truth and want to be anti-vaxxers, come what may. Wouldn't these – perhaps fictional – users have their autonomy undercut by Click-Gap if it changed their view? For all we've said, it is possible that these users would have their autonomy undercut *if Click-Gap changed their views*. But we are skeptical that Click-Gap could have an effect on such users. Click-Gap is not responding to the content of claims made by anti-vaxxers, it is simply demoting their posts. Moreover, de-emphasizing patently bad information (or misleading information) that happens to confirm antecedent views does not undermine those views per se. Rather, it mitigates unjustified

15   Dworkin, "Paternalism."

confirmation. In the end, a committed anti-vaxxer isn't likely to change their mind as a result of Click-Gap.[16] Its touch is far too light for that.

But what about a less narrowly defined group, such as committed skeptics of the medical establishment? Might they have a complaint? Again, either such skeptics are dogmatic skeptics, who will be skeptical come what may, in which case they are not likely to have their minds changed, or they are not, in which case Click-Gap will be – if anything – aiding them in their pursuit of the truth by filtering out low-quality information.

Let's now turn to freedom. Some users may not *like* what Click-Gap does, but it does not dominate them, rob them of resources to effectuate their desires, or diminish their capacity to act as agents. Under the policy, users can still post what they were able to post before, follow whomever they were able to follow before, and so on. Now, Click-Gap *does* interfere with the freedom of purveyors of low-quality content of Facebook, but that is a separate matter (one that we will deal with later). We are not arguing that Click-Gap impedes no one's freedom; we are arguing that the freedom it *does* impede is not socially valuable.

This raises a complication: Since purveyors are users, one might argue that the interference condition *does* apply in the case of Click-Gap. It is true that the interference condition is met in this special case, but this is beside the point. In the special case where the interference condition is met, the improvement condition (the condition that the intervention is taken because it will improve the welfare of the person whose freedom or autonomy is affected) is *not* met. The intervention is not taken to shield those sharing low-quality content from their own content. Rather, it is to shield potential recipients from that information.

So Click-Gap does not meet the interference and improvement conditions simultaneously. Hence, it would not be an instance of paternalism on the standard account.

But the standard account of paternalism has important limitations. The view of paternalism we wish to advance here addresses those limitations. On that conception, Click-Gap *is* an instance of paternalism. The reason we do not adopt the standard definition of paternalism is because the improvement condition itself is flawed. To see why, consider Smoke Alarm:

> **Smoke Alarm.**[17] Molly is worried about the safety of her friend, Ray. Molly knows that there is no smoke alarm in Ray's apartment and that he tends to get distracted while cooking. Molly thinks that if she were to suggest that Ray get one, he would agree. But – knowing Ray – she does not think he would actually get one. She thinks

---

[16] This is not to say that the architecture of social media sites cannot influence users in important ways. We take it that the "technological seduction" that sites like YouTube exhibit *can* encroach on autonomy by, for example, seeding and nurturing convictions that either cannot be endorsed upon reflection *or* have been seeded and nurtured through methods that agents are alienated from. See Alfano, Carter, and Cheong, "Technological Seduction and Self-Radicalization."

[17] This case is inspired by an example from Ryan, "Paternalism: An Analysis."

that if she were to offer to buy him one, he would refuse. She buys him one anyway, thinking that he will accept and install the already bought alarm.

Molly's gifting a smoke alarm does not meet the interference condition. Ray adopts no attitudes that he is alienated from and he is left free to do what he wills. Yet – intuitively – Molly acts paternalistically toward him, at least to the extent that she acts to contravene his implicit choice not to install a smoke alarm in his apartment.

Our primary reason for rejecting the standard definition is its susceptibility to counterexamples like Smoke Alarm. But there are other issues. As Shane Ryan convincingly argues, there are also issues with the non-consent and improvement conditions.[18]

Contra the non-consent condition (the condition that P φ's without the consent of S): we seem to be able to act paternalistically, even when the paternalism is welcomed. Ryan drives this point with the example of a Victorian wife who has internalized the sexist norms of her culture and wills that her husband makes her important decisions for her.[19] The Victorian wife's husband's handling of her issues is paternalistic, even though she consents to it.

Contra the improvement condition (the condition that P φ's just because it will improve the welfare of S), we can act paternalistically when we fail to improve anyone's welfare.[20] Suppose the new alarm lulls Ray into a false sense of security, which results in even more careless behavior and a cooking fire. This is not enough to show that Molly's gesture was not paternalistic. All that seems to be required is that she *thought* that buying the smoke alarm would make him better off. Whether it does is beside the point.

For these reasons, we adopt the following account of paternalism from Ryan (2016):

Paternalism*: P acts paternalistically toward S by φ'ing *iff* the following conditions are met:

Insensitivity: P does so irrespective of what P believes the wishes of S might be.
Expected improvement: P does so just because P judges that φ'ing might or will advance S's ends (S's welfare, interests, values or good).[21]

By this definition, Click-Gap could qualify as a paternalistic intervention, so long as it is motivated by Facebook's judgment that improving people's epistemic lot improves their welfare.

Now, the connection between one's epistemic lot and their welfare is contested and complicated. It is certainly true that in many instances having knowledge – say, about where the lions, tigers, and Coronaviruses are, and thus how to avoid them – is often conducive to welfare. But it is not clear that knowledge is *always* conducive to welfare. Sometimes knowledge is irrelevant to our ends: Consider Ernest Sosa's

---

[18] Ryan.
[19] Ryan.
[20] Ryan.
[21] Ryan.

example of knowing how far two randomly selected grains of sand in the Sahara are from one another.[22] Likewise, sometimes knowledge can be detrimental to our ends: Consider Thomas Kelly's example of learning how a movie ends before you see it,[23] or Bernard Williams's case of a father whose son was lost at sea but for his own sanity believes – however improbably – that his son is alive somewhere.[24]

For these reasons, we will couch the rest of our discussion in terms of *epistemic paternalism*:

> **Epistemic Paternalism:** *P* acts epistemically paternalistically toward *S* by *φ'ing iff* the following conditions are met:
>
> *Insensitivity:* *P* does so irrespective of what *P* believes the wishes of *S* might be.
> *Expected epistemic improvement:* *P* does so just because *P* judges that *φ'ing* might or will make *S* epistemically better off.

Following Kristoffer Ahlstrom-Vij we will understand agents as epistemically better off when they undergo epistemic Pareto improvements with respect to a question that is of interest to them (where *epistemic Pareto improvements* are improvements along at least one epistemic dimension of evaluation without deterioration with respect to any other epistemic dimension of evaluation).[25]

Despite failing to meet the traditional conception of paternalism, Click-Gap is an instance of epistemic paternalism. Adam Mosseri, Vice President of Facebook's News Feed, has stated that Click-Gap is part of an effort to make users better informed.[26] In other words, the policy is in place so as to make users epistemically better off (i.e., expected epistemic improvement is met). Mosseri takes it that Facebook has an obligation to stage interventions like Click-Gap in order to fight the spread of misinformation via Facebook products. In explaining this obligation, Mosseri states that "all of us – tech companies, media companies, newsrooms, teachers – have a responsibility to do our part in addressing it."[27] The comparison to teachers is apt. Teachers often must be epistemically paternalistic toward their students. That is, they often must deliver information irrespective of the wishes of their students, just because it will epistemically benefit their students. Like teachers, Facebook won't tailor its delivery of information to the exact wants of its constituency. That is, it won't abandon Click-Gap in the face of pushback or disable it for users who do not want it. So insensitivity is met. This is, in part, due to the kind of pressure Facebook is reacting to when it takes part in interventions like Click-Gap, such as pressure from the public at large and governments[28] to fight the spread of fake news.

---

[22]   Sosa, "For the Love of Truth?"
[23]   Kelly, "Epistemic Rationality as Instrumental Rationality: A Critique."
[24]   Williams, "Deciding to Believe."
[25]   Ahlstrom-Vij, *Epistemic Paternalism.*
[26]   Mosseri, "Working to Stop Misinformation and False News."
[27]   Mosseri.
[28]   Germany is proposing a law to fine Facebook for advertisements containing fake news. See Olson, "Germany Wants Facebook to Pay for Fake News."

Now that we have articulated why Click-Gap is epistemically paternalistic, let's now turn to the moral question: Is it permissible? We will address this question by exploring it from two vantage points: that of Facebook users and purveyors. Let's start by looking at the intervention from the perspective of Facebook users. What claims might users have against the policy? We have already argued that the policy is not a threat to autonomy or freedom. Further, it is not plausible that the intervention will harm users. Given this – and the fact that the intervention is driven by noble aims – it is hard to see how users could reasonably reject Click-Gap.

What about the purveyors?

They might claim that, unlike users, this policy does undermine their autonomy or freedom. But it is difficult to see how much (if any) weight can be given to this claim. Start with autonomy. Purveyors are not fed any attitudes from which they could be alienated or which undermine their epistemic competency, so any claims from procedural independence will lack teeth. Claims from substantive independence will also miss the mark. Limiting persons' ability to expose others to misinformation does nothing to undermine means of social and relational support or create impediments to one's ability to exercise de facto control over their life. Hence, this kind of epistemic paternalism undermines neither psychological nor personal autonomy.

Complaints from freedom fail in similar fashion. Click-Gap does introduce constraints on effectuating the desires of purveyors. But more is needed to show that this makes Click-Gap *wrong*. The claim that it is wrong to place any constraint on freedom is clearly false, and one our Chapter 5 account rejects. Our account says that morally considerable freedom is quality of agency, and one's quality of agency is not diminished by limitations on the ability to disseminate misinformation. That's because exercising autonomy requires the ability to advance one's interests and abide fair terms of social cooperation. Sullying the epistemic environment may advance one's interests, but it is not consonant with fair terms of social cooperation. Further, purveyors still are left otherwise free to promote their ideas on the site. One way of doing this – posting content that does well on Facebook and not elsewhere – has been made less effective, but they are left free to promote their ideas by other means.

Finally, purveyors might say they have an interest impeded by the intervention. Given that their content is still allowed on Facebook and that Click-Gap leaves open many avenues to promoting content, the interest is only somewhat impeded. Moreover, it is not a particularly weighty interest. And even though the interest is impeded, there is an open question of whether such impediments are justified. We think they are, once we consider the reasons that speak in favor of the intervention. We turn to those next.

It is reasonable to think that Click-Gap will prevent significant harms to individuals. Policies like this have been proven to be quite effective. Consider Facebook's

2016 update to the Facebook Audience Network policy, which banned fake news
from ads.[29] As a result of this ban, fake news shared among users fell by about
75 percent.[30] Since fake news is a driver of harmful movements, such as vaccine
hesitancy, there is a strong consideration in favor of the policy. After all, those who
wind up sick because of vaccine hesitancy are significantly harmed.

Harms are not the only things to consider. Policies like Click-Gap also support
user autonomy. Consider the following:

> A growing body of evidence demonstrates that consumers struggle to evaluate the
> credibility and accuracy of online content. Experimental studies find that exposure to
> online information that is critical of vaccination leads to stronger anti-vaccine beliefs,
> since individuals do not take into account the credibility of the content [...]. Survey
> evidence [...] shows that only half of low-income parents of children with special
> healthcare needs felt "comfortable determining the quality of health websites" [...].
> Since only 12% of US adults are proficient in health literacy with 36% at basic or below
> basic levels [...], Fu et al. (2016) state that [...] "low-quality antivaccine web pages [...]
> promote compelling but unsubstantiated messages [opposing vaccination]."[31]

Interventions like Click-Gap are an important element of respecting users' autonomy. The intervention, if successful, will protect users from internalizing attitudes
that would be inauthentically held.

Click-Gap is thus a policy that all parties effected could reasonably endorse.
Further, Facebook *must* engage policies like Click-Gap: Users who adopt unwarranted beliefs because of fake news and individuals who contract illnesses because of
vaccine hesitancy have a very strong claim against Facebook's taking a laissez-faire
approach to combating fake news on its site.

Interventions like Click-Gap, then, are not only permissible; they should be
common. Such interventions, however, are limited. Click-Gap might be able to
pop some users' epistemic bubbles, but they are unlikely to dismantle sturdier
structures such as echo chambers. So there is good reason to look into what we
may do to chip away at these structures, a topic to which we now turn.

6.2 DISMANTLING ECHO CHAMBERS

In fall 2017, Reddit – a social media site consisting of message boards ("subreddits")
based on interests (e.g., science, world news, gaming) – banned r/incels,[32] a message
board for "incels," people who have trouble finding romantic partners.[33] The group

---

29 Wingfield, Isaac, and Benner, "Google and Facebook Take Aim at Fake News Sites."
30 Chiou and Tucker, "Fake News and Advertising on Social Media: A Study of the Anti-Vaccination
    Movement."
31 Chiou and Tucker.
32 The URL of a subreddit begins with "reddit.com/r/." For this reason, many subreddits, such as the
    subreddit for world news, are referred to as "r/worldnews."
33 Beauchamp, "Incels: A Definition and Investigation into a Dark Internet Corner."

was banned for hosting "content that encourages, glorifies, incites, or calls for violence or physical harm against an individual or a group of people."[34] We take it that the ban was justified; banning a group is an intrusive step, but such intrusions can be justified when the stakes are high, such as when physical harm is threatened. Here, we would like to ask what Reddit may have done before the stakes were so high and what Reddit may have done before things got so out of hand.[35] We begin with some history.

The term "incel," which was derived from "involuntary celibate," was coined by "Alana Boltwood" (a pseudonym the creator of the term uses to protect her offline identity) in the early 1990s as part of Alana's Involuntary Celibacy Project, an upbeat and inclusive online support group for the romantically challenged.[36] However – as of this writing – "incel" has lost any associations with positivity or inclusiveness.

In the 2000s and early 2010s, Alana's Involuntary Celibacy Project inspired the founding of other incel websites, several of which were dominated by conversations that were "a cocktail of misery and defeatism – all mixed with a strong shot of misogyny."[37] Here are some representative comments from one such site, *Love-Shy.com*:

> The bulk of my anger is over the fact that virtually all women are dishonest to the point that even they themselves believe the lies they tell.
>
> The reality, and I make no apologies for saying this, is that the modern woman is an impossible to please, shallow, superficial creature that is only attracted to shiny things, e.g. looks and money.

By some point in the early 2010s, "incel" and "involuntary celibate" were yoked to the negative, misogynistic thread of inceldom. One turning point was a highly publicized murder spree in Isla Vista in 2014, where Elliot Rodger – a self-identified incel – murdered six college students as part of a "revolution" against women and feminism.[38] Incels are now so strongly associated with misogyny and violence that the Southern Poverty Law center describes them as part of the "online male supremacist ecosystem" and tracks them on the center's "hate map" (a geographical map of hate groups in America).[39]

An online petition that called for banning r/incels described the group as "a toxic echo chamber for its users, [...] a dark corner of the internet that finally needs to be addressed."[40] The petition details the problematic content on r/incels:

34 "Update on Site-Wide Rules Regarding Violent Content."
35 Of course, it is possible that in this particular case Reddit could not have prevented r/incels from becoming so toxic; perhaps that was inevitable. Nevertheless, we would like to explore some steps Reddit may have taken as a preventative measure.
36 Beauchamp, "Incels: A Definition and Investigation into a Dark Internet Corner."
37 Baker, "What Happens to Men Who Can't Have Sex."
38 Glasstetter, "Shooting Suspect Elliot Rodger's Misogynistic Posts Point to Motive."
39 Janik, "'I Laugh at the Death of Normies': How Incels Are Celebrating the Toronto Mass Killing."
40 Cochran, "Shut Down the Subreddit r/incels."

Violence against women is encouraged. Rape against women is justified and encouraged. [. . .] Users often canonize Elliot Rodger, [. . .] [who is] is often referred to as "Saint Elliot" with many praising his actions and claiming that they would like to follow in his path.[41]

Recall that we have described echo chambers as structures that, like epistemic bubbles, leave relevant sources of information out but, unlike epistemic bubbles, actively discredit those sources.[42] Let us now ask: Was r/incels in fact an echo chamber, as the petition claims?

We think so. r/incels did not just create a space where people with similar ideas about women and feminism congregated. It actively left dissenting voices out. As a petition to have r/incels banned states, "the moderators [of r/incels] have allowed this group to become the epicenter for misogyny on Reddit, *banning users that disagree with the hate speech that floods this forum.*"[43]

Dissent was not the only reason users were banned; some were excluded simply for being identified as women. It is difficult to run a rigorous study – it has been noted that "the community [of incels] is deeply hostile to outsiders, particularly researchers and journalists"[44] – but polls have found that r/braincels (another popular incel subreddit, which was banned in 2019) is nearly all men.[45] These demographics were kept up in part through the use of banning; it has been reported that in r/braincels, women were banned "on sight."[46] All the while outsiders (derisively referred to as "normies"[47]) and women ("femoids,"[48] "Stacys,"[49] and "Beckys"[50]) were demeaned in the conversations they were excluded from.

This is disconcerting for many reasons, not least of which is the vulnerability to misinformation about women and dating manifest in users drawn to groups like r/incels. Consider the stories of the pseudonymous "Abe" and "John," each of whom seems to be a typical incel.[51]

---

[41]   Cochran.
[42]   Nguyen, "Echo Chambers and Epistemic Bubbles."
[43]   Cochran, "Shut Down the Subreddit r/incels" (emphasis added).
[44]   Beauchamp, "Incels: A Definition and Investigation into a Dark Internet Corner."
[45]   Beauchamp.
[46]   Beauchamp.
[47]   "[A]nyone who is broadly neurotypical, average-looking and of average intelligence." See Squirrel, "A Definitive Guide to Incels."
[48]   "A portmanteau of 'female' and 'humanoid' or 'android,' this term is used to describe women as sub-human or non-human. Some incels go further and use the term 'Female Humanoid Organism,' or FHO for short." See Sonnad and Squirrell, "The Alt-Right Is Creating Its Own Dialect. Here's the Dictionary."
[49]   Women considered to be "air-headed, unintelligent, beautiful and promiscuous." See Squirrel, "A Definitive Guide to Incels."
[50]   "[T]he 'average' woman [. . .] who 'will likely die [sic] her hair green, pink, or blue after attending college' and 'posts provocative pictures because she needs attention' despite being a '6/10.'" See Jennings, "Incels Categorize Women by Personal Style and Attractiveness."
[51]   The stories of both John and Abe can be found in Beauchamp, "Incels: A Definition and Investigation into a Dark Internet Corner."

Abe, 19, is a lifelong loner who claims to have once dated someone for a month. Abe turned to the internet for support. There he found a cadre of people who were happy to reinforce his belief that the problem was his looks (this is a common incel trope – that our romantic futures are determined by superficial, genetically encoded traits such as height, the strength of one's jawline, and length of one's forehead), and "how manipulative some women can be when seeking validation" (this reflects another trope – that women are shallow, opportunistic, and cruel).[52]

One helpful way to understand this process comes from Alfano, Carter, and Cheong's notion of technological seduction, which we first encountered in the previous chapter.[53] The core idea is that people can encounter ideas that fulfill psychological needs and are consistent with personal dispositions and be attracted – *seduced* – into reading, listening, and watching more related ideas. This often happens in a way that ramps up or becomes more extreme. Users become seduced into a kind of self-radicalization. They need not have had an antecedent belief in the seductive ideas to start identifying with them. The Abe example exhibits these characteristics. He came to the incel community predisposed to think he was an especially bad case and that women were cruel. The community was happy to indulge these thoughts. He then spent more time in the community and began to adopt even more fatalistic views about his dating prospects and more cynical views about women.

John, like Abe, turned to incel groups for support due to feelings of isolation. He too thinks that immutable features of his appearance have doomed him to a life of romantic isolation:

> Most people will not be in my situation, so they can't relate. They can't comprehend someone being so ugly that they can't get a girlfriend [...] What I noticed was how similar my situation was to the other guys. I thought I was the only one in the world so inept at dating.[54]

The truth, of course, is that many – if not most – people can relate to these feelings. As Beauchamp notes, "All of us have, at one point, experienced our share of rejection or loneliness."[55] But when socially isolated young men congregate around the idea that they are uniquely a bad case, that anyone who says otherwise is an ideological foe, and when they can exclude perceived ideological foes from their universe of information (as well as anyone whom their conspiracy theories scapegoat and stereotype), the result is a toxic mix of radicalizing ideas and people vulnerable to their uptake. Note that John, too, seems to be a victim of technological seduction.

---

[52] Beauchamp.
[53] Alfano, Carter, and Cheong, "Technological Seduction and Self-Radicalization."
[54] Beauchamp, "Incels: A Definition and Investigation into a Dark Internet Corner."
[55] Beauchamp.

So what might we do to ameliorate this while respecting the autonomy of the members of groups like r/incels? In what follows we investigate two epistemically paternalistic approaches, one that involves making access to alternative points of view salient, another involves making the barriers of the echo chamber itself more porous.

6.2.1 Access to Reasons

Cass Sunstein discusses a number of remedies to echo chambers and filter bubbles that involve providing access to reasons that speak against the ideology of the chamber or bubble.[56]

One such remedy involves the introduction of an "opposing viewpoint button," inspired by an article by Geoffrey Fowler, arguing that Facebook should add a button to News Feed. This button would, in Fowler's words, "turn all the conservative viewpoints that you see liberal, or vice versa."[57] This would enable users to "realize that [their] [...] news might look nothing like [their] [...] neighbor's."[58] Such a button might not make very much sense in a subreddit, but a variation of it might. Perhaps Reddit could offer dissenting groups the opportunity to have a link posted to a subreddit's menu that would take users to a statement or page that outlines an opposing point of view.

Or, perhaps, instead of a link to a statement, subreddits could have links to deliberative domains, "spaces where people with different views can meet and exchange reasons, and have a chance to understand, as least a bit, the point of view of those who disagree with them."[59]

Whether it is via a link to a statement or a deliberative domain, both proposals involve the adding of an option to access reasons from the opposing side. Were either taken unilaterally and in the spirit of improving users' epistemic lot, they would be instances of epistemic paternalism.

Now we can ask, were Reddit to explore this option of adding access to reasons – either through an opposing viewpoint button or link to a deliberative space – would it be permissible?

We think so, and we will explain why in familiar fashion. The relevant perspective from which to view the intervention is that of the denizens of r/incels. The intervention would not limit the freedom or autonomy of any of the members of the group, nor would it harm them. They are left free to have whatever discussions they please, post whatever they'd like to, and so on. If their minds are changed by the intervention it will be through the cool exchange of reasons, a process of changing their minds from which they cannot be alienated.

---

[56]   Sunstein, *#Republic: Divided Democracy in the Age of Social Media*.
[57]   Fowler, "What If Facebook Gave Us an Opposing-Viewpoints Button?"
[58]   Fowler.
[59]   Sunstein, *#Republic: Divided Democracy in the Age of Social Media*.

6.2.2 *Inclusiveness*

While the proposals under the banner "access to reasons" are promising and permissible, such proposals might not go very far in addressing the issue of echo chambers. It's likely that many users simply wouldn't take advantage of the opportunity to use the links. And, if they did and the experience changed their mind, they would likely leave or be exited from the echo chambers they belonged to. So, while the above proposals may help an individual user escape an echo chamber, the "access to reasons" proposals – on their own – are likely not enough.

Let us, then, explore a proposal that may offer further assistance. At the moment, the moderators of subreddits (and similar entities such as Facebook groups and so on) are free to ban users from their discussions at their discretion. We saw earlier that women were banned from r/braincels "on sight."[60] This, clearly, does not help the community's distorted view of women. The power to ban gives moderators the ability to form and maintain echo chambers, as it gives them the power to literally exclude certain voices from their discussions.

Another class of interventions, then, might be aimed at limiting this power. What might this look like?

Sites like Reddit could give its users some entitlement to not being excluded from subreddits strictly for belonging to a protected class, and this could be accomplished by modifying moderators' privileges to ban users at their own discretion. The site could, for example, discourage discrimination on the basis of protected attributes by stating that it is a behavior that is not allowed on the site and (partially) enforcing this by making some kind of appeals process for bans or suspending moderators who violate the policy.

As a supplement or alternative, a similar system could be set up for bans that do not result from breaking any site-wide or explicitly stated group rules. The idea here is that groups that have moderators who want to ban ideological foes would have to at least do so openly or not at all. The hope here is that many groups would not be okay with this as an explicit policy, reducing or eliminating cases where moderators have an unofficial policy of banning ideological foes.

Anyone familiar with Reddit might object to this suggestion on practical grounds, saying that the site is too large and anonymous for this to work. There are roughly 2 million subreddits in existence, with single subreddits having tens of millions of users.[61] Further, users are typically anonymous, and it is very easy to make new accounts. As a practical matter, the objection goes, such a change to the site is just not feasible.

Reddit's scale and design do present practical difficulties for these proposals, but it does not make them unworkable. There are various ways in which the proposals can be implemented at scale. For example, the site could – for practical reasons – rule that appeals can only be made by certain accounts, such as accounts that have existed for more than a certain amount of time and have been verified. And this rule

---

[60] Beauchamp, "Incels: A Definition and Investigation into a Dark Internet Corner."
[61] Reddit Metrics, "Top Subreddits."

could, of course, be enforced using algorithms. Penalties for frivolous appeals could also be part of the policy. The site could also consider limiting investigations by only investigating moderators when patterns of appeals appear, for example, once a moderator has racked up a certain number of appeals from verified users in a certain time period. This, too, could be managed algorithmically to make the solution scalable.

Assuming that the practical objection could be addressed, we can then ask: Are these policies permissible?

We think so. To show this, let's look at the policy from the point of view that might have complaints about the proposal: the moderators. What complaints might moderators have? Their autonomy isn't being undercut, nor are they being harmed. So it does not seem that they could make complaints from autonomy or harm. However, they are being constrained in what they can do. So, perhaps, they can complain that their freedom is being encroached upon, specifically in the form of diminished quality of agency. This, it seems, is the only plausible complaint they might have. So it is the one we will explore.

But we now can return to a familiar refrain: That a course of action will limit an agent's freedom is not enough to show that it is wrong. Legal bans on murder limit our freedom, but not wrongfully so. Limiting moderator's privileges to ban users is, we think, a permissible constraint on their freedom. This is because the complaint from moderators that putting a check on banning limits their freedom is complicated by two factors. One factor is that their freedom to ban users limits users' freedom to partake in the conversations they are banned from. So their claim to the freedom to ban users butts up against the freedom of the users they will ban. The other factor is that while some bans are non-objectionable – bans made in response to violations of Reddit's site-wide ban on involuntary pornography, for example – the class of bans we are discussing here is objectionable. Users who have been banned based on their membership to a protected class can reasonably object to those bans and to a system that allows them.

6.3 CONCLUSION

Since much of the internet information environment is epistemically noxious, there is lots of room and opportunity for epistemically paternalistic interventions such as Click-Gap, opposing viewpoint buttons, and modifications to moderators' privileges. Hence, many epistemically paternalistic policies can (and should) be a perennial part of the internet information environment. What should we conclude from that? One thing is that we should recognize that developers should engage in epistemic paternalism as a matter of course. Another is that our focus in evaluating epistemically relevant interventions should not be on whether such actions are epistemically paternalistic. Rather, it should be on how they relate to other values (such as well-being, autonomy, freedom, and so on).

PART IV

The Responsibilities of Agents

7

Agency Laundering and Information Technologies

There have been numerous examples of automated decision systems going wrong in consequential ways. In 2018, an Uber-automated driving system failed to recognize a bicyclist, whom it struck and killed.[1] In 2012, the Target Corporation received international attention when, based on predictive analytics and an automated advertising system, it sent fliers targeting women seeking prenatal products to a minor before she had revealed her pregnancy to one of her parents.[2] In 2017, the news organization ProPublica was able to use Facebook's automated system to make an ad buy targeting users with anti-Semitic affiliations.[3] The system even suggested additional racist categories to make the ad purchase more effective. As we have discussed, COMPAS yields different results depending on the race and ethnicity of defendants.[4] A common element in these stories is that the technology itself plays an important role. The existence and use of technological systems are a key part of the explanation of the events. Whether (and how) the technologies are relevant in assessing moral responsibility is considerably more complex.

Our discussion so far has focused on how persons deserve to be treated in light of their autonomy and conditions necessary for people to act autonomously. This chapter instead considers the moral agency of those who deploy information technologies (as collectors of big data, users of algorithmic decision systems, developers of social media sites, and so on).

We will argue that a type of moral wrong that can arise in using automated decision tools is "agency laundering." At root, agency laundering involves obfuscating one's moral responsibility by enlisting a technology or process to take some action and letting it forestall others from demanding an account for bad outcomes that result. Laundering is not unique to information technologies. However, we

[1] Levin and Wong, "Self-Driving Uber Kills Arizona Woman in First Fatal Crash Involving Pedestrian."
[2] Duhigg, "How Companies Learn Your Secrets." Note that a number of commentators believe the story makes too close a connection between predictive analytics and pregnancy-related advertising. There are reasons to send such advertising to people who are not pregnant, the advertising may have been based on criteria unrelated to pregnancy, and others. Harford, "Big Data."
[3] Angwin, Varner, and Tobin, "Facebook Enabled Advertisers to Reach 'Jew Haters.'"
[4] Angwin et al., "Machine Bias," May 23, 2016.

argue that the concept of agency laundering helps understand important moral problems in several recent cases involving algorithmic systems. The moral concerns are not merely that values are instantiated within such systems, but that intermingling moral wrongs with morally permissible processes undermines a fundamental facet of responsibility itself.

We begin, in Section 7.1, with an account of responsibility to ground our arguments. In Section 7.2, we develop our account of agency laundering and explain its moral salience. In Sections 7.3 through 7.6, we offer several case studies that allow us to apply and further explain our conception. One is Facebook's targeted advertising system and its response to complaints that it allows users to make racist ad purchases. This is a clear case of agency laundering. Next, we consider Uber's use of algorithmic systems in its driver-management apps and show how we can distinguish cases of agency laundering from non-agency laundering in structurally similar cases. We then turn to public-sector uses, showing how school districts can launder agency in teacher-evaluation cases and how courts can avoid agency laundering by clarifying responsibility for decision systems. In Section 7.7, we explain how agency laundering is distinct from other concepts, especially the "responsibility gap."[5]

7.1 AGENCY AND RESPONSIBILITY

Our argument turns on the concept of responsibility. For a person to launder his or her agency requires that he or she be a moral agent in the first place, and being a moral agent requires that one be in some sense morally responsible. In this section, we first distinguish several facets of responsibility and how they relate to one another, which helps structure our understanding of agency laundering in the following section. Then, we offer a substantive account of responsibility, which will ground our understanding of the moral wrongs associated with agency laundering.

7.1.1 *The Structure of Responsibility*

In *Punishment and Responsibility*, H. L. A. Hart describes a ship captain who gets drunk, wrecks their ship, is convicted of criminal negligence, and whose employer is held financially liable for the loss of life and property.[6] Hart's allegory and the distinctions he offers are useful in grounding our account.[7]

To begin, a person might be responsible in virtue of a role. In Hart's example, a person is responsible for a ship's safety in virtue of the fact that they are the captain.

---

[5]   Matthias, "The Responsibility Gap: Ascribing Responsibility for the Actions of Learning Automata."
[6]   Hart, *Punishment and Responsibility; Essays in the Philosophy of Law*, 211.
[7]   Our account of the structure of responsibility follows closely those articulated by Nicole Vincent and Chris Kutz. Both Vincent and Kutz recast Hart's ship captain case to distinguish various facets of responsibility. See Vincent, "A Structured Taxonomy of Responsibility Concepts"; Kutz, "Responsibility."

A person's role requires them to anticipate events in some domain and to take actions to avoid bad outcomes in that domain.[8] A ship captain should anticipate bad weather and obstacles and plot course accordingly. Parents should anticipate their children's needs and plan ways to address them. Financial advisors should anticipate client needs and economic forecasts and guide clients' actions suitably. Although one's well-defined social roles (ship captain, parent, financial trustor) may give rise to specific responsibilities, the idea of role responsibility is broad enough to encompass general obligations one has as a moral agent. So, for example, adults have a responsibility to operate heavy machinery carefully, regardless of their specialized social roles; community members have a responsibility to pay applicable taxes; and people engaged in commerce have a responsibility to bargain in good faith.[9]

Second is *causal* responsibility or the link between an agent's action (or omission or disposition[10]) and an event that results from it. Chris Kutz calls this *explanatory* responsibility, as causation generally explains an event.[11] Any explanation of the shipwreck that ignores the captain and the captain's drinking would be inadequate. Causal responsibility in this sense does not entail moral responsibility. That is because of the third facet, capacity responsibility, which relates to whether an agent has the requisite capacities to be responsible for an outcome. One may lack capacity responsibility due to pathology or pre-reflective, non-deliberative action. In Hart's example, it is possible that a ship captain's drinking was due to extreme, clinical anxiety, in which case their intoxication is something they caused, but for which they lacked the required capacity to be responsible.[12] Alternatively, one may lack capacity due to lack of access to relevant information. That is, an agent must be in a position to access certain facts about their actions and their significance in order to be retrospectively morally responsible for them.

We can sum up the structure so far as follows. For a person to be (retrospectively) morally responsible – which is to say *morally liable* – for some event or outcome, they must have some role responsibility (either a specific duty that attaches to a social role or a general duty as a moral agent) and they must be causally responsible for the outcome (which is to say an action of theirs is a key part of the explanation of

---

[8] Antony Duff calls this "prospective" responsibility. See Duff, "Responsibility." Here we should note that we are only discussing morally justifiable roles, where the holders of role responsibility are themselves moral agents. Hence, being assigned a role within a criminal organization, or being assigned a role when one lacks the capacity to act morally, cannot confer role responsibility in the required sense.

[9] Goodin, "Responsibilities"; Goodin, "Apportioning Responsibilities"; Williams, "Responsibility as a Virtue"; Vincent, "A Structured Taxonomy of Responsibility Concepts."

[10] For the sake of simplicity, we will refer to "actions" in discussing responsibility. However, our account extends to omissions and dispositions. Note, too, that causal responsibility is complicated in overde-termination cases. But those cases do not affect our analysis here.

[11] Kutz, "Responsibility," 549.

[12] This, of course, may not absolve the captain completely. Fischer and Ravizza, *Responsibility and Control: A Theory of Moral Responsibility*, 49–51, for an explanation of "tracing" responsibility to prior actions.

the outcome). Moreover, they must have capacity responsibility. That is, their action must not be the result of some pathology or pre-reflective action, and they must in some sense have access to relevant information.[13] For the remainder of the chapter we use "moral responsibility" and "moral liability" interchangeably, and they will refer to this conjunction of role responsibility, causal responsibility, and capacity responsibility.

7.1.2 *The Content of Responsibility*

With these distinctions in mind, we can turn to the *content* of moral responsibility. In other words, once we have determined that an actor has some kind of role responsibility, is causally responsible for an outcome, and has the requisite capacity to be responsible, there is a further question about what this responsibility means. There are two key features of the view we endorse here. First, moral responsibility is fundamentally relational and grounded in social roles. Second, being morally responsible for some action means that one is accountable for (and should be able to provide an account of) their reasons for that action.

The view that moral responsibility is fundamentally relational owes a great deal to Peter Strawson's seminal article, "Freedom and Resentment."[14] Holding a person responsible by forming reactive attitudes about him or her (e.g., appreciation, admiration, disdain) is a feature of interpersonal relationships in which one regards the other as a participant. We might resent the captain for getting drunk and steering their ship onto the rocks, or we might admire them for their skill in guiding the ship to safety during a storm. However, we do not form such reactive attitudes toward entities that are not participants in relationships; resentment and admiration are not reasonable reactions to the actions of infants or machines. If an autopilot algorithm successfully steers the ship to safety, it would be appropriate to be impressed, baffled, or happy, but not to feel respect and admiration for the algorithm itself.

Despite these important insights, precisely what (if anything) justifies reactive attitudes is a further question. As Marina Oshana points out, the mere fact (if it is) that people are committed to the appropriateness of their reactive attitudes toward (some) people for (some of) their actions cannot suffice to explain why those reactions are appropriate. We do not call a person morally responsible just because others *regard them* as responsible. Rather, "we call a person an appropriate subject of reactive attitudes because the person *is* [morally] responsible."[15]

---

[13]   There remain some controversial issues, including for example Frankfurt-style cases in which one may be responsible or not regardless of whether they do or do not know how their actions will be causally effective. But the issues in those cases turn on the link between causal responsibility and the ability to do otherwise. That does not affect our arguments.

[14]   Strawson, "Freedom and Resentment."

[15]   Oshana, "Ascriptions of Responsibility," 1997, 75 (emphasis added).

While keeping in mind the important social function of responsibility attribu-tions, our view aligns with the constellation of views for which an agent's moral responsibility turns on whether they are answerable or accountable for their actions. Angela Smith, for example, argues that for an agent to be morally responsible for something is for the agent to be "open, in principle, to demands for justification regarding that thing."[16] And blame is in effect a demand that the agent "justify herself." Oshana's view is related. She articulates an accountability view according to which a person is responsible if, and only if, "it ought to be the case that the person account for her behavior." Giving such an account requires a person to provide a statement of their "beliefs or intentions" for their actions. "Thus," Oshana explains, "'X is accountable for Y' can be unpacked as 'It is appropriate that X explain her intentions in doing (or being) Y'."[17]

The key insight of the accountability views is that they identify not only who is morally responsible but what that responsibility involves. Specifically, it is justifiable to ask the responsible agent to account for their actions, omissions, or dispositions. They should be able to explain their intentions, reasons, and actions in terms that other relationship participants can understand.

7.2 AGENCY LAUNDERING

With our discussion of responsibility in mind, we can return to the chapter's central argument. Using an automated process to make decisions can allow a person to distance themself from morally suspect actions by attributing the decision to the system, thereby laundering their agency. Put slightly differently, invoking the com-plexity or automated nature of a decision system to explain an outcome allows

[16] Smith, "Attributability, Answerability, and Accountability," 577–578. Within this group of views, there is substantial debate about whether person X is responsible for Y in virtue of Y being attributable to X, of X being answerable for Y, or of X being accountable for Y. Scanlon's view focuses on attributability (Scanlon 2008). Shoemaker distinguishes between attributability, answerability, and accountability (Shoemaker 2011). Smith (like Shoemaker) distinguishes a thing being attributable to a person and that person being responsible for it; however, she views accountability as a species of answerability. What is important for our purposes is that each of the views in this constellation recognizes that the content of responsibility claims is that responsible agents are those for whom it is appropriate, or for whom it ought to be the case, that they provide an account of their intentions, interests, and reasons for an action.

[17] Oshana, "Ascriptions of Responsibility," 1997, 77. Fischer and Ravizza provide an accountability view that bridges (a) Strawson's attention to the social function of holding others responsible by way of reactive attitudes and (b) accountability views' attention to reasons. Specifically, they maintain that an agent is responsible if they are an apt target of reactive attitudes. More important here, though, is that being morally responsible for actions requires that agents exercise "guidance control." That requires that agents be at least weakly reasons-responsive, which is to say that where the agent has access to strong reasons in favor or against an action, they will act in accordance with those reasons. It also requires that the source of actions be the agent, which is to say that the reason-responsiveness is internal to the agent. Fischer and Ravizza, *Responsibility and Control: A Theory of Moral Responsibility*, 31–41.

a party to imply that the action is something for which they are not morally responsible.

Compare money laundering.[18] Where one has such large amounts of illicit cash that spending it or placing it into legitimate financial instruments would be suspicious, one can launder it by mingling it with other, legitimate streams of income so that the illicit cash appears legal. For example, one might add the illegal cash to money received in a legal, cash-dependent business.[19] The bad thing (income from an illicit source) is hidden by the existence of some other, similar phenomenon. To be clear, we are not making an argument by analogy; decisions are not like cash. Rather, the point is that it is possible to obscure the source of responsibility for actions and make them appear unsuspicious by mingling them with other actions.

Consider a minor example ("Chair"). Suppose that Cheese State University vests department chairs with control over curriculum. A chair and several members of their department would like to get rid of phlogiston studies ("P-studies") because they think it is unimportant. The chair could do this unilaterally by removing courses, reassigning instructors, and altering degree requirements but wants to avoid the wrath of the department phlogistologists. The chair therefore delegates curriculum decisions to a committee of people who they know want to eliminate P-studies. When P-partisans complain, the chair responds that it was the committee's decision, though the chair knew from the beginning what that decision would be. By impaneling a committee to ensure the results the chair wanted, the chair obscures their own role in the decision. The committee appears to be the relevant power, though it remained the chair.

There are several features of Chair to address initially. First is that the chair had legitimate institutional authority to make the decision, and if they had moved to eliminate P-studies unilaterally it would have happened. The chair's institutional authority is a form of role responsibility for their department's curriculum. The chair has the responsibility to anticipate educational needs, department resources, student demand, scholarly trends, and so forth, and to ensure that the department's offerings adequately address them. And the chair's de facto power to alter the curriculum is a form of causal responsibility; when the curriculum changes, the chair's actions are an essential part of the explanation why.

Second, although the chair has power to make the decision, they draw in a separate body by giving the committee some degree of causal responsibility. Because the curriculum change would not occur without the committee's work, the committee is an essential part of the explanation for the curriculum change. It is not the only cause, as it is mixed with the chair's actions. Third, when the chair forms the committee, they imply it is neutral, would weigh evidence fairly, and might act

---

[18] 18 U.S. Code § 1956 – Laundering of monetary instruments.
[19] Other aspects of money laundering are about concealing identities of agents, for example by routing illicit money through shell corporations and bank accounts in permissive jurisdictions.

in a way that the chair doesn't anticipate. But that's a ruse – ex hypothesi, the chair knows that the committee will act just as the chair wishes.

Fourth, the chair's actions obscure their causal responsibility with respect to the curriculum. The chair is able to obscure the fact that they orchestrated the result by making the committee partially causally responsible (i.e., a key part of the explanation) for the result. Fifth, although the chair appears to fulfill their responsibility in shepherding the curriculum, appointing the committee obscures the chair's designs to eliminate P-studies.

The following is a definition of agency laundering that incorporates these features of Chair. An agent (*a*) launders their agency where

(1) *a* is morally responsible with respect to some domain X, *and*
(2) *a* ensures that *b* (some process, person, or entity) has some causal responsibility with respect to X, *and*
(3) *a* ascribes (implicitly or explicitly) morally relevant qualities to *b*'s actions (e.g., relevance, neutrality, reliability), *and*
(4) in virtue of (2) and (3), *a* obscures the scope of their causal responsibility with respect to X, *and*
(5) in virtue of (4), *a* fails to adequately account for events within X for which they are morally responsible.

This definition only gets us so far. It sets out the structure of agency laundering, which tracks and incorporates the structure of moral responsibility from Section 7.1.1. However, it does not explain the moral problem of agency laundering itself (if there is one). That's our next task.

There are several ways in which the chair may have acted wrongly. One possibility is that it is unjustifiable to eliminate phlogistology in any case. But let's leave that aside and assume that it's permissible to eliminate it based on its substance and the context. More important is that the chair's ascription of morally relevant qualities to the committee is misleading, and they have therefore deceived people about the process involved. Regardless of whether getting rid of P-studies is justifiable, the chair's obscuring their reasons and intentions in impaneling the committee do not appear justifiable. Others with whom the chair has a relationship have a claim to understand such an important facet of their professional lives.

A still deeper moral problem is that the chair's action allows them to avoid the core demand of responsibility, which is to provide an account. Regardless of whether the chair is meeting their role responsibilities with respect to the curriculum, they are forestalling others' ability to demand an account for the chair's actions within a domain of their legitimate concern.[20] This is the defining feature of agency laundering, and it turns on the substantive account of responsibility given in

---

[20] Two other accounts addressing causal and moral responsibility in the computing context are worth noting here. First, Daniel Dennett posits that machines may be credited with (i.e., responsible for) some tasks (e.g., Deep Blue beating Kasparov) but cannot be responsible for others (e.g., murdering

Section 7.1.2. There, we explained that responsibility is first about social relations. We hold others responsible for their actions in part by forming reactive attitudes, and such reactive attitudes are key in understanding responsibility. However, our view is that moral responsibility is also a matter of whether agents are open to demands to justify their actions and whether it is appropriate for others to demand an account of their reasons and intentions.

Now we come full circle. Agency laundering involves a kind of misdirection (as in (2)–(4)). But, crucially, the misdirection undermines others' ability to demand reasons for an agent's actions. In other words, the *laundering* part of agency laundering cuts straight to the heart of *what responsibility is* by undermining the ability of others to ask the agent to provide an account.

Department members will be unable to ask the chair for their reasons and intentions in eliminating phlogistography, because the chair's actions look like formation of a committee that (apparently) deliberated about and then eliminated the subfield. Department members would reasonably believe that all the chair has to provide is an account of delegation to the committee. But an account that focused on the committee would *not* be an account of the chair's actual reasons and intentions, which are about engineering an outcome, not initiating a process to weigh things.[21]

It is worth explaining the role of condition (5) a bit further. What matters about (5) is that it distinguishes cases like Chair from structurally similar cases of delegation. Consider a variation in which the chair thinks P-studies should be eliminated, and they know that there are so few P-sympathists that any full committee will have a majority of P-eliminationists. Nonetheless, the chair delegates the curriculum decision to a committee because of their commitment to inclusive, democratic

Kasparov). Dennett, "When Hal Kills, Who's to Blame? Computer Ethics." We would argue that this difference tracks the causal/moral responsibility distinction, though that is not Dennett's claim. Helen Nissenbaum argues that the increased use of computing systems poses a threat to accountability, based on four key barriers. These include the problem of many hands, the existence of bugs that cause computing failures, the ability to use computers as scapegoats, and the separation of system ownership from legal liability for problems. In doing so she notes that distributed causal responsibility can function to obscure responsibility and blameworthiness. See Nissenbaum, "Computing and Accountability," 74. Our view of laundering can apply to each of the barriers she discusses but does not reduce to any of them. Consider the example of "blaming the computer" or pointing to the computer as the sole source of causal responsibility. That considered by itself would not seem to be a case of laundering, but instead just a straightforward denial of responsibility. If, instead, it included a process by which a party ensures the computer has causal responsibility, ascribes morally relevant qualities to the computer's actions, obscures the party's causal responsibility, and in so doing fails to adequately account for events for which the party is morally responsible, it could be laundering. In other words, merely blaming something else does not rise to laundering. Laundering is, we take it, more insidious in that it forestalls others' abilities to demand an account of actions within domains of their legitimate concern.

21   Note that agency laundering does not require that one infringe one's substantive role responsibilities (except to the extent that one's role responsibility includes being transparent about one's causal responsibility). In Chair, for example, it is plausible that the chair was fulfilling their role responsibilities with respect to the department's curriculum. We return to this point in Section 7.4.

department governance. As in Chair, (1)–(3) obtain. And (4) plausibly obtains, as the chair's causal responsibility in forming the committee may obscure their causal role in deciding to review P-studies. But the key difference is that the committee formation in "Democratic Chair" is not a sham, constructed so that the chair can avoid having to account for their actions regarding the curriculum. Just as in the original example, department members will reasonably believe that the action for which the chair should provide an account is the formation of the committee. But in democratic chair, that *is* the only action for which the chair should provide an account.

So that's the account. Let's turn to some cases. These will help us understand how predictive, automated decision systems can launder agency.

7.3 FACEBOOK AND ANTI-SEMITIC ADVERTISING

In 2017, ProPublica published a report detailing an investigation into Facebook-targeted advertising practices.[22] Using Facebook's automated system, the ProPublica team found a user-generated category called "Jew hater" with more than 2,200 members. While two thousand Facebook users choosing to identify as "Jew hater" in their profiles seems like a lot, Facebook's platform helpfully informed the ProPublica team that it was too small an audience for an effective ad buy. To help ProPublica find a larger audience (and hence have a better ad purchase), Facebook suggested a number of additional categories. For example, it suggested including the category "Second Amendment," presumably because of some overlap in users' choices of interests in their profiles. ProPublica used the platform to select other profiles displaying anti-Semitic categories, and Facebook approved ProPublica's ad with minor changes.

Facebook's platform also allows clients to target ads by excluding profiles by age, geographic, and race and ethnic categories. For example, advertisers can target users in specific places and income ranges while excluding people with specific "ethnic affinities." Many of these affiliations are generated automatically, based on content users and their friends have liked or shared. In some cases it is not the category that creates a problem, but the purpose of the ad. Targeting an ad by age makes sense in some contexts (life insurance, toys) but is discriminatory in others (job recruitment).[23]

When ProPublica revealed the anti-Semitic categories and other news outlets reported similarly odious categories,[24] Facebook responded by explaining that algorithms had created the categories based on user responses to target fields (e.g., answers to questions about education and hobbies). It also pledged to address the

---

[22] Angwin, Varner, and Tobin, "Facebook Enabled Advertisers to Reach 'Jew Haters.'"
[23] Note that Facebook has recently taken measures aimed at reducing discriminatory advertising (Levin 2019).
[24] Oremus and Carey, "Facebook's Offensive Ad Targeting Options Go Far beyond 'Jew Haters.'"

issue. But Facebook was loath to claim it had responsibility. Chief Operating Officer Sheryl Sandberg claimed in a public response that "[w]e never intended or anticipated this functionality being used this way."[25] That is no doubt true, though Facebook wishes to both sell advertising and employ as little labor as possible to monitor how that advertising functions.

Is it agency laundering? An agent (Facebook) launders its agency where

(1) Facebook has moral responsibility with respect to targeted advertising, *and*
(2) Facebook ensures that its algorithmic advertising process has some causal responsibility with respect to targeted advertising on its platform, *and*
(3) Facebook ascribes morally relevant qualities to its algorithmic advertising process's actions, *and*
(4) in virtue of (2) and (3), Facebook obscures the scope of its causal responsibility with respect to targeted advertising on its platform, *and*
(5) in virtue of (4) Facebook fails to adequately account for events within a domain for which it is morally responsible: specifically, the way in which its advertising platform helps target advertising to racists.

Each of these conditions appears to obtain. Certainly, Facebook has causal responsibility with respect to targeted advertising on its platform. A more difficult question is whether Facebook has role, or prospective, responsibility. The clearest sense in which they have role responsibility is that they have de jure authority over their platform, and they have a *general* responsibility to be good members of the broad community of people who use the platform. More specifically, they have (in our view) a *specific* responsibility to ensure that their platform does not facilitate racists to easily find an audience to whom they can advertise.

The claims that Facebook has such specific moral responsibilities will no doubt be controversial. Others may argue that Facebook has a moral responsibility to be a mere conduit of communication among members.[26] That is unconvincing for a couple of reasons. For one, this case is about advertising. Any claims about how Facebook should structure information between end users tell us nothing about Facebook's responsibility vis-à-vis advertisers. Moreover, Facebook already acts as if it has responsibilities with respect to both content and advertising. It has community

---

[25] Sandberg, "Last Week We Temporarily Disabled Some of Our Ads Tools."

[26] Note that this is a possible moral claim that one might make about Facebook and other media organizations. This is a distinct question from what kinds of legal rights and obligations information intermediaries have in light of (inter alia) 104th United States Congress; an act to promote competition and reduce regulation in order to secure lower prices and higher quality services for telecommunication consumers and encourage the rapid deployment of new telecommunications technologies; European Union, Directive 2000/31/EC of the European Parliament and of the Council of 8 June 2000 on certain legal aspects of information society services, in particular electronic commerce, in the internal market (directive on electronic commerce); European Union, Regulation (EU) 2016/679 of the European Parliament and of the Council of 27 April 2016 on the protection of natural persons with regard to the processing of personal data and on the free movement of such data, and repealing Directive 95/46/EC (General Data Protection Regulation). Keller, "The Right Tools."

standards, by which it judges and removes content, and it restricts certain kinds of advertising.[27] In any case, agency laundering only requires that Facebook have general responsibilities within this domain.

Facebook's categories are derived in part by automated systems. It takes a hands-off approach, letting users generate profile information, letting an algorithm pick out characteristics from user profiles, letting advertisers peruse those categories, and letting an algorithm suggest compatible categories to build better ad target groups. Thus, Facebook ensures that an algorithmic process has causal responsibility (i.e., is a key part of the explanation) for what ads appear to whom on Facebook's platform. That's condition (2).

Facebook's business model includes allowing advertisers to target groups of people narrowly and effectively. It does this in a way that avoids the labor costs associated with human approval of ad targets or human oversight of ad categories and purchases. In so doing, Facebook implies that its algorithmically generated categories and suggestions are relevant to advertisers (otherwise, advertisers would have no reason to purchase ads). And the fact that one can place ads based on those categories without oversight implies that Facebook believes (at least implicitly) that whatever ads served to whatever audience are appropriate. These are morally relevant qualities, as per our third condition. The algorithms' causal responsibility and implication that they are appropriate obscure the scope of Facebook's causal responsibility (condition (4)).

Finally, in automating its advertising process, Facebook is able to claim that it "never intended or anticipated this functionality being used this way." It effectively distances itself from the fact that a system for which it is (causally and morally) responsible allows noxious (and in the case of discriminatory categories, illegal) advertising. That is, the causal responsibility of the algorithm's suggestions deflects from Facebook's causal responsibility in creating a platform that uses the algorithm, minimizes the labor that would be required to better monitor advertising categories, and profits from the automated system. Its attribution of morally salient characteristics (relevance, usefulness) presupposes that its optimization is consistent with Facebook's responsibilities, though it is not.

Here is where understanding Facebook's actions as agency laundering is a difference-maker. Conditions (1)–(4) describe several important moral features. But the crux of laundering is condition (5). The fact that Facebook is morally responsible with respect to targeted advertising means that it is appropriate to demand that Facebook provide an account of its intentions and reasons in facilitating racists in easily finding an audience to whom they can advertise. Facebook has inserted an automated procedure into its advertisement purchasing procedure, and it suggests that the *algorithms* are the natural object to scrutinize rather than Facebook's reasons and intentions with respect to building a system that deploys

[27] See, e.g., Facebook, "Community Standards Enforcement."

them and lets them run with minimal supervision. In doing so, Facebook undermines the central feature of responsibility by deflecting demands for an account of Facebook's reasons, intentions, and actions in helping racists target advertise. Hence, the automated process is a mechanism by which Facebook launders its agency.

There are several potential rejoinders to our argument here. One might disagree about what Facebook's responsibilities are. One might argue instead that it is advertisers and users who bear responsibility for populating Facebook's categories with racist characteristics. Certainly, it is true that users populating categories with anti-Semitic and other racist ads bear responsibility for those actions, and any advertiser targeting ads based on such categories bears responsibility for doing so. But, as in Chair, that others have acted wrongly does not tell us much about Facebook's responsibility. One might further argue that Facebook has not laundered its agency because it has agreed to address the problem. But the fact that Facebook has indicated an intention to address these problems demonstrates that it is a problem within Facebook's control.

A related objection concerns the degree, or the severity, of Facebook's failure to fulfill its responsibilities (assuming that it has some). Perhaps Facebook knew of problems in how its algorithms functioned to allow malignant actions. But perhaps instead it was merely negligent.[28] This is no doubt an area others will reasonably dispute. It does not matter for our analysis of laundering, though. Facebook laundered *whatever degree of agency it had*. Moreover, it can launder its agency even if it meets its substantive role responsibilities. That the advertising platform afforded the opportunity to target advertising in a racist way is something for which detailed explanation of intentions, reasons, and actions is warranted.

Another potential objection is that it may well be that no particular Facebook contractor or developer acted with discriminatory intent, alleviating any potential moral responsibility any of them might have for the outcome.[29] However, Facebook's role responsibility is not reducible to any particular individual developer within Facebook. Rather, the company's responsibility is better understood as widely distributed across its contractors, employees, and other stakeholders. Moreover, Facebook's platform is complex, and the consequences of its operations over time

---

[28]   One can frame this as a question of capacity responsibility. That is, if Facebook did not have epistemic access to the relevant information about the possibility of misuse, it would not have the necessary capacity to be morally responsible. Note here that epistemic access is not limited to actual knowledge, but the ability to garner it under reasonable conditions. Hence, Facebook's moral responsibility will turn on the degree to which it could reasonably have known about potential for misuse. And that would define its degree of agency laundering.

One further complicating issue is mitigation. Facebook or another social media company might use its suggestion system to better understand relations among (for example) racists or purveyors of disinformation to promote anti-racist or epistemically sound information. The degree to which that would mitigate or deepen laundering is a question beyond what we can cover here. Thanks to an anonymous reviewer for making this point.

[29]   Binns, "Fairness in Machine Learning: Lessons from Political Philosophy."

are impossible to predict. Coeckelbergh and Wackers argue that organizations deploying such complex, vulnerable systems have obligations to manage their operations not only legally, but with a certain positive "imagination" regarding systemic crises or other harms.[30] In other words, it is unjustifiable to simply let such complex systems run their course and cause harm.

There is a further, related question about whether the conception of responsibility we have outlined here is properly attributable to collectives. There is significant philosophical debate about collective responsibility, and we cannot do it justice here. But we can note two things. First, the accounts of responsibility we outline in Section 7.2 need not be limited to individual wills. Certainly, we do have reactive attitudes toward collections of people, and those targets may be apt. Further, it seems plausible to attribute reasons to groups, in which case it seems plausible that such a group may be responsible in the sense that it ought to be the case that the collective be accountable. Second, even if it is the case that a collective's responsibility is reducible to the responsibility of its individual members, this would imply that those individuals have laundered their agency. In any case, whatever responsibility there is, Facebook's reliance on algorithms to do work and to explain its failures is (on the conception outlined here) an instance of agency laundering.

7.4 UBER AND DRIVER MANAGEMENT

Another private-sector example shows how our concept of agency laundering can distinguish between structurally similar cases. The ride-hailing company Uber has received substantial social, regulatory, and academic criticism based on its AI-driven, algorithmic systems. Uber uses such systems to map routes, track passengers, monitor drivers, anticipate demand, steer driver behavior, and (at one point) identify and deceive regulators. Many of these uses have been criticized elsewhere on the grounds that they are deceptive, unfair, opaque, or even illegal.[31] Our task here, though, is to consider whether any are instances of agency laundering and, if so, whether analyzing them as agency laundering sheds light on moral concerns with Uber's practices.

Recall two issues that we touched on in Chapter 5: how Uber uses algorithmic systems to keep its drivers working. One way is by providing reminders of individual drivers' goals. For example, the Uber app might display a message that the driver is very close to their goal of earning \$50 for their shift, which may induce them to take more riders. Similarly, Uber at times sends drivers their next ride requests before

---

[30] Coeckelbergh and Wackers, "Imagination, Distributed Responsibility and Vulnerable Technological Systems: The Case of Snorre A."

[31] One tool, named "Greyball," was developed to surreptitiously ban users who Uber believed were violating the company's terms of service. Uber eventually used Greyball to surreptitiously ban people Uber believed to be government regulators investigating whether Uber was operating illegally. See Isaac 2017.

they have delivered their current rider. This creates a kind of "queue effect," much like video platforms that keep people watching by immediately starting the next episode of a series.[32] A number of critics – including drivers – object to these practices on the grounds that they rely on nonrational mechanisms or are manipulative.[33]

Another way that Uber gets drivers to keep working involves the prospect of dynamically priced fares, which allows drivers to increase their per-hour earnings by driving during high-demand/low-supply periods. When there are lots of passengers seeking rides and relatively few drivers working, Uber will charge higher (surge) prices and drivers thus earn more. Uber's driver app will often prompt drivers to work at times that Uber anticipates will be high demand. So, it might say that, for example New Year's Eve will probably have surge pricing.[34] However, such prompts do not guarantee surge pricing, and drivers do not know when they accept a ride whether it will be surge-priced. In some cases, the Uber app estimates surge pricing, but fares during that period are normal, either because demand does not materialize or because enough drivers are working to offset the demand.[35]

These two cases are structurally similar: app-based mechanisms that prompt drivers to work somewhat more than they would have otherwise. Recall our argument that only surge pricing interferes with people's valuable freedoms. Relatedly, only the surge pricing appears to be a case of agency laundering. To see this, begin by running both through our understanding of laundering.

(1) Uber has moral responsibility with respect to fielding drivers, *and*
(2) Uber ensures that its algorithm has some causal responsibility with respect to fielding drivers, *and*
(3) Uber ascribes morally relevant qualities to its app-based prompts to drivers, *and*
(4) In virtue of (2) and (3), Uber obscures the scope of its causal responsibility with respect to fielding drivers, *and*
(5) In virtue of (4), Uber fails to adequately account for events within a domain for which it is morally responsible: specifically, the way in which its interface induces driving.

Conditions (1) and (2) are clear enough. Although Uber claims to be a technology company merely connecting riders and drivers through a platform, it nonetheless plays a large role in getting people to both drive and ride. It enters into contractual relationships with drivers and riders, maintains standards for drivers and equipment, subjects drivers to background checks, adjudicates disputes, and so forth. And there is no question that its algorithms are a key part of the explanation of which drivers are driving when. Uber ascribes morally relevant features to the algorithms: that they

[32] Scheiber, "How Uber Uses Psychological Tricks to Push Its Drivers' Buttons."
[33] Scheiber; Calo and Rosenblat, "The Taking Economy: Uber, Information, and Power."
[34] Rosenblat, *Uberland*, 128–132.
[35] Rosenblat, 98–100.

reflect drivers' own goals, that they are reliable, that they are based on a neutral assessment of facts on the ground (condition (3)).

The differences in the cases concern conditions (4) and (5).

Begin with the case of goal-reminders and queuing effects. It is difficult to see how Uber obscures its causal responsibility in incentivizing driving when it uses these tactics to spur drivers into taking more rides. Certainly, Uber is drawing on (or even exploiting) behavioral psychology, and behavioral psychology is an essential part of the explanation of drivers' decisions to drive. But that fact, and the fact that Uber has set up a system in which algorithms instantiate such strategies, is not obscured.

Now consider condition (5). Here, too, it is difficult to see how Uber fails to adequately account for events within a domain for which it is morally responsible. As a provider of ride-hailing services, Uber has an interest in keeping enough drivers on the road, and it is using a straightforward tactic to promote this interest. Further, Uber has been clear about the practice. In a recent *New York Times* article, a spokesperson for Uber describes goal-reminding and queuing as ways to incentivize driving.[36] As far as we can tell, Uber does not launder its agency when it uses goal-reminders and queuing.

One plausible counterargument here is that, at least in extreme cases, using such tools undermines drivers' wills so much that it obscures the scope of Uber's causal responsibility. Perhaps the interface is sufficiently gamified that users have hallmarks of addiction, or perhaps the quality of drivers' wills is so degraded that decisions to drive do not count as drivers' own. In that case, Uber's causal responsibility would be far greater than it appears and any adequate account of Uber's responsibility would include an explanation of how it circumvents drivers' wills. That possibility is worth both empirical and philosophical examination. Nonetheless, at least weaker forms of nudging seem well within the range of responsible employer behavior and not cases of agency laundering.

Contrast the goal-reminders and queuing with the surge-pricing case. Uber uses machine learning techniques to predict high-demand/low-supply times and uses those predictions to prompt drivers to work. This *does* seem to obscure Uber's causal responsibility in fielding drivers, per condition (4). The judgment that surge pricing is likely to occur appears to be an inference about how the world outside Uber is operating, and Uber is merely reacting to it. Indeed, in comments pertaining to the phenomenon of surge pricing, Travis Kalanick (Uber's cofounder and former CEO) said, "We are not setting the price. The market is setting the price."[37] In fact, Uber is causally responsible for setting up a system in which there are pay differentials (where driving at surge times is more attractive to drivers) and then using those facts to induce driving. Surge periods are not a natural feature about the world that Uber measures, but a period defined and deployed by Uber.

[36]   Scheiber, "How Uber Uses Psychological Tricks to Push Its Drivers' Buttons."
[37]   Clark, "Uber Denies Researchers' 'Phantom Cars' Map Claim."

More important, though, is condition (5). By predicting surge pricing and signaling the likelihood of surge pricing to drivers, Uber simultaneously exploits surge
pricing and makes it less likely. In other words, by using surge pricing as an
inducement to drivers seeking a better wage, Uber helps ensure that supply matches
demand more closely. Thus, it creates for drivers reasonable expectations of better
pay and fails to meet them. Then, when the prices are not offered, Uber tells the
drivers it is the market that is making the decision, not Uber. But this is a failure to
account for the situation a driver finds themself in when, for example, they have
driven to Times Square on New Year's Eve under Uber's advice that there will be
a surge and then find that the surge has disappeared. As Alex Rosenblat observes,
"When drivers follow this advice and find that they have been dispatched to pick up
a passenger for a nonpremium-priced ride, meaning that surge pricing has disappeared, they feel tricked."[38] It is not the market that reached out to the driver to quell
the surge. It is not the market that decided how Uber's payment system works.
Rather, it is Uber that sets up a system where a driver who responds to its enticements
may not get surge rates if the campaign to get drivers to an area has worked. And this
is the action within its domain of moral responsibility for which Uber owes an
account. Uber's claim that it is simply the market's doing is an inadequate account,
satisfying condition (5). Thus, Uber launders its agency.

So our conception of agency laundering is sensitive enough to distinguish
between different uses of algorithmic systems to influence driver behavior. The
next question is whether analyzing each in terms of agency laundering adds something of value beyond simply analyzing Uber's responsibilities to its employees. We
believe that it does. The laundering analysis emphasizes the fact that use of tools
(committees, bureaucracies, technologies) may be a way to simultaneously violate
duties and undermine accountability. This is a way to show that laundering adds
something. By calling it laundering, we can make clear what is happening. But more
importantly, our argument picks out a discrete moral infirmity, viz., eroding others'
ability to demand Uber provide an account of its reasons and intentions. In Uber's
case, use of a tool to both predict surge pricing and induce drivers looks similar to use
of other prompts. One might be tempted to think of it as a case of nudging (or
perhaps of manipulation). But that would miss the fact that by tying the process to
a prediction about facts on the ground, Uber can deflect attention from its own
responsibility for creating a situation in which it simultaneously predicts surge
pricing and makes it less likely.

7.5 VAMS AND TEACHER EVALUATION

Facebook, Uber, and other large technology firms receive substantial attention. It
would be a mistake, however, to think that agency laundering is primarily the

---

[38] *Uberland*, p. 129.

province of the private sector. The depth and importance of agency laundering may be even greater in public agencies. To demonstrate, we will reexamine Houston Schools' use of EVAAS. Recall that EVAAS is in practice not auditable for two interrelated reasons. First, all of its scores are so deeply interconnected with other scores that the only way to recalculate a score is to recalculate them all. Second, recalculating all of the scores is a complex task and thus very costly.

Despite its shortcomings, Houston Schools defended its use of EVAAS on the grounds that it reliably measures student progress.[39] But this claim, even if true, is largely irrelevant to the question of whether the use of EVAAS is justified. Student progress and the contributions an individual teacher makes to student progress are distinct quantities. To measure one is not to measure the other. Indeed, the American Statistical Association (ASA) issued a statement in 2014 pointing out that most studies conclude that teachers have only a marginal effect on the test scores that VAMs (such as EVAAS) take as inputs.[40] So, even if EVAAS reliably measures student progress, this is a poor proxy for teacher effectiveness.

Has the school district laundered its responsibility for firing teachers? We think so.

(1) Houston Schools is morally responsible with respect to hiring, firing, and promoting teachers, *and*

(2) Houston Schools ensures that EVAAS has some causal responsibility in making those determinations, *and*

(3) Houston Schools ascribes morally relevant qualities to EVAAS, *and*

(4) In virtue of (2) and (3), Houston Schools obscures the scope of its causal responsibility with respect to hiring, firing, and promoting teachers, *and*

(5) In virtue of (4), Houston Schools fails to adequately account for events within a domain for which it is morally responsible: specifically, the "exiting" of teachers deemed ineffective through EVAAS.

In virtue of Houston Schools' role as an employer, the first condition is met. When Houston Schools implements EVAAS to aide in personnel decisions it meets the second condition. Houston Schools meets the third condition implicitly by using EVAAS for high-stakes decisions. It meets the third condition explicitly by invoking EVAAS's reliability in measuring student progress as a reason in favor of using EVAAS. The fourth condition is met when Houston Schools repeatedly refers to one good thing that EVAAS does (measure student progress) to obscure the fact that Houston Schools is implementing a system in which teachers are fired based on measures for which the teachers are not responsible (recall the statement from the ASA mentioned earlier). Finally, the fifth is met because teachers who are fired on account of their EVAAS scores are given a faulty accounting of why they were fired. They are told they are being fired for being ineffective, when, given EVAAS's flaws,

---

[39] "Defendant's Original Answer and Defenses," in *Houston Fed of Teachers, Local 2415 v. Houston Ind Sch Dist*, 251 F. Supp. 3d.

[40] Morganstein and Wasserstein, "ASA Statement on Value-Added Models," 2.

this is likely not the case. Hence, understanding Houston Schools' actions as laundering shows us that there is something going on beyond lack of transparency; the mechanism of evaluation positively misdirects those who would seek reasons for how teachers are treated. It forestalls teachers' ability to demand an account for the school district's actions, within a domain of their legitimate concern.

Note that Houston Schools uses EVAAS while fulfilling its public function of managing an education system. That means that the public has a collective stake in how the system functions and has an interest in the actions Houston Schools undertakes. Hence, the fact that Houston Schools' laundering makes accountability all the more difficult matters in a way that accountability of private firms does not; it suggests that use of EVAAS must conform to standards of public reason, rather than aligning only to the isolated wishes of the district.[41]

7.6 COMPAS AND CRIMINAL SENTENCING

So far, we have described agency laundering in both private-sector and public-sector cases. And in the Uber case we saw how use of algorithmic decision systems will not be agency laundering where the agent does not obscure their causal responsibility for outcomes. We will return to *Loomis* to demonstrate how a public entity can avoid agency laundering by making clear their moral responsibility for an outcome.

Loomis and COMPAS have been the subjects of significant criticism. However, we think that the Wisconsin Supreme Court's opinion in the case shows how actors can *avoid* agency laundering in deploying algorithmic systems. Hence, the case shows that our understanding of agency laundering is not so broad as to be meaningless.

A trial court launders its agency where

(1) the trial court has moral responsibility with respect to sentencing, *and*
(2) the trial court ensures that COMPAS has some causal responsibility with respect to sentencing, *and*
(3) the trial court ascribes morally relevant qualities to COMPAS, *and*
(4) in virtue of (2) and (3), the trial court obscures the scope of its causal responsibility with respect to sentencing, *and*
(5) in virtue of (4), the trial court fails to adequately account for decisions pertaining to sentencing, specifically the decision to sentence Loomis in the maximum range.

The trial court certainly has moral responsibility with respect to sentencing. But did the trial court ensure that COMPAS had some causal responsibility with respect to sentencing? The judge referenced Loomis's risk scores and they plausibly had an effect on sentencing. This, though, was only one of the factors the judge described.

[41] Binns, "Algorithmic Accountability and Public Reason."

He also considered important the conduct Loomis admitted as part of the read-in charges and Loomis's conduct while under prior supervision. Let's interpret this as giving some degree of causal responsibility to COMPAS. It is, after all, at least plausible that the COMPAS score is a key part of the explanation for Loomis's sentence. The court's use of COMPAS implies that it is useful, reliable, and fair, which are morally relevant qualities, per condition (3).

The question of agency laundering in *Loomis* turns on conditions (4) and (5). Although the judge in the case referenced the COMPAS assessment in his decision, he also indicated that his own judgment (based on Loomis's conduct and history) led him to a similar conclusion. There is some possibility that the judge was confabulating by ascribing his own reasons to the outcome COMPAS reached. If that's true, it would not be that the use of COMPAS obscures the trial court's causal responsibility. Rather, it would be that the court's description of its reasons obscures the scope of COMPAS's causal responsibility.

The key issue, though, is whether the trial court fails to adequately account for decisions pertaining to sentencing. Consider the following from the Wisconsin Supreme Court's decision.

> We determine that because the circuit court explained that its consideration of the COMPAS risk scores was supported by other independent factors, its use was not determinative in deciding whether Loomis could be supervised safely and effectively in the community. Therefore, the circuit court did not erroneously exercise its discretion.[42]

The passage makes clear that tools like COMPAS cannot be used alone, and use of such scores has to be supported by other factors that are independent of the tool. Similarly, the court required that courts weigh all relevant factors in order to sentence an individual defendant,[43] and it prohibited trial courts from using scores to determine whether to incarcerate a person or not, to determine the length and severity of sentence, and to determine aggravating or mitigating factors in sentencing.[44] And the court required that any PSI that uses a COMPAS report carry a number of warnings about the limitations of such reports.

The supreme court's *Loomis* opinion places responsibility squarely on the trial court in using tools like COMPAS. It prohibits trial courts from relying completely on the COMPAS algorithm, and it requires trial courts to use other factors to support any use of risk assessment algorithms. Hence, the court forecloses the ability of trial courts to use algorithms as a way to distance themselves from responsibility. Thus, *Loomis* addresses condition (5), and it is not a case of agency laundering.[45]

42 *Wisconsin v. Loomis*, 881 N.W.2d paragraph 9.
43 *Wisconsin v. Loomis*, 881 N.W.2d paragraph 74.
44 *Wisconsin v. Loomis*, 881 N.W.2d paragraphs 88–98.
45 Note that *Loomis* demonstrates another way one can launder even while fulfilling one's substantive role responsibilities. Imagine that the trial court had deliberated about its decision but did not explain

Deploying tools like COMPAS could certainly be a means by which courts (and others in the criminal justice system) can launder their agency. However, the *Loomis* decision is tailored precisely to avoid that. Hence, it appears to be a good test case for our view. It is the use of an algorithmic system where one does not launder their agency. As a result, it can demonstrate how other actors may fail in their moral responsibilities, even where their actions superficially resemble the *Loomis* court's. The court did not forestall others' ability to demand an account for its actions within a domain of their legitimate concern, but a different court (or different actor within a criminal justice system) might do so by failing to provide its own reasons for decisions.

7.7 RELATED CONCEPTS AND CONCERNS

7.7.1 *The Responsibility Gap*

Agency laundering can help shed light on some other concepts related to moral issues in technology. One of these is the "responsibility gap." In a 2004 article, Andreas Matthias argued that in some cases a technological system may be sufficiently sophisticated that no person or persons are responsible for the outcomes it causes.[46] The idea is that machine learning systems may be so opaque to human developers and users that it is impossible to predict how those systems will behave. Where such systems cause harm, it may be (on Matthias's view) a mistake to attribute responsibility to the developer, the owner, or any other person. The rules by which machine learning systems act "are not fixed during the production process, but can be changed during the operation of the machine, *by the machine itself*."[47] These actions do not mesh with traditional accounts of responsibility "because nobody has enough *control* over the machine's actions to be able to assume the responsibility for them."[48] He provides several examples. One is an elevator system that, having used an AI system to adapt to use patterns over time, leaves an executive stranded and late for a meeting. Another is a machine learning system to diagnose lung cancer, but which has a high false-positive rate (and causes emotional and financial stress to people diagnosed). Yet another is an AI children's toy that, in learning to navigate a new home environment, injures a child.

There has been a great deal of discussion of the responsibility gap in the years since Matthias's article was first published. Here, we want to illustrate how agency

---

its reasoning for the sentence. Suppose instead it merely wrote that it agreed with the COMPAS report's assessment with no further comment. That would obscure the scope of the court's causal responsibility and would fail to provide an adequate account of the decision. But in that case, the court would not have violated some other substantive role responsibility.

[46] Matthias, "The Responsibility Gap: Ascribing Responsibility for the Actions of Learning Automata."

[47] Matthias, 177 (emphasis in original).

[48] Matthias, 177.

laundering is distinct from responsibility gaps and how it can explain where responsibility fits in the gaps.

Note first that Matthias's conception of the responsibility gap focuses on an automated system's causal responsibility for some outcome. In the toy case, Matthias posits that the responsibility gap pertains to the action of knocking over and injuring the child. Our account of agency laundering, however, considers a wider range of actions. Imagine that the toy manufacturer developed, marketed, and sold the toy without fully testing its ability to knock over and injure a toddler. The manufacturer would seem to have causal and role responsibility with respect to whether its toys injure children (condition (1)). It would also ensure that the toy has causal responsibility for whether it injures children (as Matthias describes the case, the child's injury is explicable only by describing how the toy operates) (condition (2)). By selling the toy, the manufacturer attributes morally relevant qualities to the toy (age appropriateness, safety) (condition (3)). It would also be difficult to provide an adequate account of a toy manufacturer's distribution of a toy that has the affordances (size, weight, mobility, unpredictability) to knock over a small child (condition (5)).

The question, then, is whether the manufacturer obscures the scope of its causal responsibility with respect to the injury (condition (4)). Nothing in the example (either Matthias's version or ours) suggests that it does. However, if the manufacturer were to *posit* a responsibility gap (e.g., by saying that the machine learning process was opaque, and hence the manufacturer could not anticipate injury), that would fulfill condition (4) and be an instance of agency laundering. In other words, invoking the idea of a responsibility gap is a mechanism by which people may launder their agency.

There are other possibilities as well. One might set up a system expressly to avoid being held to account. Such a scenario would appear to be a form of preemptive laundering, and it would be advanced by whatever responsibility gap it creates. A different possibility is that one creates a gap between one's actions and outcomes for good reasons but, in so doing, ensures that there will be a responsibility gap. Suppose, for example, an agency responsible for assessing how likely persons accused of a crime are to reoffend. To address a known problem of arbitrary assessments by human decision-makers, it deploys a system similar to COMPAS (while acknowledging biases similar to those in COMPAS). This would look like a case similar to democratic chair in Section 7.3. The agency's use of the system would not be a means to avoid having to account for some other action. Rather, it is the decision to deploy the system that requires an account, and that decision is not obscured.[49]

We leave open whether there are genuine cases of responsibility gaps – that's a topic others have addressed more thoroughly than we can do here.[50] But our analysis of agency laundering requires thinking about role and causal responsibilities of people who deploy technologies like those Matthias contemplates. That

[49]   Thanks to a reviewer here for pointing out these possibilities and noting their similarities to "Chair" and "Democratic Chair."
[50]   Johnson and Verdicchio, "Reframing AI Discourse."

forces one to consider a wider range of actions than the operations of an AI system and can help distinguish genuine responsibility gaps from responsibility obfuscation and agency laundering.

7.7.2 *Bias Laundering, Masking, and Humans in the Loop*

At a 2016 conference sponsored by the Society for the Advancement of Socio-Economics, Maciej Cegłowski stated that "machine learning [is] an ingenious way of disclaiming responsibility for anything. Machine learning is like money laundering for bias."[51] Although Cegłowski does not spell out what laundering is or why it matters morally, there do seem to be some points of similarity and difference worth noting. What Cegłowski's comment picks out is the ability to obscure something important and deflect disapproval. So if an algorithm (e.g., for predictive policing) is built on criminal justice data, which is itself based on over-policing Black communities, the algorithm may be a mathematically neutral tool that reflects biases that already exist. The tool's neutrality can appear neutral tout court to the extent that one fails to examine the bias in the underlying data sources.

However, our understanding of agency laundering is a general account of laundering, and it is broad enough that it encompasses bias laundering. Agency laundering can obscure many different kinds of wrongs and limiting the concept to bias laundering would fail to capture them. Likewise, there is no need to link laundering tightly with machine learning or algorithmic decision-making. As we've explained, any process or socio-technical system can be a mechanism for laundering. More importantly, our account explains just how laundering is related to responsibility, both structurally and morally. Finally, in our view the thing that is laundered is typically agency, and that is typically the appropriate target of analysis.[52] One might at times act as an agent, yet launder responsibility, but in any case *these* are the things laundered. Thus, while we agree that machine learning can be a means of disclaiming responsibility, just what it means to "disclaim responsibility" and just what it is that one is responsible for are difficult questions to answer. This chapter is an attempt to do just that.

A similar concept is "masking" or the intentional use of algorithmic systems to obfuscate discrimination.[53] Barocas and Selbst describe masking as a way of using data mining to return discriminatory results while hiding whatever discriminatory

---

[51] Cegłowski, "The Moral Economy of Tech." Thanks to Suresh Venkatasubramanian for pointing us to this talk.
[52] We appreciate an anonymous reviewer raising the question of whether there are cases where one maintains agency but launders accountability instead. Our sense is that any such case would involve minimizing one's agency. In other words, accountability is the thing that is avoided, and one avoids it by laundering the degree to which one is (morally) responsible, which is in turn a function of a person's agency in a process. Likewise, money laundering is a way to forestall accountability, and it is the laundering of some other thing (viz., money) that helps avoid the accountability.
[53] Barocas and Selbst, "Big Data's Disparate Impact," 692–693, 712–714.

intent one might have behind an information system. Certainly, masking could be part of laundering. However, the other elements of laundering – relevant role responsibilities, ascription of morally relevant qualities, tension with fundamental aspects of responsibility (viz., accountability) – are not necessarily elements of masking.

There is a third important issue related to socio-technical systems, responsibility, and moral liability. The distinction between systems with humans in and out of the loop are well established. Systems employing humans in the loop include things like automated cars that provide for human override, autonomous weapons systems that require humans to approve strikes, and content moderation in which humans help teach algorithms what content is objectionable and make decisions in cases for which automated systems are not yet adept. Control in such systems is itself a complicated concept, and there is an active area of scholarship surrounding whether (and if so, how) there can be meaningful human control even for systems that leave humans out of particular decision loops.[54]

Of particular importance for our project is that having humans in the loop may itself obscure causal and moral responsibility. Ben Wagner notes that there are many purportedly automated systems that rely on humans to take an active role, fix mistakes, or replace system decisions.[55] However, he argues that the actual human role may be compromised by the design of the system. For example, there may be insufficient time to make decisions, they may grow weary or inured to a process, or they may lack sufficient training and experience to make good decisions. He outlines a number of criteria important in determining whether systems are "quasi-autonomous," such that humans in the loop "have responsibility but little agency" (or, in our usage, humans have causal but not capacity responsibility, and hence cannot be morally liable).

Madeleine Elish considers similar scenarios in which human actors have a causal role within socio-technical systems (including AI).[56] She argues that responsibility for outcomes may be misattributed to human actors within such systems, creating a kind of "moral crumple zone" that protects the system from attributions of responsibility. In our conception, humans' causal responsibility could obscure the causal responsibility of a technical system (of course it cannot obscure the *moral* responsibility of a technical system, for such a system does not have capacity responsibility).

The systems that Wagner and Elish envision are ones that could potentially launder agency (though not necessarily). Suppose, for example, an autonomous vehicle has a human in the loop, but the human has too little time to respond when needed and causes an accident. That would seem to fulfill the conditions (1) and (2):

54 Santoni de Sio and van den Hoven, "Meaningful Human Control over Autonomous Systems: A Philosophical Account."
55 Wagner, "Liable, but Not in Control?"
56 Elish, "Moral Crumple Zones."

some entity with moral responsibility has ensured a human has causal responsibility. The questions are whether placing a human in the loop attributes morally relevant qualities to the human's actions (efficacy, perhaps), whether doing so obscures the causal responsibility of the larger system and thereby fails to adequately account for the moral responsibility of the larger entity. What is key for our view, though, is that the mechanism for laundering need not be technological at all; that is, humans in the loop can be a means of laundering just as well as automation itself.

7.7.3 Concerns

One potential objection to our conception of agency laundering is that it is merely a metaphor and as such does not add a great deal to our ability to analyze and evaluate the relationship between information technologies and responsibility. There are a couple of reasons to think otherwise. Using the concept of laundering takes its cue from the idea of money laundering, which is of course metaphorical. Crooks do not literally wash money. Rather, they obscure its sources by mixing it with money from legitimate sources. Hence, whatever actions work to obscure the source of illicit funds also serve to launder those funds. Laundering is a way of obscuring the source of morally weighty states of affairs by mixing actions with technologies, procedures, or bureaucracies. Part of the value of using the laundering metaphor (for both money and agency) is that it plays a "descriptive role in helping a lay person understand" what the underlying phenomenon is.[57] That is, a metaphor can help capture the gist of a concept and, in this case, give people an intuitive grasp of the underlying concerns before following the entire argument.

Note, too, that the concept of agency laundering can help us both to make judgments in difficult cases and to explicate antecedent moral wrongs more fully. So, for example, in the Facebook case, it is unclear just what the moral wrong is in using an automated targeted advertising system that bad actors can exploit. It is plausible that Facebook did not act wrongly in developing and using such a system. However, the advertising platform is still within a domain for which Facebook has moral responsibility, and its conflation of its actions with an automated system's actions undermines the foundation of responsibility, viz., providing an account.

Similarly, the concept of agency laundering can explain why Uber acts wrongly in some cases (surge pricing) but not in others (goal prompts, queuing).[58] Both actions are within Uber's domain of responsibility, and both are actions where there is an open question about whether Uber infringes its substantive role responsibility. Our account of agency laundering can help evaluate what, if anything, Uber does wrong.

---

[57] Thanks to an anonymous reviewer for this language and description. In this signaling respect, our use of a metaphor here works similarly to the "crumple zone" metaphor in Elish, discussed in Section 8.2.
[58] Note that there may be other, non-laundering moral wrongs involved in goal prompts and queuing, as discussed in Section 7.5.

The account may be of particular use in public-facing cases, where organizations have a remit to serve the public and derive legitimacy from public trust and support. In cases like *Houston* and *Loomis*, the possibility of socio-technical systems forestalling persons' abilities to demand an account of organizations' actions within a domain of legitimate concern is particularly important. Drawing on the metaphor of laundering here helps capture content of the concept.

A further advantage of our account is that it may help in understanding what kinds of rights to explanation people have in the context of automated or algorithmic decision systems, for example in the GDPR.[59] As we discussed in Chapter 4, such a right (if there is one) is generally discussed as an individual right in the face of adverse decisions.[60] But agency laundering is a problem not just for individuals whose interests have been affected. It is also a general problem, and our arguments about laundering and forestalling others' abilities to demand an account within areas of their legitimate interest extend further. After all, how a massive social media company helps target ads, how an international employer of drivers with millions of users and drivers induces use, how a school district evaluates and fires teachers, and how a criminal justice system wields its power are areas of general legitimate interest, regardless of whether a particular individual has a claim to an explanation of a discrete event.

7.8 CONCLUSION

Our goals in this chapter were to, first, explain a type of wrong that arises when agents obscure responsibility for their actions. We have outlined this type of wrong and called it "agency laundering." Second was to draw on several cases to help specify our account of agency laundering. We have argued that some of these (Facebook advertising, Uber's surge-pricing prompts, Houston Schools' use of EVAAS) involve laundering and two (other Uber prompts, use of COMPAS in the *Loomis* case) do not. Third, we have argued that analyzing these cases in terms of agency laundering both helps understand the cases and adds something morally. Lastly, we have distinguished agency laundering from other relevant concepts.

We have not given the final word on agency laundering here. One further question concerns the degree to which laundering must be intentional. In other words, can a person who uses a tool to make decisions launder their agency inadvertently? This appears compatible with our definition of agency, though the moral importance of such laundering warrants further consideration. Another

---

[59] Regulation (EU) 2016/679 of the European Parliament and the Council of 27 April 2016 on the protection of natural persons with regard to the processing of personal data and on the free movement of such data and repealing Directive 95/46/EC (General Data Protection Regulation), 2016 O.J. (L 119).

[60] Wachter, Mittelstadt, and Russell, "Counterfactual Explanations without Opening the Black Box: Automated Decisions and the GDPR"; Selbst and Powles, "Meaningful Information and the Right to Explanation"; Kaminski, "The Right to Explanation, Explained."

question concerns how widely the concept of agency laundering applies. A few people with whom we've discussed this project have asked whether large-scale social processes (e.g., political events and movements) can serve either as mechanisms or as sites of laundering. Perhaps so, though that would involve sorting through complex issues of causal responsibility and conceptual questions of capacity responsibility.

8

Democratic Obligations and Technological Threats to Legitimacy

8.1 TWO NEW TECHNOLOGIES

In 2011, UCLA anthropology professor Jeff Brantingham launched PredPol, which is an algorithmic system for predicting and preventing crime. The idea at the heart of PredPol is that crimes follow predictable, geographic patterns.[1] Thus, it may be possible to reduce crime by deploying police resources to places where predictive analytics suggests crime will occur. To facilitate this, PredPol has a graphical interface that overlays a red box (indicating a predicted crime "hotspot") on top of a city map. This allows police to concentrate on those areas in the hopes of deterring crime.

There is evidence that PredPol is effective in some respects, especially in addressing property crime. And it has a degree of support. *Time* magazine called predictive policing[2] one of the "50 Best Inventions" of 2011.[3] Today, PredPol is a national leader in predictive policing technology and dozens of cities across the United States use it.[4]

---

[1] The analogies advocates use to explain PredPol are varied and tend to liken crime to phenomena outside of complex, modern society. One analogy is with earthquakes. After an earthquake, it is likely that there will be another one in the same area, an aftershock. Similarly for crime on this theory, certain "place-based" crimes (such as a burglary) are followed by crimes in the same area. See Goode, "Sending the Police before There's a Crime." Another analogy is to hunter-gatherers, in part because the PredPol grew out of Brantingham's work using computer models to understand hunter-gatherers. Brantingham states that "[c]riminals are effectively foragers ... [c]hoosing what car to steal is like choosing which animal to hunt. The same decision-making processes go into both of these choices." See Hoff, "Professor Helps Develop Predictive Policing by Using Trends to Predict, Prevent Crimes." We are not convinced that these analogies are helpful beyond the fact that some kinds of crime exhibit geographic patterns.

[2] Note that in this chapter we will use "predictive policing" to refer to "place-based" predictive policing, which focuses on forecasting *where* crimes will occur. This is often contrasted with "person-based" predictive policing. Person-based predictive policing raises similar concerns, but we will not focus on it here. For an excellent overview of these issues, see Ferguson, *The Rise of Big Data Policing*, chapter 3.

[3] Grossman et al., "The 50 Best Inventions."

[4] Ferguson, *The Rise of Big Data Policing*, 65–67.

There are, however, several important criticisms of the technology. One is that its ability to predict property crimes may not translate well to predicting (much less preventing) other crimes. Another concern is that predictive policing in general simply recreates biases in policing practices and that predictive tools will be deployed in ways that harm communities of color, much in the same way that stop-and-frisk policies, pretrial detention, and sentencing do.[5]

Not long after PredPol was getting off the ground, a different set of algorithmic systems was developing in a way that would have profound implications for electoral politics. The political data analytics firm Cambridge Analytica began building specialized personal profiles and using large datasets collected from social media to stage political influence operations at scale. While use of profiling and data to influence politics is nothing new, Cambridge Analytica's actions are novel in several ways. The data on which their operation was built was massive and obtained in intrusive ways (including by gaining access via friends' permissions in Facebook). In addition, the data was collected under the imprimatur of a prestigious academic institution (Cambridge University). Finally, the kinds of information pushed to users were difficult for others to see, as it was targeted on social media. This left fewer obvious trails as it was happening than, say, television or mail ads. In parallel with the Cambridge Analytica efforts was a Russia-sponsored disinformation campaign, also making use of social media and recommendation systems. This was carried out by an organization called the Internet Research Agency (IRA).

Although PredPol and Cambridge Analytica/IRA address fundamentally different parts of modern life, they both have important implications for democratic governance. PredPol is a tool that helps structure how governments exercise their enormous power to investigate and sanction crime. The ability of the state to visit harms upon its constituents is at the heart of liberal theorists' commitments to limit state power.[6] This concern about state-sanctioned harm is sharpened by concerns about unsanctioned state violence that is often unaccountable.[7] Cambridge Analytica, in contrast, is not primarily about how a state deploys its power. Rather, it is about the connection (or disconnection) between democratic processes and governance. Put differently, it is about the necessary conditions for democratic processes to provide grounds for governments to hold power and implement policy decisions.[8]

Questions about justifying exercise of power via policing and questions about democratic processes and justifying power are, at root, about political legitimacy. So far in this book, we have examined algorithmic decision systems from three autonomy-based

[5] Edwards, "Predictive Policing Software Is More Accurate at Predicting Policing than Predicting Crime"; Ferguson, *The Rise of Big Data Policing*, 73–74.
[6] Shklar, "The Liberalism of Fear."
[7] Schwartz, "After Qualified Immunity."
[8] For the purposes of this chapter we won't draw sharp distinctions between government actions, decisions, policies, and laws. While they can be distinguished (both legally and philosophically) and different justificatory burdens may be appropriate to each, our concern here is about legitimacy and legitimation at a general level that is applicable to each.

perspectives: in terms of what we owe autonomous agents (Chapters 3 and 4), in terms of the conditions required for people to act autonomously (Chapters 5 and 6), and in terms of the responsibilities of agents (Chapter 7). Political legitimacy is another way in which autonomy and responsibility are linked. This relationship is the basis of the current chapter, and it is important in understanding the moral salience of algorithmic systems. We will draw the connection as follows: In Section 8.2 we will outline a conception of political legitimacy. In Section 8.3 we will explain that the connection between political legitimacy and autonomy is that legitimacy is grounded in legitimating processes, which are in turn based on autonomy. Algorithmic systems – among them PredPol and the Cambridge Analytica-Facebook amalgam – can hinder that legitimation process and conflict with democratic legitimacy, as we argue in Section 8.4. We will conclude by returning to our old friends, *Loomis*, *Wagner*, and *Houston Schools*.

8.2 POLITICAL LEGITIMACY: THREE CONCEPTIONS AND A HYBRID VIEW

Governments exercise enormous power over their denizens and expend vast resources promoting a range of policies (education, transportation infrastructure, defense, public health, commercial regulation, scientific research, information collection, parklands, safety and policing, and on and on). Those powers can be exerted in ways that are justifiable or unjustifiable, that are good or bad, and that are useful and not useful. The exercise of political authority can, in other words, be legitimate or not. In its broadest sense, political legitimacy refers to the justification of political authority, where "authority" just means having a certain political right to act coercively. But what constitutes such a right, and how could anyone ever acquire it? In this section, we discuss three conceptions of legitimacy – descriptive, demo-cratic (or "will" based), and epistemic (or "normative authority" based) – and then offer our own, hybrid view based on a recent account from Fabienne Peter.

8.2.1 *Legitimacy and Descriptive Criteria*

One family of views distinguishes legitimate from illegitimate authority in terms of purely descriptive (or empirical), as opposed to normative, criteria. This sort of view, which finds its roots in Max Weber's work,[9] is often associated with the social sciences. Such descriptive accounts examine how authority (understood as people recognizing a body's ability to exert power) can be established and maintained.[10]

Weber himself offered three methods of establishing and maintaining the ability to exert power: through tradition, through charisma, and through rational appeal. In other words, the continuity of traditional leadership, the transformative personal

---

[9] Weber, *Economy and Society*.
[10] This is a question of internal legitimacy or legitimacy within a state. There may be questions as to whether a state can justify itself internationally. See Peter, *Democratic Legitimacy*, chapter 1.

characteristics of charismatic rulers, and the inherent rationality of law can each, for better or worse, contribute to establishing and maintaining a political regime. Later theorists have refined Weber's list, distinguishing, for example, claims of traditional authority staked on "convention" from those staked on "sacredness" and distinguishing claims of charismatic authority based on "personal ties" from those based on "personal qualities."[11] In the context of algorithmic systems, Ari Waldman provides an account of this descriptive sense of legitimacy as "the socially constructed propriety of authority to make decisions for others."[12] Given that "[t]he managerial ethos inside corporations operating in a permissive, neoliberal regulatory environment will twist process to serve corporate ends," legitimacy requires that regulators "go beyond process to rebalance the structures of power."[13]

Work on this process of establishing recognition of a right to exert authority is important (and we will return to it in Section 8.3). However, it addresses different questions than those about the *normative* foundation of authority. The mere fact (if it is) that people are willing to recognize a government's authority to exert power on the basis of, say, a leader's charisma does not tell us anything at all about whether the government's actions are justifiable. To understand this, we must also understand how a right to exert authority could be justified by moral or political principles.[14]

8.2.2 *Legitimacy and Democratic Criteria*

One normative conception of legitimacy holds that it is a function of democratic consent. Legitimacy in this sense depends on some sort of approval of authority by a state's citizens. This can be cached out in a couple of different ways.

On one view, approval requires the kind of epistemic competence and non-alienation that are conditions of what we called psychological autonomy in Chapter 2. Most people never agree to be governed in this way, of course, so explicit consent cannot be the requirement for legitimacy. One might then consider hypothetical agreement as the grounds for legitimacy, arguing that a sufficient condition of legitimate authority is that reasonable persons could consent to it, or one might argue that it is a necessary condition of legitimate authority that people could consent to it. Indeed, the account of psychological autonomy from John Christman that we use as an exemplar in Chapter 2 links autonomy to legitimacy in this fashion. Christman writes that "the test for legitimacy of political principles should be the following: principles are legitimate only if the (reasonable) citizens to whom they apply would not be *understandably*

---

[11]   Matheson, "Weber and the Classification of Forms of Legitimacy."
[12]   Waldman, "Power, Process, and Automated Decision-Making," 614.
[13]   Waldman, 616.
[14]   For a helpful and recent overview of the topic of the grounds of political legitimacy, see Peter, "The Grounds of Political Legitimacy."

alienated from them.”[15] What matters is not explicit agreement, but whether people would identify with political principles if given adequate opportunity to reflect on them in light of their values and the sources and history of those values.

Another view linking autonomy to legitimacy is based on the degree to which political bodies and decisions reflect constituent wills. What is important in legitimacy is that persons subject to authority have some say in how that authority is constituted and deployed. In this way, what Marina Oshana calls “political autonomy” more closely reflects her sense of personal autonomy than psychological autonomy.[16] Legitimacy in this sense turns on the degree to which political processes afford citizens the genuine opportunity to participate, rather than principles reflecting their wills.

Both views of autonomy ground legitimacy in democratic will. Rawls, for instance, offers a principle of legitimacy that is defined in terms of “public reason.” On this view, political power is justified “when it is exercised in accordance with a constitution the essentials of which all citizens as free and equal may reasonably be expected to endorse in the light of principles and ideals acceptable to their common human reason.”[17] Similarly, Pettit’s account is grounded in “popular control.” He argues that political power is justified when all citizens have equal access to the prevailing system of influence over the government and that system imposes a direction welcomed by all.[18] In both cases, the account of legitimacy is premised on the notion of individuals as the “self-originating sources of valid claims” in the sense that “their claims have weight apart from being derived from duties or obligations specified by the political conception of justice, for example, from duties and obligations owed to society.”[19] What gives their claims this sort of weight is their autonomous wills.

Both Rawls’s and Pettit’s views align with descriptive accounts in that both Rawls and Pettit acknowledge that legitimacy is tied to stability. However, they diverge from descriptive accounts in maintaining that legitimacy requires that political authority meet normative criteria as well. Specifically, political authority must obey certain rules and democratic procedures. Rawls describes the ideal of political legitimacy not in terms of stability per se (i.e., in terms of a “modus vivendi”), but in terms of “stability for the right reasons,” where each citizen is compelled to obey the public constitution from their own individual perspective rather than merely out of self-interest. And Pettit describes the ideal of legitimacy in terms of passing a “tough luck” test, according to which authority is legitimate when people can think that “when public structures and policies and decisions frustrate their personal

[15] Christman, *The Politics of Persons: Individual Autonomy and Socio-Historical Selves*, 239 (emphasis in original).
[16] Oshana, *Personal Autonomy in Society*, 97–100.
[17] Rawls, *Political Liberalism*, 137.
[18] Pettit, *Just Freedom*, chapter 5.
[19] Rawls, “Justice as Fairness,” 242.

preferences, that is just tough luck."²⁰ Note that these normative criteria for political legitimacy are versions of the reasonable endorsement principles we outline in Chapter 3. Since these principles index the degree of legitimacy to facts about the wills of constituents, we can, following Fabienne Peter, call them "will" principles of legitimacy.

8.2.3 *Legitimacy and Epistemic Criteria*

A third view of legitimacy ties it to whether systems or decisions meet *epistemic* criteria.

To understand this set of views, it is useful to start with what Peter calls the "normative facts" view. On this conception, what matters for legitimacy turns on whether political decisions track the truth of the matter as to what is morally right to do. That is, the normative facts view assumes something akin to moral realism, thinks that propositions about what governments should do can be true or false, and pegs legitimacy to whether such decisions indeed track those normative facts. And they do so *regardless* of what people's beliefs about them are.

The problem of a normative facts view is that it leaves out the link between legitimacy and autonomy. That is, legitimate decisions need not be ratified in any sense by the people subject to them. Peter explains this as a violation of what she calls the "access constraint": Political legitimacy, whatever it is, must "be such that it can settle political deliberation (at least temporarily)," and to do this, it "must involve the attitudes of at least some citizens." Therefore, if normative facts are relevant to our political decision-making, it will be "through our beliefs about them."²¹

In this vein (i.e., bridging normative facts and beliefs about normative facts), Raz offers a "service" conception of legitimacy. On this view political authority is legitimate only if it is made in service of people's underlying reasons. The "normal" justification for authority, in other words, is that authority done right does nothing more than guide people according to the reasons they already have. As Raz puts it, "[T]he normal way to establish that a person has authority over another person involves showing that the alleged subject is likely better to comply with reasons which apply to him [...] if he accepts the directives of the alleged authority as authoritatively binding and tries to follow them, rather than by trying to follow the reasons which apply to him directly."²² Later theorists following Raz have explained further how this sort of epistemic preemption might work.

David Enoch, for instance, extends Raz's notion of a duty as a special sort of reason, describing authority as giving rise to obligation when there is some "normative structure in the background" allowing the authority to give its subject those sorts

²⁰ Pettit, *Just Freedom*, 112.
²¹ Peter, "The Grounds of Political Legitimacy," 377.
²² Raz, *The Morality of Freedom*, 53.

of reasons.[23] On wildlife tours, the tour guide often serves (and expects to serve) as this sort of preemptive decision-maker. The guide is the authority on, for instance, when the group needs to leave a group of animals behind rather than continue to take pictures – because of the dangerous nature of the circumstances and the special knowledge the guide has acquired through experience over time.

In any case, when the normal justification is present, Raz argues, the duties prescribed by the authority can override even the dictates of the democratic will and thus can offer grounds for "a ready embrace of various paternalistic measures," which would not pass democratic muster.[24] Here, we might find the justification for such policies as smoking bans, bans on trans fats, helmet laws, and mask mandates.

8.2.4 *The Disjunctive Conception of Legitimacy*

As Peter points out, neither the democratic nor the epistemic criteria seem on their own to fully encapsulate the normative grounds of political legitimacy.[25] If we accept what she calls a "will-based" conception of political legitimacy, exemplified by Rawls's and Pettit's democratic criteria, we run into what Peter calls the arbitrariness objection: that "[t]he validity of at least some practical claims depends on third-personal sources of validity," and thus that these will-based conceptions "support undue arbitrariness in political decision-making." We cannot hold the wills of all citizens to be politically relevant; individuals are not self-originating sources of valid claims but are instead often deeply irrational or unreasonable. Hence, democratic processes (via voting, consensus, public reason, or the like) are not sufficient on their own to justify exercise of political authority. There are, in other words, exercises of authority that are illegitimate even if they genuinely reflect citizen will. They may be so ill-conceived and so harmful, or they may be so detrimental to democratic processes and structures themselves, that they can not be legitimated by democratic processes.

A purely "belief-based" conception of political legitimacy (corresponding to Raz's and Enoch's epistemic criteria) is also inadequate. Peters argues that these accounts run the problem of "epistemic underdetermination." Specifically, there are few (if any) political decisions for which there is sufficient evidence to ensure that they are optimal. As Peter puts it, "[T]he epistemic circumstances of politics are such that for most political decisions, there will not be a decisive normative authority."[26] So even if we reject democratic adjudication as the univocal source of normative authority, the epistemic circumstances are often so complex and uncertain that normative authority remains difficult or impossible to establish. The main tension is that persons' wills and epistemic criteria both seem to be key conditions of justifiable

---

[23] Enoch, "Authority and Reason-Giving," 31.
[24] Raz, The Morality of Freedom, 422.
[25] Peter, "The Grounds of Political Legitimacy."
[26] For a longer discussion of this problem, see Peter, "The Epistemic Circumstances of Democracy."

exercise of political authority. Thus, the determinative question seems to be how to incorporate the autonomous wills and beliefs of citizens, given the need for policy that is appropriately responsive to facts.[27]

To address these issues, Peter defends a hybrid account of the normative grounds of political legitimacy. This account holds that legitimacy includes "both responsiveness to normative authority and adjudication between valid, but conflicting, claims as grounds of legitimacy." The conception itself is "disjunctive," which is to say that legitimacy can derive from either will or belief. Moreover, it favors normative authority over democratic processes; legitimacy is tied to "how the decision reflects normative authority, when normative authority can be established, or, when normative authority cannot be established, [. . .] how it adjudicates between the conflicting, but valid claims made by the citizens." In other words, democratic adjudication is secondary; it is a source of legitimacy only "as a response to difficulties with establishing normative authority."

Peter's hybrid account of the grounds of legitimacy is on the right track, but we want to refine it slightly. We cannot define our way out of the threats to legitimacy presented by our most difficult and contentious cases simply through disjunctive addition. It is not as if the arbitrariness problem somehow disappears in cases where normative authority cannot be established. (Indeed, it seems more likely that the two problems are self-reinforcing and thus run together.) It may well be possible to balance power among parties to a conflict in some cases where normative authority is epistemically underdetermined, but we should not mistake this modus vivendi for an arrangement that is genuinely politically legitimate.

Peter's concern with securing a secondary ground of legitimacy beyond normative authority is connected to her concern with the function of political legitimacy. She writes that "[a] plausible conception of political legitimacy should be able to settle which decisions are and which are not legitimate even under unfavourable epistemic circumstances," and this is something that can often only be settled by the balancing of wills. Nor, she argues, can we "claim that all decisions made in the absence of decisive normative authority would be illegitimate," because this "would itself amount to a political decision about which we could ask whether it is legitimate," leading to a regress.

Peter considers the secondary role of democratic adjudication in the context of a well-entrenched topic of disagreement: abortion. If we grant for the sake of argument that there is no decisive normative authority on that issue, it is not clear that any political method of adjudicating the conflicting claims on the issue will ever be able to provide the sort of consolation that might soothe parties who have been disenfranchised by "tough luck," to say nothing of providing stability for the right reasons. This seems like precisely the sort of issue that democratic adjudication can settle, but not in the "right" way.

---

[27] Estlund, *Democratic Authority: A Philosophical Framework.*

To see the grounds and function of political legitimacy correctly, we need to keep the secondary notion of democratic adjudication separate from the primary notion of normative authority. This is because there are political decisions, systems, or regimes that might be democratically ratified, but that are illegitimate in the epistemic, normative authority sense. Thus, there will be some policies that *appear* legitimate in the democratic sense but are not legitimate in the normative authority sense. Our view is similar to Peter's hybrid model, with the caveat that policies can be legitimate via a combination of normative authority and democratic will. As evidence of good policy increases (i.e., as it becomes increasingly evident that some policy, law, or action is justified via normative authority), then the stringency of the democratic facet of legitimacy is weaker.

8.3 LEGITIMATING PROCESSES

As we explained in the previous section, there are two facets to normative legitimacy. One, characterized by "will" theories generally, is vulnerable to arbitrariness. The other is characterized by normative authority, which is in turn a function of justified belief in structures, policies, and actions of states that are in fact good. This second facet is not vulnerable to arbitrariness in the way that will theories are. That is because justification is baked into the definition. Any policy, structure, or action that is both correct and justifiably believed to be correct is, ipso facto, legitimate. The primary limitation of the normative authority facet of legitimacy is epistemic; determining what is in fact the right policy or action is difficult, to say the least (cf., Section 1.5).

When we consider technological threats to legitimacy – gaming of algorithms in social media, use of algorithms in predictive policing, for example – it is tempting to move straight from a conception of legitimacy to a claim that some set of institutions, policies, or structures are themselves illegitimate, all things considered. It will no doubt be true that some political actions will fail to meet both the will conditions and the normative authority conditions for legitimacy and those actions will thus be unjustifiable exercises of authority. However, for any particular policy taking place within a complex set of social and political structures against background facts that are themselves challenging to interpret, all-things-considered judgments about legitimacy will be difficult. Hence, it is a far larger task than we can address here. Moreover, making that kind of final judgment about legitimacy itself would take us too far afield from the subject of this book, which is about autonomy. Finally, legitimacy (like autonomy) is not a binary, success concept. It is not something that an institution, polity, law, or action simply has or lacks. There is a spectrum of legitimacy, and limitations based on will or based on normative authority will often diminish legitimacy without warranting a conclusion that a policy decision crosses some floor below which it is illegitimate.

For these reasons, our focus here is on legitimation.[28] Will theories, normative authority theories, Peter's disjunctive theory, and our hybrid interpretation of Peter's view all rely on exercises of persons' autonomy as a foundation for legitimacy of governments, laws, policies, and the like. That process of exercising autonomy, either through will or through justified beliefs about normative claims (or both), is the mechanism by which use of political authority is justified. And in turn, members of a polity have the responsibility to use their autonomy to understand and support (or not support) actions by their government.[29] It is that process of legitimation that algorithmic systems can disrupt. In other words, algorithmic systems may in some cases hinder people from fulfilling their responsibilities of legitimating government policies, actions, laws, and the like.

Our argument for the centrality of autonomy to legitimacy begins with the conception of legitimacy outlined earlier. For political authority to be justified, it must be based on either democratic will or normative authority (i.e., where the exercise of political authority is good and there is justified belief that it is good), or a degree of both. As normative authority increases – that is, where policy is good and there is excellent epistemic justification for it – the degree to which it must be supported by mere will decreases.

Both paths to legitimate authority are based on a process of legitimation, each of which is itself grounded in autonomy. We explained in Section 8.2.2 that will-based theories are based on some version of agreement, public reason, or hypothetical consent and that Christman and Oshana explicitly link legitimacy to their conceptions of autonomy. The idea is straightforward. For one's agreement to a system of governance and to the actions, policies, and decisions of a government to carry force, the agreement must be based on conditions that meet the criteria of autonomy and freedom. One must be epistemically competent, the reasoning upon which one's agreement is based must satisfy authenticity conditions (as Christman puts it, one must not be understandably alienated from them). One should have the room to determine whether to support political decisions by having a degree of substantive independence. Moreover, people performing their legitimating responsibilities should be free of substantial impediments to the quality of their agency. As we explained in Chapter 5, one's agency may be impaired by affective, deliberative, and social challenges. Where the quality of their agency is sufficiently challenged in

---

[28] Note that "legitimation" in this normative sense is different from, though related to, the descriptive sense of legitimation in descriptive accounts of legitimacy. The descriptive sense of legitimation refers to the processes by which a governing entity establishes and maintains power, regardless of whether those processes justify that power. Descriptive legitimation may be necessary for normatively legitimate policies to function.

[29] To be clear, it is neither possible nor desirable that every member of a polity understand every kind of government institution, law, and action. Rather, there are some broad states of affairs that most any member of society has a responsibility to understand and support (or not): some conception of fair representation and enfranchisement, basic human rights. Others will have responsibilities based on their communities, experiences, and expertise. The responsibility is to exercise autonomy (properly understood as social and relational) in *some* facets of social life.

those ways, their ability to fulfill the responsibility of legitimating government policies is limited.

The link between autonomy and legitimation by normative authority is not as intuitively clear as between autonomy and will theories. Normative authority requires, first, that a policy, law, or action by a government be a good one. But the mere fact that a policy is good cannot confer legitimacy because of what Peter calls the "access constraint." Legitimacy demands that people believe that the policy is good and that they do so for sound reasons. Put another way, the legitimation process requires that people have sufficient information and understanding to assess a policy and believe that it is justified on its merits. The ability to do that is based on autonomy. To form justified beliefs about whether a policy is good, one must be epistemically competent, they must have some sense of value from which they are not alienated, and their reasoning must be substantively independent enough that their ability to reason is not compromised. Finally, the quality of their agency should not be so diminished that it undermines the degree to which their beliefs and actions are indeed their own.

8.4 TECHNOLOGICAL THREATS TO LEGITIMACY

Before we apply our arguments about legitimacy, legitimation, and autonomy to algorithmic systems, let's summarize the conception of legitimacy that we have developed.

1. For a government policy, law, or action to be normatively politically legitimate, requires either (a) normative authority, (b) democratic will (within certain bounds, dictated by (a)), or (c) some combination of both (a) and (b).
2. For a policy, law, or action to be legitimate via normative authority requires that the policy, law, or action in fact be good, *and* meet the access constraint.
3. The access constraint functions to ensure that autonomy enters the process by having belief-forming mechanisms in place under sufficient quality of agency.
4. For a policy, law, or action to be legitimate via democratic will requires some process of voting or public reason.
5. For a process of voting or public reason to confer legitimacy requires that persons engaged in that process do so autonomously.

With that in mind, let's return to PredPol, Cambridge Analytica, and the IRA.

8.4.1 *PredPol, Normative Authority, and Legitimation*

Our analysis of PredPol and legitimation is centered on legitimacy through normative authority. Recall that legitimacy via normative authority involves both normative claims (i.e., that some policy is in fact a good one) and the access constraint. The access constraint requires that the reason some policy is implemented is that people implementing it have epistemically sound reason to believe that the policy is in fact good. Based on these criteria, there are four key questions for determining whether a policy is legitimate based on the normative authority view: (1) Is the policy a good one? (2) Is there ample evidence that the policy is a good one? (3) Does the evidence that the policy is good drive the beliefs about the policy? and (4) Do the beliefs about the policy reflect the actual implementation of the policy?

We will consider the first two questions together, since we cannot address the question of whether the policy is good independent of evidence for it. So, is use of PredPol in fact good policy? Certainly, reduction in crime is a worthwhile objective. Hence, whether use of PredPol is good policy will turn on whether it is effective, whether it has bad consequences that offset any good ones, or whether it impinges other claims. There is some evidence PredPol is effective. In a July 2011 pilot test, the Santa Cruz, CA police department piloted a crime-deterrence program using PredPol. Zach Friend, the department's crime analyst, reported encouraging results. Burglaries in 2011 were down 27 percent that July, compared with July in the previous year. Speaking to the question of effectiveness, Friend added, "The worst-case scenario is that it doesn't work and we're no worse off" (though who the "we" refers to is unclear).[30]

However, the evidence of PredPol's efficacy is equivocal. Santa Cruz's drop in burglaries in 2011 is not enough to conclude that PredPol was the cause; after all, cities are complex entities and a one-year drop in one category of crime does not warrant a conclusion about a single cause and tells us nothing about other crimes. There have been only a few academic studies on predictive systems like PredPol. Those that exist yield mixed results, with some showing predictive methods having some crime-reducing effects, but others showing it has no effect at all.[31] For example, a study by the RAND Corporation testing a place-based system like PredPol found that the predictive system had no statistically significant effect on crime overall.[32]

There is also reason to think that use of PredPol has negative effects that offset whatever advantages in crime reduction it confers. Several cities using predictive policing technology have found that police simply stay in the locations indicated by the algorithm. That is, they stayed in the "red box" that PredPol overlays on a map. Susan Merritt, San Francisco Police Department's chief information officer, remarked that "[i]n L.A. I heard that many officers were only patrolling the red boxes, not other areas [. . .] People became too focused on the boxes, and they had to come up with a slogan, 'Think outside the box'."[33] And there is evidence that this has deleterious effects. Patrol officers stayed in the "red boxed" areas and engaged in "intelligence gathering," for example questioning people, running people's records,

[30]   Goode, "Sending the Police before There's a Crime."
[31]   Ferguson, *The Rise of Big Data Policing*, 72; Meijer and Wessels, "Predictive Policing: Review of Benefits and Drawbacks."
[32]   Hunt, Saunders, and Hollywood, "Evaluation of the Shreveport Predictive Policing Experiment."
[33]   Bond-Graham, "All Tomorrow's Crimes"; Ferguson, *The Rise of Big Data Policing*, 79.

investigating for potential (though unreported) narcotics use, and so forth. This, in turn, had the effect of slowing response times to emergencies.[34]

A further consequence that offsets whatever benefits PredPol has is disproportionate use. The Los Angeles Police Department (LAPD) has used predictive methods as a reason to deploy helicopters (as opposed to patrol cars) to the 500 foot by 500 foot boxes that denote "hot spots." These practices outrun the design of the predictive tool for several reasons. For one, it is difficult to discern unspecified criminal activity from a helicopter. And helicopters' deterrent effect is fleeting. Criminologist Geoffrey Alpert – a specialist in the use of helicopters in policing – says that helicopters, which are loud and obvious, will at best deter criminals while they are overhead but that criminals will simply return when the helicopters are not around.[35] Moreover, accommodating helicopter flight paths, the search area had to be expanded well beyond the "red box," conflicting with the purported specificity of PredPol.[36] Add to this the annoyance residents experience having loud helicopters overhead, and there are several negative consequences offsetting PredPol's advantages.

Finally, there are potential rights impingements relevant in determining whether PredPol is good policy. Predictive models indicating a "high crime area" can be a factor in determining whether police have legal authority to stop and frisk a person.[37] Hence, people may be stopped and frisked more often in a PredPol-designated area, and such stops are more likely to be permissible under the Fourth Amendment. However, it is another question whether merely being in a high-crime area can help morally justify a stop. And because of the source of data, the patterns of high-crime areas are skewed toward neighborhoods in which residents are predominantly from racial and ethnic minorities.

So, even if use of PredPol has some positive effects on a justifiable policy goal, it is not warranted to conclude that it is good policy overall and that there is ample evidence for it being good policy. Let's assume that the answer to the third question – whether evidence that the policy is good drives beliefs about the policy – is yes. That is not to say that the inference is correct; the access constraint merely requires a connection between evidence and belief on the assumption that the policy is good and justifiable.

The legitimation problem for use of PredPol comes in steps (3) and (4). It is possible that what evidence there is that PredPol can help reduce some types of crime grounds municipalities' use of the technology. However, the actual implementation of PredPol does not appear to reflect the evidence of its efficacy. Even if PredPol is well suited for predicting some kinds of crimes, the evidence for that does

---

[34] Ferguson, *The Rise of Big Data Policing*, 79; Hunt, Saunders, and Hollywood, "Evaluation of the Shreveport Predictive Policing Experiment."

[35] Mather and Winton, "LAPD Uses Its Helicopters to Stop Crimes before They Start."

[36] Ferguson, *The Rise of Big Data Policing*, 81; Mather and Winton, "LAPD Uses Its Helicopters to Stop Crimes before They Start."

[37] Ferguson, *The Rise of Big Data Policing*. For example, in *Illinois v. Wardlow*, 528 U.S. 119, the Supreme Court determined that simply being in high-crime area did not suffice to justify a *Terry* stop, but it can be relevant in determining whether other facts are sufficiently suspicious for a stop.

not warrant belief about PredPol's use as a general law enforcement tool, much less as a reason to park police officers in red-boxed areas or to act as general investigators (and slow responses to emergencies). It likewise does not support belief that deploying helicopters to fly over red-boxed and surrounding areas is warranted. It also does not provide grounds for thinking that individual persons who happen to be in red-boxed areas are themselves engaged in criminal activity. To reiterate, the access constraint is the requirement that belief in a policy's justification be based on the fact (if it is a fact) that the policy is a good one. Here, the fact that PredPol is effective in one area instead grounds the apparent belief that it is a good tool for intensive policing of discrete areas and conducting stops of individuals. In this way, the evidence for PredPol's efficacy in one area actually circumvents an important legitimating process. The evidence for its efficacy in one area stands in for evidence of efficacy for the tasks in which it is actually used. This is a barrier for citizens in being able to form beliefs about whether a policy is a good one. In other words, deploying PredPol well outside the range of circumstances for which there is evidence of its efficacy undermines citizens' abilities to fulfill their responsibility of exercising their autonomy in legitimating policy.

Here we want to be very clear about the limitations of this discussion. The mere fact that a policy is not good does not render it illegitimate. Any kind of policymaking (broadly construed) is complex, takes place under epistemic limitations, and will affect lots of people with considerable interests in the policy. Moreover, for a policy to be "good" in the strong sense necessary for it to be legitimate via normative authority is a very tall order. And the fact that use of PredPol does not seem to clear that threshold is therefore unsurprising. Use of PredPol might instead be legitimate based on the democratic, will-based view. Hence, our argument is emphatically *not* an attempt to make an all-things-considered judgment that using PredPol is not democratically legitimate (perhaps it is, perhaps it isn't). Rather, as we emphasized earlier, our purpose here is to examine autonomy and the process of legitimation. And on that question, PredPol is an informative case because it precludes citizens' abilities to legitimate predictive policing by undercutting their ability to assess its policy rationale.

8.4.2 *Cambridge Analytica, the IRA, and Will-Based Authority*

What are often referred to as the "Cambridge Analytica scandal" and "Russian hacking case" are in fact an interconnected, overlapping, and confusing welter of activities, organizations, tools, and technologies that grew up before and became widely known in the wake of the 2016 UK Brexit campaign and the 2016 US presidential election. The events are well documented in that there have been multiple tell-all books,[38]

[38] Wylie, *Mindf*ck: Cambridge Analytica and the Plot to Break America*; Kaiser, *Targeted: The Cambridge Analytica Whistleblower's Inside Story of How Big Data, Trump, and Facebook Broke Democracy and How It Can Happen Again*.

government investigations,[39] academic reports,[40] and news stories.[41] However, the interwoven stories are obscured by their very complexity, redactions in official reports and indictments, disinformation and deflection campaigns, and failures of public institutions to follow through with further investigations. Given the scope of the stories, we cannot possibly do them justice here. However, we can pull out a few important threads to ground our arguments about legitimation.

Cambridge Analytica is a data analytics and political consultancy firm based in London, UK. It is an offshoot of the SCL Group. In the years before the Brexit campaign and the 2016 US presidential election, the firm became interested in using the gigantic, rich datasets generated on social media platforms – particularly Facebook – to build ever more sophisticated models of voters and behavior. In order to pursue this work, they partnered with Cambridge University psychologist Aleksandr Kogan, who was already collecting social media information for his own research. Kogan had developed (along with other researchers) a personality app called "This Is Your Digital Life." The app, which included a "lengthy psychological questionnaire,"[42] was actually only downloaded by around 270,000 users, but it ultimately harvested user data from those users *and from their friends*, a group that might number up to 87 million.[43] This data was shared with Cambridge Analytica. On the basis of psychological profiles and data about Facebook users, Cambridge Analytica offered micro-targeted advertising based on their data-driven psychometrics. They did this first for Republican Party nomination seeker Ted Cruz.[44] When Cruz dropped out of the nomination race, they shifted their operation to candidate Donald Trump.

The targeted advertising and social media campaign spearheaded by Cambridge Analytica is of particular note. Christopher Wylie is a data scientist and former employee of Cambridge Analytica who eventually became a whistleblower and author of a book about the company. He describes several key features of the company's strategies. For example, he describes a project targeting African American voters with messages designed to decrease their motivation for voting.

[39] U.S. Department of Justice, "Report on the Investigation into Russian Interference in the 2016 Presidential Election, Volume I ('Mueller Report')"; Select Committee on Intelligence, United States Senate, "Report of the Select Committee on Intelligence, United States Senate, on Russian Active Measures Campaigns and Interference in the 2016 U.S. Election, Volume I: Russian Efforts against Election Infrastructure with Additional Views."

[40] Howard et al., "Social Media, News and Political Information during the US Election: Was Polarizing Content Concentrated in Swing States?"; DiResta et al., "The Tactics & Tropes of the Internet Research Agency."

[41] Cadwalladr and Graham-Harrison, "Revealed: 50 Million Facebook Profiles Harvested for Cambridge Analytica in Major Data Breach"; Kang and Frenkel, "Facebook Says Cambridge Analytica Harvested Data of up to 87 Million Users."

[42] Confessore, "Cambridge Analytica and Facebook."

[43] Kang and Frenkel, "Facebook Says Cambridge Analytica Harvested Data of up to 87 Million Users."

[44] Davies, "Ted Cruz Campaign Using Firm That Harvested Data on Millions of Unwitting Facebook Users."

He also describes using the techniques of using its influence to create in-person meetings of angry citizens.[45] As Wylie put things, in the original report published by *The Guardian*: "We exploited Facebook to harvest millions of people's profiles. And built models to exploit what we knew about them and target their inner demons. That was the basis the entire company was built on."[46]

The Russian Internet Research Agency (IRA) is a Russian state-supported organization that was established in 2013. It operates "like a sophisticated marketing agency," has trained "over a thousand people to engage in round-the-clock influence operations," and has targeted citizens in a variety of places, including Russia, Ukraine, and the United States.[47] In February 2018, the U.S. Department of Justice indicted the IRA and a number of Russian nationals who worked with the IRA for conspiracy to commit fraud, wire fraud, and bank fraud.[48]

The charges were based in part on disinformation "active measures" carried out on social media.[49] These measures included creation of fictitious groups that engaged social media users with inflammatory and divisive content. The IRA created fake profiles that followed other IRA sites and groups, thereby increasing their footprint and visibility to real people on social media platforms. To reach larger audiences, the IRA purchased Facebook ads that were then placed in potential followers' Facebook newsfeeds.[50] The inflammatory, divisive content promoted by the IRA sought to engage with social media from a range of political affiliations. The U.S. Senate Select Committee on Intelligence found that the IRA's targeting was particularly intensive toward African Americans. It writes, "By far, race and related issues were the preferred target of the information warfare campaign designed to divide the country in 2016."[51] It did this by creating pages and groups that sought to engage users that the social media platform identified as African American and by targeting geographic areas that are predominantly African American. These include pages such as "Blacktivist" and social media posts related to police shootings and NFL player kneeling protests of police shootings.[52] Other groups the IRA targeted with incendiary messaging include groups with names that imply a range of political dispositions ("Being Patriotic," "Stop All Immigrants," "Secured Borders," "Tea Party News," "Black Matters," "Don't Shoot Us," "LGBT United," and "United

45   Wylie, *Mindf*ck: Cambridge Analytica and the Plot to Break America*, 127–129.
46   Cadwalladr and Graham-Harrison, "Revealed: 50 Million Facebook Profiles Harvested for Cambridge Analytica in Major Data Breach."
47   DiResta et al., "The Tactics & Tropes of the Internet Research Agency," 6.
48   *U.S. v. Internet Research Agency, LLC* (Indictment, February 16, 2018).
49   *U.S. v. Internet Research Agency, LLC* (Indictment, February 16, 2018).
50   U.S. Department of Justice, "Report on the Investigation into Russian Interference in the 2016 Presidential Election, Volume I ('Mueller Report')," 25.
51   Select Committee on Intelligence, United States Senate, "Report of the Select Committee on Intelligence, United States Senate, on Russian Active Measures Campaigns and Interference in the 2016 U.S. Election, Volume II: Russia's Use of Social Media and Additional Views," 6.
52   Select Committee on Intelligence, United States Senate, 6–7.

Muslims of America").[53] The IRA's social media accounts "reached tens of millions of U.S. persons" and had "hundreds of thousands of followers."[54]

These accounts were used to organize in-person rallies, recruit activists to perform political tasks, and promote IRA content.[55] The IRA's activity is linked to social media users being exposed to a great deal of misinformation. A study of Twitter by the Oxford Internet Institute found that in the run-up to the 2016 presidential election, "users got more misinformation; polarizing, and conspiratorial content than professionally produced news."[56]

The breadth of activities by the IRA is striking. Its activities range across social media platforms, including Facebook, YouTube, Instagram, and Twitter. It targets groups from a range of social and political perspectives. Its tactics include aiming to suppress votes, aiming to direct voters toward third parties, aiming to depress turnout, encouraging secessionist movements (including in Texas and in California, comparing them to Brexit), and denigrating a range of leaders across parties.[57] They also aimed both to seed news media with content generated by Russian disinformation campaigns and to undermine trust in traditional news media.[58]

There is no official recognition or definitive documentation connecting Cambridge Analytica and Russian active measures. In his book, Wylie recounts Cambridge Analytica's involvement with Russian actors, message-testing about Vladimir Putin, close connections to people involved with pro-Russia factions in Ukraine politics,[59] and involvement with Russian oil firm Lukoil.[60] SCL's promotional materials indicate that they did work for Russia. However, SCL denies being involved in political campaigns at the behest of Russia, insisting that their work in Russia was for "private" interests.[61] It is worth noting here that the distinction between state and nominally private interests in kleptocracy is blurry.

So the existence and nature of the connection between the IRA and Cambridge Analytica are unclear. However, what matters here is not whether there was a single group of people acting in concert to sow anger and seed disinformation in the United States and elsewhere. Rather, our focus here is on the nexus of intrusive data collection (itself possible based on Facebook's weak privacy protections and permissive terms of service (themselves difficult to comprehend and rarely read),

53 U.S. Department of Justice, "Report on the Investigation into Russian Interference in the 2016 Presidential Election, Volume I ('Mueller Report')," 24–25.
54 U.S. Department of Justice, 26.
55 U.S. Department of Justice, 31–32.
56 Howard et al., "Social Media, News and Political Information during the US Election: Was Polarizing Content Concentrated in Swing States?" 1.
57 DiResta et al., "The Tactics & Tropes of the Internet Research Agency," 8–10.
58 DiResta et al., 65–66.
59 Wylie, *Mindf*ck: Cambridge Analytica and the Plot to Break America*, 142.
60 Wylie, 141, 155–156.
61 Hakim and Rosenberg, "Data Firm Tied to Trump Campaign Talked Business with Russians"; Wylie, *Mindf*ck: Cambridge Analytica and the Plot to Break America*, 139–159.

and the imprimatur of Cambridge University), predictive analytics using that data to better target influence, and algorithmic systems that suggest advertising to clients (see Section 7.4) and promote content to users. That is, our concern here is a socio-technical, big-data, and algorithmically aided group of systems that affect the attitudes, beliefs, dispositions, and actions of people within democratic states. Whether Cambridge Analytica entered into agreements or acted in explicit concert with the IRA is neither here nor there for our purposes in this chapter.

We should also emphasize that the effect of Cambridge Analytica's and the IRA's actions on the outcomes of particular elections is unclear, and no single set of events could ever be said to be the sole cause of complex phenomena like election outcomes and broad policy-making. It is disputed just how well these kinds of tactics actually work. Kogan argued that the "accuracy" of the data was exaggerated in media reports and that "[w]hat Cambridge has tried to sell is magic."[62] At first, the Cruz campaign credited the data-driven approach with its win in the 2016 Iowa caucus,[63] but NPR reports that, as the election cycle moved forward, the campaign grew more skeptical and eventually phased out the psychological profiling after later losing the South Carolina primary.[64]

Nonetheless, the tactics are important from the standpoint of political legitimacy. As a team of psychologists have recently shown, there is an increasing amount of evidence for "the effectiveness of psychological targeting in the context of real-life digital mass persuasion," and "tailoring persuasive appeals to the psychological profiles of large groups of people allowed us to influence their actual behaviors and choices."[65] The Cambridge Analytica case, they comment, "illustrates clearly how psychological mass persuasion could be abused to manipulate people to behave in ways that are neither in their best interest nor in the best interest of society."[66]

This creates a problem of legitimacy. Whereas in the PredPol case we consider the normative authority path to legitimacy, here our concern is the will or democratic path. Recall that this path relies on persons' agreement (whether tacit, hypothetical, public reason, or voting processes) to be governed and to the actions, policies, and decisions of a government, and for citizens' agreement to carry force, it must be based on conditions that meet the criteria of autonomy. And, again, our concern here is not an all-things-considered judgment about legitimacy, but about the ability of citizens to fulfill their responsibilities of legitimation.

There are several ways in which the exploitation of data, psychological profiles, social media, and algorithmic systems creates a drag on legitimation. Consider first Christman's test for legitimacy, which requires that political principles be such that reasonable citizens would not be understandably alienated from them.[67] The fake

[62] Weaver, "Facebook Scandal: I Am Being Used as Scapegoat – Academic Who Mined Data."
[63] Hamburger, "Cruz Campaign Credits Psychological Data and Analytics for Its Rising Success."
[64] Detrow, "What Did Cambridge Analytica Do during the 2016 Election?"
[65] Matz et al., "Psychological Targeting as an Effective Approach to Digital Mass Persuasion," 12717.
[66] Matz et al., 12717.
[67] Christman, *The Politics of Persons: Individual Autonomy and Socio-Historical Selves*, 239 (emphasis in original).

groups that the IRA created and advertised were promoted by fake user profiles but eventually were followed by real people, referenced real issues, and mimicked names and language of genuine social, religious, and political groups (e.g., Stop All Immigrants, Blacktivist, LGBTQ United). The language, the titles, and linking to real issues and groups drew in people who came to express their views and wills on topics with real stakes. However, by joining, engaging with, and thereby amplifying those groups and messages (and in some cases populating in-person events[68]), it is likely that their wills were not autonomous because the expression is one from which people would be alienated. That is, if people were to "engage in sustained critical reflection," which requires reflecting on how they came to their commitment, the expressions would be incompatible with their sense of self and practical identity over time.[69] And, if a person earnestly engaged in political debates about policing, rights of LGBTQ+ persons, and immigration were to reflect on the fact that Facebook groups like Stop All Immigrants, Blacktivist, and LGBTQ United were ersatz communities built by Russian agents to exploit and enrage them, they would in all likelihood be alienated from their support. In other words, the social media campaigns undermine the legitimation process by undermining the authenticity condition for autonomy.

Consider next the ways in which psychological profiling and targeting on social media works. It works, first, to engage people by keeping them scrolling on social media feeds.[70] It also seeks to create sustained engagement. One mechanism for creating such engagement is provoking strong emotions – including affinity for a cause *and* anger at opponents. The tactics draw people in and exploit their emotions. These tactics, for reasons we described in Chapter 5.2, are instances of the affective, deliberative, and social challenges to agency. They thus undermine the quality of people's agency and thereby conflict with their autonomy. This diminishes people's ability to perform their legitimating responsibilities.

The fake accounts also promoted falsehoods. First, they promoted falsehoods about the nature of the groups themselves. But they also promulgated false claims. This circumvents persons' autonomy by undermining its epistemic requirements. And it creates yet another drag on the legitimation process.

---

[68] Wylie recounts that in summer 2014, Cambridge Analytica began creating fake Facebook and other social media pages and groups with politically charged identities that were tailored to be fed into the news feeds of susceptible users by recommendation algorithms. As people joined the groups, Cambridge Analytica would set up meetings in small spaces (in order to make the group feel big). Because of the nature of the groups, and the nature of the content fed into the groups, "[p]eople would show up and find a fellowship of anger and paranoia." Wylie, *Mindf*ck: Cambridge Analytica and the Plot to Break America*, 128. These groups would, when large enough and prompted by Cambridge Analytica, meld with similar groups, creating a network of engaged, angry people who felt they were under siege. Wylie, 127–129.

[69] Christman, *The Politics of Persons: Individual Autonomy and Socio-Historical Selves*, 155.

[70] Wylie, *Mindf*ck: Cambridge Analytica and the Plot to Break America*, 127; Eyal, *Hooked: How to Build Habit-Forming Products*.

Finally, there is an issue that goes back to Feinberg's understanding of "ideal" autonomy and to social/relational conceptions of autonomy.[71] People are not isolated, atomistic individuals. They are parts of families, communities, and social groups. Such groups are vital to autonomy both in the sense that they are important in causing people to flourish and to develop their autonomy and in the sense that autonomy involves the ability to act and realize one's values within communities. The tactics of Cambridge Analytica and the IRA undermine that. They specifically seek to create ersatz communities that displace genuine ones and to rend broader communities into factions that neither trust nor communicate effectively with each other. Deep disputes are an important and ever-present facet of democratic polities. However, encouraging disparate groups to further distrust others and undermining the ability of those groups to communicate conflicts with the social facet of autonomy and, hence, with the legitimation process.

8.5 ONCE MORE PAST THE POLE

The issue of legitimation in the cases of PredPol, Cambridge Analytica, and the IRA is momentous. How police exercise their power to put others in harm's way, efforts to affect an election via social profiling, and interference of a hostile nation in a US presidential election cut to the quick of democratic legitimacy. But issues of political authority and legitimation are not limited to matters at the heart of democratic procedures and at the far reaches of state-sanctioned exercise of power. They extend also to ordinary administrative tasks as well, among them risk assessment and teacher evaluation.

COMPAS raises similar issues to PredPol on the normative authority arm of political legitimacy. It is no doubt true that efficient allocation of scarce resources for supervising people in the criminal justice system is good policy. There are substantial open questions about that system overall, of course. But if we accept the premises that the state should sanction some kinds of actions with a range of penalties and that supervision and resources (e.g., drug and alcohol treatment, job programs, counseling, housing) are appropriate responses, assessing persons for placement within those programs would appear to be a reasonable approach. But, as we explained in Section 3.4.3, the use for which COMPAS is designed and suited is different than the use to which it is put in *Loomis*. Hence, even if there is evidence that COMPAS is well calibrated in assessing risk, that same evidence does not underwrite use for sentencing purposes. As with PredPol, there is a disconnect between evidence and tool use, and that creates a drag on the epistemic facet of legitimation via normative authority.

The VAM cases are a bit simpler in that the tool itself has substantial flaws, as we discussed in Sections 1.1 and 3.4. Evaluating teachers is a reasonable policy goal.

---

[71] See Sections 2.2.2, 2.6, and 3.3.

However, the fact that the tools to do so have such big flaws precludes use of EVAAS and TVAAS from legitimation via normative authority. There is not a similar impediment to legitimation via democratic will. Note two things, though. First, that some institution, government, law, or policy is legitimate – which is to say based on a justified exercise of political power – is not the same as it being morally justified. Political legitimacy is in that sense a lower bar. Second, the fact that the algorithmic systems in these cases do not place a drag on the legitimation process is not a sufficient condition to ensure legitimacy. As we made clear in Section 8.4, our concern is that some kinds of algorithmic systems hinder citizens' abilities to exercise their responsibility to legitimate policies. VAMs do not obviously hinder fulfilling that responsibility.

8.6 CONCLUSION

Autonomy is foundational for political legitimacy. It grounds each of the accounts we canvassed in Section 8.2, including the hybrid account we endorse. We argued that one component part of legitimacy is the process of legitimation. That is, citizens have a responsibility to exercise their autonomy to legitimate governments, policies, laws, and actions. Algorithmic systems can impede citizens from fulfilling those responsibilities. PredPol (and to an extent COMPAS) is an example of an impediment to legitimation via normative authority. Whatever evidence there is of PredPol advancing a good policy goal (and there is some), that deflects from assessing how PredPol is actually used. That conflicts with the access condition, whereby belief in a policy's value has to be linked to evidence for its actual value.

The cases of Cambridge Analytica and the IRA undermine the second arm of political legitimacy. They create conditions where citizens would be alienated from the source of their beliefs and attitudes; they substitute ersatz involvement for genuine involvement and generate false beliefs.

But we should reiterate here that political legitimacy goes much further than the process of legitimation. For one, there are questions about different levels or targets of legitimacy. The fact, if it is, that policies using particular technologies create a drag on legitimation or, worse, are not legitimate all-things-considered does not tell us whether the agencies using the technologies, the municipalities, states, or nations using those technologies are legitimate or much else. It is important not to over-interpret drags on legitimation to make broader conclusions and legitimacy per se. Related is that legitimate authority can get things wrong and still retain legitimacy to exercise authority. That breadth of legitimacy is why our conclusions here are limited to the ability of citizens to exercise their responsibilities.

9

Conclusions and Caveats

It is fitting that the last example we introduced in the book was about the Internet Research Agency's (IRA) use of social media, analytics, and recommendation systems to wage disinformation campaigns and sow anger and social discord on the ground. At first glance, it seems odd to think of that as primarily an issue of technology. Disinformation campaigns are ancient, after all; the IRA's tactics are old wine in new boxes. That, however, is the point. What matters most is not particular features of technologies. Rather, it is how a range of technologies affect things of value in overlapping ways. The core thesis of our book is that understanding the moral salience of algorithmic decision systems requires understanding how such systems relate to an important value, viz., persons' autonomy. Hence, the primary through line of the book is the value itself, and we have organized it to emphasize distinct facets of autonomy and used algorithmic systems as case studies.

To review, we have argued that three broad facets of autonomy are affected by algorithmic systems. First, algorithmic systems are relevant to what we owe each other as autonomous agents. That is the focus of Chapters 3 and 4. In Chapter 3 we addressed the material conditions that we owe others and argued that respecting people as autonomous demands that any algorithmic system they are subjected to must be one that they can reasonably endorse. It does not require that they value particular outcomes or that they not be made worse off by such systems. Rather, systems must either comport with agents' own ends or be consistent with fair terms of social cooperation. We argued that persons being able to reasonably endorse a system turns on the system's reliability, responsibility, stakes, and relative burden. Chapter 4 turned to the issues of what information we owe others. There we argued that people are owed information as a function of their practical agency (i.e., their ability to act and carry out plans in accord with their values) and as a function of their cognitive agency (i.e., their ability to exercise evaluative control over mental states, including beliefs, desires, and reactive responses). We offered several principles for information access grounded in agency.

The second connection between algorithmic systems and autonomy is ensuring the conditions under which people are autonomous. In Chapter 5 we considered the relationship between algorithmic systems and freedom. We explained that algorithms bear upon negative, positive, and republican freedom and offered a general account of freedom as ecological non-domination. Key to understanding that ecology is recognizing three key challenges to freedom: affective challenges, deliberative challenges, and social challenges. In Chapter 6 we offered some suggestions for addressing some facets of those challenges. Specifically, we argue that a kind of epistemic paternalism is both permissible and (under some conditions) obligatory.

Chapters 7 and 8 shift focus to the responsibilities *of* agents in light of the fact that they are autonomous. In Chapter 7 we argue that algorithmic systems allow agents deploying such systems to undermine a key component of responsibility, viz., providing an account for actions for which they are responsible. Specifically, we argue that complex systems create an opportunity for "agency laundering," which involves a failure to meet one's moral responsibility for an outcome by attributing causal responsibility to another person, group, process, or technology. Chapter 8 addresses a different facet of responsibility. Citizens within democratic states have a responsibility to exercise their autonomy in order to legitimate political authority. That is, they have a responsibility to help ensure that governments, laws, policies, and practices are justifiable. However, some kinds of algorithmic systems hinder citizens' abilities to do that. They can do so by undermining the epistemic conditions necessary to underwrite the "normative authority" path to legitimacy or by undermining the exercise of autonomy necessary to underwrite the "democratic will" path to legitimacy.

9.1 FURTHER WORK

In one sense, that is a lot of terrain to have covered. And yet even within the scope of autonomy and algorithmic systems, there is much more work to do. Throughout the book, we pause to point out how various topics bear upon one another. There are, however, connections across the chapters that warrant more attention.

In Chapter 4 we address informational components to autonomy, and we argue that people have claims to information about algorithmic systems based on practical agency, cognitive agency, and democratic agency. There is a question, though, about whether such information is a condition for people to be able to reasonably endorse systems. That is, the precise relationship between what we owe people materially (per Chapter 3 and the Reasonable Endorsement Test) and what we owe people informationally (per the principles of informed practical and cognitive agency) is worth examining. Similar concerns arise in understanding the relationship between practical, cognitive, and democratic agency and political legitimacy. We note in Chapters 4 and 8 that the ability to exercise democratic agency is a component of the legitimating process. We explain how that relationship functions within the normative authority and democratic will "arms" of legitimacy. But a number of questions remain. Just what kinds of processes are subject to legitimation at all? Certainly, direct actions of government agents can be legitimate or not, but what about private actions? Or what about private actors whose influence on state affairs is enormous? Moreover, what is the extent of information necessary for citizens to fulfill their legitimating responsibilities?

There are further connections to be drawn between Chapter 5's discussion of quality of agency and other facets of autonomy. To the extent that the challenges to freedom limit people's quality of agency (and hence, positive freedom), are they also limitations on people's ability to reasonably endorse states of affairs? It also seems plausible that such challenges are an impediment to exercising practical, cognitive, and democratic agency. It is therefore worth exploring whether even greater epistemically paternalistic actions are justifiable (or even obligatory) than those we outline in Chapter 6.

We should also point out that the relevance of agency laundering may be even broader than we outline in Chapter 7. Laundering may be applicable in other cases we discuss throughout the book. For example, it would be worth considering it in background checks (Chapter 4) and predictive policing (Chapter 8). When presenting on the topic of agency laundering to academic audiences, we have often received questions about whether it could be applied to political actions (e.g., Brexit). While we cannot do justice to that question here, we can say that the use of sophisticated profiling and influence operations is a plausible mechanism for laundering. Hence, examining influence campaigns as potential sites of laundering is worthwhile.

And moving beyond the topics we've covered, the range of open questions is vast. Driverless vehicles, for example, raise numerous issues with respect to responsibility, human control, and worker displacement. Robots, including those that interact with humans, provide care and companionship, and displace labor are a topic of growing philosophical and moral concern. Weapons of war raise numerous issues relevant to human control and responsibility.

9.2 CAVEATS: BASELINE ISSUES

An important question that one might raise about this project concerns baseline comparisons. So, while COMPAS, EVAAS, TVAAS, PredPol, and other systems may have important problems with respect to autonomy, one might argue that despite those issues, the technologies are better than the relevant alternatives. What matters is not that algorithmic systems have flaws compared to some ideal, but whether they are meaningfully better than relevant alternatives. Having a system like COMPAS that assesses risk may be better than humans, who have well-known biases, who act arbitrarily, and who are harder to audit.

That's a reasonable criticism. However, it does not undercut the project for a number of reasons. First, even if it is the case that algorithmic systems are better than systems that precede them, it does not follow that they are justifiable. So, even if it is the case that using COMPAS is better than judges at determining likelihood of reoffense, it does not follow that use of COMPAS is itself justifiable. The space of reasonable alternatives need not be some antecedent system and some novel algorithmic system. There could be better algorithms; lower-stakes algorithms; algorithms that do not impose disparate relative burdens; that respect practical, cognitive, and democratic agency; that preserve quality of agency; that do not serve to launder agency; that allow citizens to fulfill their responsibilities of legitimation; and so forth.

Second, even where technologies are better than some alternatives, they may reveal underlying moral concerns. Consider a study from October 2019.[1] Obermeyer et al. studied a machine learning system that examined health records in order to predict which patients were in "high risk" categories and either defaulted them into a care program or referred them for screening into a care program. The study determined that Black patients identified as high risk were significantly less healthy than White patients so-identified; that is, Black patients had higher numbers of chronic conditions than similarly categorized White patients. This entailed Black patients were less likely to receive appropriate care than White patients. The reason for the difference, according to the researchers, is that the machine learning algorithm reflected health-care expenditures. That is, risk levels were correlated with the amount of care and treatment that patients received in prior years. As the authors put it, "Black patients generate lesser medical expenses, conditional on health, even when we account for specific comorbidities. As a result, accurate prediction of costs necessarily means being racially biased on health."[2] That disparity may arise for a couple of reasons. One is that poor patients (who are disproportionately Black) face substantial barriers to receiving healthcare, even if they are insured. For example, transportation time to care facilities may be greater and they may face greater difficulty in getting time off of work. There are also social barriers, including worse treatment of Black patients by care providers and distrust of health-care providers.

Notice, though, that the algorithm at work in the Obermeyer study is likely better than a system that did not use sophisticated technologies to identify high-risk patients and nudge them toward care programs. That is, it was likely better for Black patients as well as White patients and worse for no one. It was just *more* advantageous for White patients. But there is nonetheless a moral problem with the algorithm. Hence, "better than a prior baseline" should not end our inquiries. In the health system case, the study's authors developed a different analysis that sorted patients into high-risk groups based on underlying health conditions, and it performed similarly well for Black and for White patients. Our conclusions in this book, we hope, can provide grounds for analyzing what better algorithmic systems would look like.

9.3 BIGGER PICTURES

A further objection to many of our arguments in the book will have to do with background conditions and structures and whether we have properly identified the

---

[1] Obermeyer et al., "Dissecting Racial Bias in an Algorithm Used to Manage the Health of Populations."
[2] Obermeyer et al., 450.

most morally salient features of cases. In the case of COMPAS and *Loomis*, one might argue that the US criminal justice system has so many infirmities that focusing on use of a single tool is beside the point. In *Loomis*, one could argue that plea deals generally are unjust, in virtue of the fact that they take place in a system where alternatives to plea deals are trials with either expensive counsel or overstretched public defenders, high conviction rates for cases reaching jury verdicts, and long sentences for guilty verdicts. Plea deals to long sentences are common, in other words, because of other kinds of injustices and statutory penalties that outpace what is necessary for either deterrence or desert. Likewise, one might argue that the appropriate focus in analyzing use of VAMs to evaluate K-12 teachers is on issues such as school funding, the vast differences in resources available in wealthy and poor school districts, how those differences track race and ethnicity, the need to ensure excellent teaching, and administrative pressures on teachers generally. One might argue that background checks are a symptom of broader problems of wealth and income inequality, the austere state of healthcare for many Americans, and the fact that landlords have much greater legal power than tenants.

It is certainly the case that one can focus on different facets of problems, be they in criminal justice, education, rental markets, social media, disinformation campaigns, or anything else. But note that how criminal justice systems assess risk, allocate supervisory resources, and sentence people convicted of crimes are constitutive parts of the criminal justice system, not discrete actions. And different, constitutive parts of the criminal justice system may warrant different analyses, and it is not clear that overall systems are best analyzed in a univocal way. And in any case, our work here should be seen as sitting alongside other work on criminal justice, education, social media, disinformation, and so on. Systemic arguments and narrower arguments may be complementary rather than conflicting.

Finally, perhaps the biggest limitation to the project is that the sand is shifting beneath our feet. New ways of using technology continue apace, and some of the systems we discuss over the course of the book will soon have their problems resolved, change, or be replaced by new ones. But those newer algorithmic systems could also be used in ways that fail to respect autonomy, inhibit practical and cognitive agency, limit freedom, launder agency, and create drags on legitimation. That brings us full circle. What matters is not the particular technologies or the specific ways that those technologies are used. Rather, the underlying moral questions are a better anchor. Autonomy is certainly not the only moral value, and the nature, scope, and value of autonomy are contested. Moreover, the ways autonomy interacts with other values require continual reassessment. But, as we stated in Chapter 1, a rock-bottom assumption of this book is that autonomy matters – hopefully, considering autonomy helps us sort through a number of questions about technologies on the ground.

References

91st United States Congress. An Act to amend the Federal Deposit Insurance Act to require insured banks to maintain certain records, to require that certain transactions in U.S. currency be reported to the Department of the Treasury, and for other purposes., 15 U.S.C. § 1681 (1970).

104th United States Congress. An Act to promote competition and reduce regulation in order to secure lower prices and higher quality services for telecommunications consumers and encourage the rapid deployment of new telecommunications technologies., 47 U.S. C. section 230 (1996).

AAA Foundation for Traffic Safety. "Aggressive Driving | AAA Exchange." Accessed May 12, 2020. https://exchange.aaa.com/safety/driving-advice/aggressive-driving/.

Abrams, Rachel. "Target to Pay $18.5 Million to 47 States in Security Breach Settlement." *The New York Times*, May 23, 2017. www.nytimes.com/2017/05/23/business/target-security-breach-settlement.html.

Ahlstrom-Vij, Kristoffer. *Epistemic Paternalism: A Defence*. Basingstoke: Palgrave Macmillan, 2013.

Alfano, Mark J., Adam Carter, and Marc Cheong. "Technological Seduction and Self-Radicalization." *Journal of the American Philosophical Association* 4, no. 3 (2018): 298–322.

Algorithmic Accountability Act of 2019, H.R. 2231 § 116th Congress (2019–2020) (2019).

Algorithmic Accountability Act of 2019, S. 1108 § 116th Congress (2019–2020) (2019).

American Statistical Association, "ASA Statement on Using Value-Added Models for Educational Assessment," April 8, 2014. www.amstat.org/asa/files/pdfs/POL-ASAVAM-Statement.pdf.

Amrein-Beardsley, Audrey. "Evidence of Grade and Subject-Level Bias in Value-Added Measures: Article Published in TCR." VAMboozled! (blog), 2015. http://vamboozled.com/evidence-of-grade-and-subject-level-bias-in-value-added-measures-article-published-in-tcr/.

Rethinking Value-Added Models in Education. 1st ed. New York: Routledge, 2014.

Anderson, Elizabeth. *Private Government: How Employers Rule Our Lives*. Princeton, NJ: Princeton University Press, 2017.

Angwin, Julia, Jeff Larson, Surya Mattu, and Lauren Kirchner. "Machine Bias." *ProPublica*, May 23, 2016. www.propublica.org/article/machine-bias-risk-assessments-in-criminal-sentencing.

Angwin, Julia, Madeleine Varner, and Ariana Tobin. "Facebook Enabled Advertisers to Reach 'Jew Haters.'" *ProPublica*, September 14, 2017. www.propublica.org/article/facebook-enabled-advertisers-to-reach-jew-haters.

Appiah, Kwame Anthony. "The Case for Capitalizing the 'B' in Black." *The Atlantic*, June 18, 2020. www.theatlantic.com/ideas/archive/2020/06/time-to-capitalize-blackand-white /613159/.

Arthur, Charles. "Facebook Forces Instagram Users to Allow It to Sell Their Uploaded Photos." *The Guardian*, December 18, 2012. www.theguardian.com/technology/2012/ dec/18/facebook-instagram-sell-uploaded-photos.

Aslund, Anders. *Russia's Crony Capitalism: The Path from Market Economy to Kleptocracy.* New Haven, CT: Yale University Press, 2019.

Association for Computing Machinery, US Public Policy Council. "Statement on Algorithmic Transparency and Accountability." January 12, 2017. www.acm.org/binar ies/content/assets/public-policy/2017_usacm_statement_algorithms.pdf.

Baier, Annette. *Postures of the Mind: Essays on Mind and Morals.* Minnesota Archive Edition. Minneapolis: University of Minnesota Press, 1985.

Baker, Peter. "What Happens to Men Who Can't Have Sex." *Elle*, February 29, 2016. www .elle.com/life-love/sex-relationships/a33782/involuntary-celibacy/.

Bakos, Yannis, Florencia Marotta-Wurgler, and David R. Trossen. "Does Anyone Read the Fine Print? Consumer Attention to Standard-Form Contracts." *The Journal of Legal Studies* 43, no. 1 (2014): 1–35. https://doi.org/10.1086/674424.

Barnhill, Anne. "What Is Manipulation?" In *Manipulation: Theory and Practice*, edited by Christian Coons and Michael Weber, 51–72. Oxford; New York: Oxford University Press, 2014.

Barocas, Solon and Andrew D. Selbst. "Big Data's Disparate Impact." *California Law Review* 104, no. 3 (June 2016): 671–732.

Baron, Marcia. "The Mens Rea and Moral Status of Manipulation." In *Manipulation: Theory and Practice*, edited by Christian Coons and Michael Weber, 98–120. Oxford; New York: Oxford University Press, 2014.

BBC News. "Russian Businessman Buys Chelsea." July 2, 2003. http://news.bbc.co.uk/2/hi/ 3036838.stm.

"S Korean Dies after Games Session." August 10, 2005. http://news.bbc.co.uk/2/hi/technol ogy/4137782.stm.

Beauchamp, Zack. "Incels: A Definition and Investigation into a Dark Internet Corner." *Vox*, April 23, 2019. www.vox.com/the-highlight/2019/4/16/18287446/incel-definition-reddit.

Belgian Gaming Commission. "Loot Boxes in Three Video Games in Violation of Gambling Legislation," 2018. www.koengeens.be/news/2018/04/25/loot-boxen-in-drie-videogames-in-strijd-met-kansspelwetgeving.

Benoliel, Uri and Samuel Becher. "The Duty to Read the Unreadable." *Boston College Law Review* 60, no. 8 (January 1, 2019): 2255–2296.

Benson, Paul. "Taking Ownership: Authority and Voice in Autonomous Agency." In *Autonomy and the Challenges to Liberalism: New Essays*, edited by Joel Anderson and John Christman, 101–126. Cambridge: Cambridge University Press, 2005.

Berlin, Isaiah. "Two Concepts of Liberty." In *Liberty: Incorporating Four Essays on Liberty*, edited by Henry Hardy, 2nd ed., 166–217. Oxford: Oxford University Press, 2002.

Binns, Reuben. "Algorithmic Accountability and Public Reason." *Philosophy & Technology* 31, no. 4 (December 1, 2018): 543–556.

"Fairness in Machine Learning: Lessons from Political Philosophy." *Proceedings of Machine Learning Research* 81 (2018): 149–159.

Bond-Graham, Darwin. "All Tomorrow's Crimes: The Future of Policing Looks a Lot like Good Branding." *SF Weekly*, October 30, 2013. www.sfweekly.com/news/all-tomorrows-crimes-the-future-of-policing-looks-a-lot-like-good-branding/.

Bostrom, Nick. *Superintelligence: Paths, Dangers, Strategies*. Reprint. Oxford; New York: Oxford University Press, 2016.

Bratman, Michael. *Intention, Plans, and Practical Reason*. New edition. Center for the Study of Language and Information, Stanford: Stanford University Press, 1999.

Brennan, Tim, William Dieterich, and Beate Ehret. "Evaluating the Predictive Validity of the COMPAS Risk and Needs Assessment System." *Criminal Justice and Behavior* 36, no. 1 (January 1, 2009): 21–40.

Brighouse, Harry. *School Choice and Social Justice*. Oxford: Oxford University Press, 2003.

Buss, Sarah and Andrea Westlund. "Personal Autonomy." In *The Stanford Encyclopedia of Philosophy*, edited by Edward N. Zalta. Metaphysics Research Lab, Stanford: Stanford University Press, 2018.

Butt, Daniel. *Rectifying International Injustice: Principles of Compensation and Restitution between Nations*. New York: Oxford University Press, 2008.

Cadwalladr, Carole and Emma Graham-Harrison. "Revealed: 50 Million Facebook Profiles Harvested for Cambridge Analytica in Major Data Breach." *The Guardian*, March 17, 2018. www.theguardian.com/news/2018/mar/17/cambridge-analytica-facebook-influence-us-election.

Caldwell, Leigh Ann and Alex Moe. "Republican Justin Amash Stands by Position to Start Impeachment Proceedings." NBC News, May 28, 2019. www.nbcnews.com/news/us-news/republican-justin-amash-stands-position-start-impeachment-proceedings-despite-criticism-n1011176.

Calo, Ryan and Alex Rosenblat. "The Taking Economy: Uber, Information, and Power." *Columbia Law Review* 117, no. 6 (March 9, 2017): 1623–1690.

Campolo, Alex, Madelyn Sanfilippo, Meredith Whittaker, and Kate Crawford. "AI Now 2017 Report." New York: AI Now Institute, 2017. https://ainowinstitute.org/AI_Now_2017_Report.pdf.

Castro, Clinton. "Just Machines," n.d.

Castro, Clinton and Adam Pham. "Is the Attention Economy Noxious?" *Philosophers' Imprint* 20, no. 17 (2020): 1–13.

Cegłowski, Maciej. "The Moral Economy of Tech." Presented at the Moral Economies, Economic Moralities, Society for the Advancement of Socio-Economics, Berkeley, CA, June 24, 2016. https://sase.org/event/2016-berkeley/.

Chiou, Lesley and Catherine Tucker. "Fake News and Advertising on Social Media: A Study of the Anti-Vaccination Movement." Working Paper, National Bureau of Economic Research, November 2018. www.nber.org/papers/w25223.pdf.

Christman, John. "Saving Positive Freedom." *Political Theory* 33, no. 1 (2005): 79–88.
The Politics of Persons: Individual Autonomy and Socio-Historical Selves. Reissue edition. Cambridge: Cambridge University Press, 2011.

Citron, Danielle Keats. "Technological Due Process." *Washington University Law Review* 85, no. 6 (2008): 1249–1314.

Citron, Danielle and Frank Pasquale. "The Scored Society: Due Process for Automated Predictions." *Washington Law Review* 89, no. 1 (March 1, 2014): 1–33.

Clark, Liat. "Uber Denies Researchers' 'Phantom Cars' Map Claim." *Wired UK*, July 28, 2015. www.wired.co.uk/article/uber-cars-always-in-real-time.

Cochran, Donald. "Shut Down the Subreddit r/Incels." Change.org. Accessed July 7, 2020. www.change.org/p/reddit-com-shut-down-the-subreddit-r-incels.

Coeckelbergh, Mark and Ger Wackers. "Imagination, Distributed Responsibility and Vulnerable Technological Systems: The Case of Snorre A." *Science & Engineering Ethics* 13, no. 2 (June 2007): 235–248.

Cohen, G. A. "Freedom and Money." In *On the Currency of Egalitarian Justice, and Other Essays in Political Philosophy*, edited by G. A. Cohen, 166–200. Princeton: Princeton University Press, 2011.

Confessore, Nicholas. "Cambridge Analytica and Facebook: The Scandal and the Fallout so Far." *The New York Times*, April 4, 2018. www.nytimes.com/2018/04/04/us/politics/cambridge-analytica-scandal-fallout.html.

Connecticut Fair Hous. Ctr. v. Corelogic Rental Prop. Sols., LLC, 369 F. Supp. 3d 362 (D. Conn. 2020).

Corbett-Davies, Sam and Sharad Goel. "The Measure and Mismeasure of Fairness: A Critical Review of Fair Machine Learning." *ArXiv:1808.00023 [Cs]*, July 31, 2018. http://arxiv.org/abs/1808.00023.

Corbett-Davies, Sam, Emma Pierson, Avi Feller, Sharad Goel, and Aziz Huq. "Algorithmic Decision Making and the Cost of Fairness." *KDD '17: Proceedings of the 23rd ACM SIGKDD International Conference on Knowledge Discovery and Data Mining*, June 9, 2017, 797–806.

Cramb, Auslan. "Scotland's Most Expensive Sporting Estate Bought by Russian Vodka Billionaire." *The Telegraph*, March 30, 2017.

Danaher, John. "The Threat of Algocracy: Reality, Resistance and Accommodation." *Philosophy & Technology* 29, no. 3 (September 1, 2016): 245–268.

"Toward an Ethics of AI Assistants: An Initial Framework." *Philosophy & Technology* 31, no. 4 (December 1, 2018): 629–653. https://doi.org/10.1007/s13347-018-0317-3.

"Freedom in an Age of Algocracy." In Oxford Handbook of Philosophy of Technology, edited by Shannon Vallor Oxford Handbook of Philosophy of Technology. Oxford, UK: Oxford University Press, forthcoming.

Davidson, Donald. *Essays on Actions and Events*. 2nd ed. Oxford: New York: Clarendon Press, 2001.

Davies, Harry. "Ted Cruz Campaign Using Firm That Harvested Data on Millions of Unwitting Facebook Users." *The Guardian*, December 11, 2015. www.theguardian.com/us-news/2015/dec/11/senator-ted-cruz-president-campaign-facebook-user-data.

DeepMind. "About DeepMind." Accessed July 15, 2020. https://deepmind.com/about.

DeMichele, Matthew, Peter Baumgartner, Michael Wenger, Kelle Barrick, Megan Comfort, and Shilpi Misra. "The Public Safety Assessment: A Re-Validation and Assessment of Predictive Utility and Differential Prediction by Race and Gender in Kentucky." *SSRN Electronic Journal*, January 1, 2018. https://dx.doi.org/10.2139/ssrn.3168452.

Dennett, Daniel C. "When Hal Kills, Who's to Blame? Computer Ethics." In *Hal's Legacy: 2001's Computer as Dream and Reality*, edited by D. Stork, 351–365. Cambridge: MIT Press, 1997.

Detrow, Scott. "What Did Cambridge Analytica Do During the 2016 Election?" NPR. Accessed June 17, 2020. www.npr.org/2018/03/20/595338116/what-did-cambridge-analytica-do-during-the-2016-election.

Dieterich, William, Christina Mendoza, and Tim Brennan. "COMPAS Risk Scales: Demonstrating Accuracy Equity and Predictive Parity." Performance of the COMPAS Risk Scales in Broward County. Northpointe Inc. Research Department, July 8, 2016.

DiResta, Renee, Kris Shaffer, Becky Ruppel, David Sullivan, Robert Matney, Ryan Fox, Jonathan Albright, and Ben Johnson. "The Tactics & Tropes of the Internet Research Agency." U.S. Senate Documents, October 1, 2019.

Duff, R. A. "Responsibility." *Routledge Encyclopedia of Philosophy*, 1998. https://doi.org/10.4324/9780415249126-L085-1.

Duhigg, Charles. "How Companies Learn Your Secrets." *The New York Times Magazine*, February 16, 2012. www.nytimes.com/2012/02/19/magazine/shopping-habits.html.

Dworkin, Gerald. "Paternalism." In *The Stanford Encyclopedia of Philosophy*, edited by Edward N. Zalta, Summer 2020. Metaphysics Research Lab, Stanford University, 2020.

The Theory and Practice of Autonomy. Cambridge; New York: Cambridge University Press, 1988.

Edwards, Ezekiel. "Predictive Policing Software Is More Accurate at Predicting Policing than Predicting Crime." American Civil Liberties Union (blog). Accessed July 8, 2020. www.aclu.org/blog/criminal-law-reform/reforming-police/predictive-policing-software-more-accurate-predicting.

Elish, Madeleine Clare. "Moral Crumple Zones: Cautionary Tales in Human-Robot Interaction." *Engaging Science, Technology, and Society* 5 (March 23, 2019): 40–60.

Enoch, David. "Authority and Reason-Giving." *Philosophy and Phenomenological Research* 89, no. 2 (2014): 296–332.

Estlund, David M. *Democratic Authority: A Philosophical Framework*. Princeton, NJ: Princeton University Press, 2008.

Eubanks, Virginia. *Automating Inequality: How High-Tech Tools Profile, Police, and Punish the Poor*. New York, NY: St. Martin's Press, 2018.

European Union. Directive 2000/31/EC of the European Parliament and of the Council of 8 June 2000 on certain legal aspects of information society services, in particular electronic commerce, in the Internal Market (Directive on electronic commerce), 2000 O.J. (L 178) 1 § (2000).

Regulation (EU) 2016/679 of the European Parliament and of the Council of 27 April 2016 on the protection of natural persons with regard to the processing of personal data and on the free movement of such data, and repealing Directive 95/46/EC (General Data Protection Regulation), 2016 O.J. (L 119) 1 § (2016).

Eyal, Nir. *Hooked: How to Build Habit-Forming Products*. Edited by Ryan Hoover. 1st ed. New York, NY: Portfolio, 2014.

Facebook. "Community Standards Enforcement," May 2018. https://transparency.facebook.com/communitystandards-enforcement.

"News Feed." Accessed July 15, 2020. www.facebook.com/facebookmedia/solutions/news-feed.

Feinberg, Joel. "Autonomy." In *The Inner Citadel: Essays on Individual Autonomy*, edited by John Christman. New York: Oxford University Press, 1989.

Harm to Self: The Moral Limits of the Criminal Law. Reprint. Vol. 3. New York: Oxford University Press USA, 1989.

Ferguson, Andrew Guthrie. *The Rise of Big Data Policing: Surveillance, Race, and the Future of Law Enforcement*. New York: NYU Press, 2017.

Finlay, Steven. *Predictive Analytics, Data Mining and Big Data*. New York: Palgrave Macmillan, 2014.

Fischer, John Martin, and Mark S. J. Ravizza. *Responsibility and Control: A Theory of Moral Responsibility*. Cambridge, UK; New York: Cambridge University Press, 1998.

Floyd v. City of New York, 959 F. Supp. 2d 540 (S.D.N.Y. 2013).

Fowler, Geoffrey. "What If Facebook Gave Us an Opposing-Viewpoints Button?" *The Wall Street Journal*, May 18, 2016. www.wsj.com/articles/what-if-facebook-gave-us-an-opposing-viewpoints-button-1463573101.

Fox-Brewster, Tom. "Londoners Give up Eldest Children in Public Wi-Fi Security Horror Show." The Guardian, September 29, 2014. www.theguardian.com/technology/2014/sep/29/londoners-wi-fi-security-herod-clause.

Frankfurt, Harry G. "Freedom of the Will and the Concept of a Person." *The Journal of Philosophy* 68, no. 1 (1971): 5–20.

Friedman, Marilyn. *Autonomy, Gender, Politics.* New York: Oxford University Press, 2003.

Fry, Hannah. *Hello World: Being Human in the Age of Algorithms.* 1st ed. New York, NY: W. W. Norton & Company, 2018.

Gardner v. Florida, 430 U.S. 349 (1977).

Garvie, Jonathan, and Clare Frankle. "Facial-Recognition Software Might Have a Racial Bias Problem." *The Atlantic*, April 7, 2016. www.theatlantic.com/technology/archive/2016/04/the-underlying-bias-of-facial-recognition-systems/476991/.

Glasstetter, Josh. "Shooting Suspect Elliot Rodger's Misogynistic Posts Point to Motive." *Southern Poverty Law Center* (blog). Accessed July 7, 2020. www.splcenter.org/hatewatch/2014/05/23/shooting-suspect-elliot-rodgers-misogynistic-posts-point-motive.

Goldman, Alvin I. *Theory of Human Action.* Princeton, NJ: Princeton University Press, 1977.

Goode, Erica. "Sending the Police Before There's a Crime." *The New York Times*, August 15, 2011. www.nytimes.com/2011/08/16/us/16police.html.

Goodin, Robert E. "Apportioning Responsibilities." *Law & Philosophy* 6 (August 1987): 167–185. https://doi.org/10.1007/BF00145427.

"Responsibilities." *Philosophical Quarterly* 36, no. 142 (January 1986): 50–56.

Gorin, Moti. "Do Manipulators Always Threaten Rationality?" *American Philosophical Quarterly* 51, no. 1 (2014): 51–61.

Grant, David, Jeff Behrends, and John Basl, "What We Owe to Decision Subjects: Beyond Transparency and Explanation in Automated Decision-Making," (manuscript under review), n.d.

Grossman, Lev, Mark Thompson, Jeffrey Kluger, Alice Park, Bryan Walsh, Claire Suddath, Eric Dodds, et al. "The 50 Best Inventions." *Time*, November 28, 2011.

Guardian Staff. "Sistema Boss Arrested in Russia on Money-Laundering Charges." *The Guardian*, September 17, 2014. www.theguardian.com/world/2014/sep/17/sistema-russia-money-laundering-charges.

Gutmann, Amy. *Democratic Education.* Revised. Princeton: Princeton University Press, 1999.

Hakim, Danny and Matthew Rosenberg. "Data Firm Tied to Trump Campaign Talked Business with Russians." *The New York Times*, March 17, 2018. www.nytimes.com/2018/03/17/us/politics/cambridge-analytica-russia.html.

Hamburger, Tom. "Cruz Campaign Credits Psychological Data and Analytics for Its Rising Success." *Washington Post*, December 13, 2015. www.washingtonpost.com/politics/cruz-campaign-credits-psychological-data-and-analytics-for-its-rising-success/2015/12/13/4cb0baf8-9dc5-11e5-bce4-708fe33e3288_story.html.

Harford, Tim. "Big Data: Are We Making a Big Mistake?" *Financial Times US*, March 28, 2014. www.ft.com/content/21a6e7d8-b479-11e3-a09a-00144feabdc0.

Hart, H. L. A. *Punishment and Responsibility; Essays in the Philosophy of Law.* New York: Oxford University Press, 1968.

Hayek, F. A. *The Constitution of Liberty.* Chicago: The University of Chicago Press, 1978.

Herington, Jonathan. "Measuring Fairness in an Unfair World." In *Proceedings of the AAAI/ACM Conference on AI, Ethics, and Society*, 286–292. AIES '20. New York, NY, USA: Association for Computing Machinery, 2020.

Hern, Alex. "I Read All the Small Print on the Internet and It Made Me Want to Die." *The Guardian*, June 15, 2015. www.theguardian.com/technology/2015/jun/15/i-read-all-the-small-print-on-the-internet.

Hieronymi, Pamela. "Two Kinds of Agency." In *Mental Actions*, edited by Lucy O'Brien and Matthew Soteriou. New York: Oxford University Press, 2009.

Hill, Jr., Thomas. "Autonomy and Benevolent Lies." *The Journal of Value Inquiry* 18, no. 4 (December 1, 1984): 251–267.

"The Kantian Conception of Autonomy." In *The Inner Citidel: Essays on Individual Autonomy*, edited by John Christman, 91–105. Oxford: Oxford University Press, 1989.

Hoff, Sam. "Professor Helps Develop Predictive Policing by Using Trends to Predict, Prevent Crimes." *The Daily Bruin*, April 26, 2013. https://web.archive.org/web/20191216105955/ https://dailybruin.com/2013/04/26/professor-helps-develop-predictive-policing-by-using-trends-to-predict-prevent-crimes/.

Holloway, Jessica. "Evidence of Grade and Subject-Level Bias in Value-Added Measures." Teachers College Record, July 8, 2015. www.tcrecord.org/Content.asp?ContentID=17987.

Hooker, Brad. "Fairness." *Ethical Theory and Moral Practice* 8, no. 4 (2005): 329–352.

Houston Fed of Teachers, Local 2415 v. Houston Ind Sch Dist, 251 F. Supp. 3d 1168 (S.D. Tex. 2017).

Houston Independent School District. "EVAAS/Value-Added Frequently Asked Questions," 2015. http://static.battelleforkids.org/documents/HISD/EVAAS-Value-Added-FAQs-Final-2015–02-02.pdf.

Howard, Philip N., Bence Kollanyi, Samantha Bradshaw, and Lisa-Maria Neudert. "Social Media, News and Political Information during the US Election: Was Polarizing Content Concentrated in Swing States?" *Oxford Internet Institute, Project on Computational Propaganda*, 2017.

Hunt, Priscilla, Jessica Saunders, and John Hollywood. "Evaluation of the Shreveport Predictive Policing Experiment." Santa Monica, CA: RAND Corporation, 2014. www .rand.org/pubs/research_reports/RR531.html.

Hussain, Azhar, Syed Ali, Madiha Ahmed, and Sheharyar Hussain. "The Anti-Vaccination Movement: A Regression in Modern Medicine." *Cureus* 10, no. 7 (July 3, 2018): e2919.

Ideastream. "Grading the Teachers: Teachers in Richer Schools Score Higher on Value-Added Measure," June 18, 2013. www.ideastream.org/stateimpact/2013/06/18/grading-the-teachers-teachers-in-richer-schools-score-higher-on-value-added-measure.

Illinois v. Wardlow, 528 U.S. 119 (2000).

Isenberg, Eric, and Heinrich Hock. "Measuring School and Teacher Value Added in DC, 2011–2012 School Year." Mathematica Policy Research, Inc, August 31, 2012. https://eric .ed.gov/?id=ED565712.

Janik, Rachel. "'I Laugh at the Death of Normies': How Incels Are Celebrating the Toronto Mass Killing." *Southern Poverty Law Center* (blog), 2018. www.splcenter.org/hatewatch/ 2018/04/24/i-laugh-death-normies-how-incels-are-celebrating-toronto-mass-killing.

Japanese Society for Artificial Intelligence. "Ethical Guidelines," 2017. http://ai-elsi.org/wp-content/uploads/2017/05/JSAI-Ethical-Guidelines-1.pdf.

Jennings, Rebecca. "Incels Categorize Women by Personal Style and Attractiveness." Vox, April 28, 2018. www.vox.com/2018/4/28/17290256/incel-chad-stacy-becky.

Johnson, Deborah G., and Mario Verdicchio. "Reframing AI Discourse." *Minds and Machines* 27, no. 4 (December 1, 2017): 575–590.

Joy, Kevin. "What's Causing the 2019 Current Measles Outbreak?" *Michigan Health Lab*, 2019. https://healthblog.uofmhealth.org/whats-causing-2019-measles-outbreak-symptoms -perfcon.

Jungen, Anne. "Vang Gets 10 Years in Prison for Drive-by Shooting." *La Crosse Tribune*. October 23, 2013.

Kagan, Shelly. "The Additive Fallacy." *Ethics* 99, no. 1 (October 1, 1988): 5–31.

Kahneman, Daniel, Jack L. Knetsch, and Richard H. Thaler. "Experimental Tests of the Endowment Effect and the Coase Theorem." *Journal of Political Economy* 98, no. 6 (1990): 1325–1348.

Kaiser, Brittany. *Targeted: The Cambridge Analytica Whistleblower's Inside Story of How Big Data, Trump, and Facebook Broke Democracy and How It Can Happen Again*. Harper, 2019.

Kaiser, Jonas, and Adrian Rauchfleisch. "Unite the Right? How YouTube's Recommendation Algorithm Connects the U.S. Far-Right." *Medium* (blog), April 11, 2018. https://medium.com/@MediaManipulation/unite-the-right-how-youtubes-recommendation-algorithm-connects-the-u-s-far-right-9f1387ccfabd.

Kaminski, Margot E. "The Right to Explanation, Explained." *Berkeley Technology Law Journal* 34, no. 189 (2019).

Kang, Cecilia, and Sheera Frenkel. "Facebook Says Cambridge Analytica Harvested Data of up to 87 Million Users." *The New York Times*, April 4, 2018. www.nytimes.com/2018/04/04/technology/mark-zuckerberg-testify-congress.html.

Kant, Immanuel. *Groundwork of the Metaphysics of Morals*. Translated by H. J. Paton. New York, NY: HarpPeren, 1964.

Kar, Robin Bradley, and Margaret Jane Radin. "Pseudo-Contract & Shared Meaning Analysis." *Harvard Law Review* 132, no. 4 (2019): 1135–1219.

Keller, Daphne. "The Right Tools: Europe's Intermediary Liability Laws and the EU 2016 General Data Protection Regulation." *Berkeley Technology Law Journal* 33, no. 1 (2018): 287.

Keller, Evelyn Fox. *Reflections on Gender and Science*. Anniversary edition. New Haven: Yale University Press, 1996.

Kelly, Thomas. "Epistemic Rationality as Instrumental Rationality: A Critique." *Philosophy and Phenomenological Research* 66, no. 3 (2003): 612–640.

Kirchner, Lauren, and Matthew Goldstein. "Access Denied: Faulty Automated Background Checks Freeze Out Renters," May 28, 2020. https://themarkup.org/locked-out/2020/05/28/access-denied-faulty-automated-background-checks-freeze-out-renters.

Kitchin, Rob. "Big Data, New Epistemologies and Paradigm Shifts." *Big Data & Society* 1, no. 1 (January 1, 2014): 1–12.

Korsgaard, Christine M., G. A. Cohen, Raymond Geuss, Thomas Nagel, and Bernard Williams. *The Sources of Normativity*. Edited by Onora O'Neill. Cambridge; New York: Cambridge University Press, 1996.

Kumar, Rahul. "Defending the Moral Moderate: Contractualism and Common Sense." *Philosophy & Public Affairs* 28, no. 4 (1999): 275–309.

"Reasonable Reasons in Contractualist Moral Argument." *Ethics* 114, no. 1 (2003): 6–37.

Kutz, Christopher. "Responsibility." In *Oxford Handbook of Jurisprudence and Philosophy of Law*, edited by Jules Coleman, Scott Shapiro, and Kenneth Einar Himma, 548–587. Oxford: Oxford University Press, 2004.

Lanier, Jaron. *Ten Arguments for Deleting Your Social Media Accounts Right Now*. New York: Henry Holt and Co., 2018.

Lanzing, Marjolein. "'Strongly Recommended' Revisiting Decisional Privacy to Judge Hypernudging in Self-Tracking Technologies." *Philosophy & Technology* 32, no. 3 (September 1, 2019): 549–568.

Lee, Dami. "Duolingo Redesigned Its Owl to Guilt-Trip You Even Harder." *The Verge*, December 13, 2018. www.theverge.com/2018/12/13/18137843/duolingo-owl-redesign-language-learning-app.

Levin, Sam, and Julia Carrie Wong. "Self-Driving Uber Kills Arizona Woman in First Fatal Crash Involving Pedestrian." *The Guardian*, March 19, 2018. www.theguardian.com/technology/2018/mar/19/uber-self-driving-car-kills-woman-arizona-tempe.

Lewis, Paul. "'Fiction Is Outperforming Reality': How YouTube's Algorithm Distorts Truth." The Guardian, 2018. www.theguardian.com/technology/2018/feb/02/how-youtubes-algorithm-distorts-truth.

Lin, Zi. *New Perspectives on the Moral Significance of Coercion, Manipulation, and Bodily Violence*. Doctoral Dissertation, University of Wisconsin-Madison, 2019.

MacCallum, Gerald C. "Negative and Positive Freedom." *The Philosophical Review* 76, no. 3 (1967): 312–334.

Mackenzie, Catriona. "Relational Autonomy, Normative Authority and Perfectionism." *Journal of Social Philosophy* 39, no. 4 (2008): 512–533.

Mackenzie, Catriona, and Natalie Stoljar, eds. *Relational Autonomy: Feminist Perspectives on Autonomy, Agency, and the Social Self*. 1st ed. New York: Oxford University Press, 2000.

Maheshwari, Sapna. "On YouTube Kids, Startling Videos Slip Past Filters." *The New York Times*, November 4, 2017. www.nytimes.com/2017/11/04/business/media/youtube-kids-paw-patrol.html.

Marcus, Gary. "Deep Learning: A Critical Appraisal." *ArXiv:1801.00631 [Cs, Stat]*, January 2, 2018, http://arxiv.org/abs/1801.00631.

Martin, Kirsten E. "Ethical Issues in the Big Data Industry." *MIS Quarterly Executive* 14, no. 2 (April 25, 2015): 67–85.

Mather, Kate, and Richard Winton. "LAPD Uses Its Helicopters to Stop Crimes Before They Start." *Los Angeles Times*, March 7, 2015. www.latimes.com/local/crime/la-me-lapd-helicopter-20150308-story.html.

Matheson, Craig. "Weber and the Classification of Forms of Legitimacy." *The British Journal of Sociology* 38, no. 2 (1987): 199–215.

Matthias, Andreas. "The Responsibility Gap: Ascribing Responsibility for the Actions of Learning Automata." *Ethics and Information Technology* 6, no. 3 (September 1, 2004): 175–183.

Matz, Sandra C., Michal Kosinski, Gideon Nave, and David J. Stillwell. "Psychological Targeting as an Effective Approach to Digital Mass Persuasion" 114, no. 48 (2017): 12714–12719.

Meijer, Albert, and Martijn Wessels. "Predictive Policing: Review of Benefits and Drawbacks." *International Journal of Public Administration* 42, no. 12 (September 10, 2019): 1031–1039.

Mendoza, Isak, and Lee Bygrave. "The Right Not to Be Subject to Automated Decisions Based on Profiling." In *EU Internet Law: Regulation and Enforcement*, edited by Tatiani-Eleni Synodinou, Philippe Jougleux, Christiana Markou, and Thalia Prastitou, 77–98, 2017.

Meyers, Diana T. "Personal Autonomy and the Paradox of Feminine Socialization." *The Journal of Philosophy* 84, no. 11 (1987): 619–628.

Self, Society, and Personal Choice. 1st edition. New York: Columbia University Press, 1989.

Mill, John Stuart. *On Liberty*. Edited by Elizabeth Rapaport. Indianapolis, IN; Cambridge, UK: Hackett Publishing Company, 1978.

Mittelstadt, Brent Daniel, Patrick Allo, Mariarosaria Taddeo, Sandra Wachter, and Luciano Floridi. "The Ethics of Algorithms: Mapping the Debate." *Big Data & Society* 3, no. 2 (November 1, 2016): 1–21.

Morganstein, David, and Ron Wasserstein. "ASA Statement on Value-Added Models." *Statistics and Public Policy* 1, no. 1 (December 22, 2014): 108–110.

Mosseri, Adam. "Working to Stop Misinformation and False News." Facebook Newsroom (blog), 2017. https://about.fb.com/news/2017/04/working-to-stop-misinformation-and-false-news/.

National Science and Technology Council. "Preparing for the Future of Artificial Intelligence." Washington, DC, October 30, 2016.

Nedelsky, Jennifer. "Reconceiving Autonomy: Sources, Thoughts and Possibilities." *Yale Journal of Law and Feminism* 1, no. 1 (1989): 7–36.

Nelson, Ariel. "Broken Records Redux: How Errors by Criminal Background Check Companies Continue to Harm Consumers Seeking Jobs and Housing." Boston, MA: National Consumer Law Center, December 6, 2019.

Netherlands Gaming Authority. "Study into Loot Boxes: A Treasure or a Burden?" Netherlands Gaming Authority, April 10, 2018. https://kansspelautoriteit.nl/publish/pages/8676/study_into_loot_boxes_-_a_treasure_or_a_burden_-_eng.pdf.

Nguyen, C. Thi. "Echo Chambers and Epistemic Bubbles." *Episteme* 17, no. 2 (June 2020): 141–161.

Nissenbaum, Helen. "Computing and Accountability." *Communications of the ACM* 37, no. 1 (January 2, 1994): 72–80.

Noble, Safiya Umoja. *Algorithms of Oppression: How Search Engines Reinforce Racism.* New York: New York University Press, 2018.

Northpointe, Inc. "Practitioner's Guide to COMPAS Core," March 19, 2015. www.northpointeinc.com/files/technical_documents/Practitioners-Guide-COMPAS-Core-_031915.pdf.

Nyholm, Sven. *Humans and Robots: Ethics, Agency, and Anthropomorphism.* London; New York: Rowman & Littlefield Publishers, 2020.

Obermeyer, Ziad, Brian Powers, Christine Vogeli, and Sendhil Mullainathan. "Dissecting Racial Bias in an Algorithm Used to Manage the Health of Populations." *Science* 366, no. 6464 (October 25, 2019): 447–453.

Olson, Parmy. "Germany Wants Facebook to Pay for Fake News." *Forbes*, December 19, 2016. www.forbes.com/sites/parmyolson/2016/12/19/germany-wants-facebook-to-pay-for-fake-news/?sh=1c22d48f2dcc.

O'Neil, Cathy. *Weapons of Math Destruction: How Big Data Increases Inequality and Threatens Democracy.* 1st ed. New York: Crown, 2016.

OpenAI. "About OpenAI." Accessed July 15, 2020. https://openai.com/about/.

Oremus, Will, and Bill Carey. "Facebook's Offensive Ad Targeting Options Go Far Beyond 'Jew Haters.'" Slate, September 14, 2017. www.slate.com/blogs/future_tense/2017/09/14/facebook_let_advertisers_target_jew_haters_it_doesn_t_end_there.html.

Orphanides, K. G. "Children's YouTube Is Still Churning out Blood, Suicide and Cannibalism." *Wired UK*, March 23, 2018. www.wired.co.uk/article/youtube-for-kids-videos-problems-algorithm-recommend.

Oshana, Marina. "Ascriptions of Responsibility." *American Philosophical Quarterly* 34, no. 1 (1997): 71–83.

　　Personal Autonomy in Society. 1st ed. Aldershot, Hants, England; Burlington, VT: Routledge, 2006.

Parfit, Derek. *On What Matters.* Oxford; New York: Oxford University Press, 2011.

Pariser, Eli. *The Filter Bubble: How the New Personalized Web Is Changing What We Read and How We Think.* Reprint edition. New York, NY: Penguin Books, 2012.

Pasquale, Frank. *The Black Box Society: The Secret Algorithms That Control Money and Information.* Cambridge, MA: Harvard University Press, 2016.

Peter, Fabienne. *Democratic Legitimacy.* New York: Routledge, 2008.

　　"The Epistemic Circumstances of Democracy." In *The Epistemic Life of Groups: Essays in the Epistemology of Collectives*, edited by Miranda Fricker and Michael Brady, 133–149. Oxford: Oxford University Press, 2016.

"The Grounds of Political Legitimacy" *Journal of the American Philosophical Association* 6, no. 3 (Fall 2020): 372–390.

Pettit, Philip. "Freedom as Antipower." *Ethics* 106, no. 3 (April 1996): 576–604.

Just Freedom: A Moral Compass for a Complex World. 1st edition. New York: W. W. Norton & Company, 2014.

Pham, Adam, and Clinton Castro. "The Moral Limits of the Market: The Case of Consumer Scoring Data." *Ethics and Information Technology* 21, no. 2 (March 18, 2019): 117–126.

Piper, Mark. "Autonomy: Normative." In *Internet Encyclopedia of Philosophy.* Accessed July 8, 2020. www.iep.utm.edu/aut-norm/.

Quick, Kimberly. "The Unfair Effects of IMPACT on Teachers with the Toughest Jobs." *The Century Foundation* (blog), October 16, 2015. https://tcf.org/content/commentary/the-unfair-effects-of-impact-on-teachers-with-the-toughest-jobs/.

Rawls, John. *A Theory of Justice.* Cambridge, MA: Belknap Press of Harvard University Press, 1999.

"Justice as Fairness: Political Not Metaphysical." *Philosophy & Public Affairs* 14, no. 3 (1985): 223–251.

Political Liberalism. New York: Columbia University Press, 2005.

Raz, Joseph. *The Morality of Freedom.* Oxford: Oxford University Press, 1988.

Reddit. "Update on Site-Wide Rules Regarding Violent Content." Accessed July 7, 2020. www.reddit.com/r/modnews/comments/78p7bz/update_on_sitewide_rules_regarding_vio lent_content/.

Reddit Metrics. "Top Subreddits." Accessed July 15, 2020. https://redditmetrics.com/top.

Regan, Tom. "Introduction to Moral Reasoning." In *Information Ethics: Privacy, Property, and Power,* edited by Adam D. Moore, 30–46. Seattle: University of Washington Press, 2005.

Roberts, Sarah T. *Behind the Screen: Content Moderation in the Shadows of Social Media.* New Haven: Yale University Press, 2019.

Roose, Kevin. "The Making of a YouTube Radical." *The New York Times,* June 8, 2019. www.nytimes.com/interactive/2019/06/08/technology/youtube-radical.html.

Rosen, Guy, and Tessa Lyons. "Remove, Reduce, Inform: New Steps to Manage Problematic Content." *Facebook Newsroom* (blog), April 10, 2019. https://about.fb.com/news/2019/04/remove-reduce-inform-new-steps/.

Rosenblat, Alex. *Uberland: How Algorithms Are Rewriting the Rules of Work.* Oakland, CA: University of California Press, 2018.

Rothbard, Murray N. *For a New Liberty: The Libertarian Manifesto.* 2nd ed. Auburn, AL: Ludwig von Mises Institute, 2006.

Rubel, Alan. "Privacy and Positive Intellectual Freedom." *Journal of Social Philosophy* 45, no. 3 (September 1, 2014): 390–407.

"Privacy and the USA Patriot Act: Rights, the Value of Rights, and Autonomy." *Law and Philosophy* 26, no. 2 (2007): 119–159.

Rubel, Alan, Clinton Castro, and Adam Pham. "Agency Laundering and Information Technologies." *Ethical Theory and Moral Practice* 22 (2019): 1017–1041.

"Algorithms, Agency, and Respect for Persons." *Social Theory & Practice* 43, no. 3 (July 2020): 547–572.

Ryan, Shane. "Paternalism: An Analysis." *Utilitas* 28, no. 2 (June 2016): 123–135.

Sandberg, Sheryl. "Last Week We Temporarily Disabled Some of Our Ads Tools." Facebook, September 20, 2017. www.facebook.com/sheryl/posts/10159255449515177.

Sandel, Michael J. *Liberalism and the Limits of Justice.* Cambridge, UK; New York: Cambridge University Press, 1998.

Santoni de Sio, Filippo, and Jeroen van den Hoven. "Meaningful Human Control over Autonomous Systems: A Philosophical Account." *Frontiers in Robotics and AI* 5 (2018).

Satz, Debra. *Why Some Things Should Not Be for Sale: The Moral Limits of Markets*. Reprint edition. New York: Oxford University Press, 2012.

Scanlon, T. M. *What We Owe to Each Other*. Revised edition. Cambridge, MA: Belknap Press, 2000.

Scheiber, Noam. "How Uber Uses Psychological Tricks to Push Its Drivers' Buttons." *The New York Times*, April 2, 2017. www.nytimes.com/interactive/2017/04/02/technology/uber-drivers-psychological-tricks.html.

Schwartz, Barry. *The Paradox of Choice: Why More Is Less*. Revised edition. HarperCollins e-books, 2009.

Schwartz, Joanna C. "After Qualified Immunity." *Columbia Law Review* 120, no. 2 (2020): 309–388.

Segal, David. "A Russian Oligarch's $500 Million Yacht Is in the Middle of Britain's Costliest Divorce." *The New York Times*, June 6, 2018. www.nytimes.com/2018/06/06/business/britain-divorce-farkhad-akhmedov.html.

Selbst, Andrew D., and Julia Powles. "Meaningful Information and the Right to Explanation." *International Data Privacy Law* 7, no. 4 (November 1, 2017): 233–242.

Select Committee on Artificial Intelligence. *"AI in the UK: Ready, Willing and Able?"* HL 100 2017–2019. London: House of Lords, 2018.

Select Committee on Intelligence, United States Senate. "Report of the Select Committee on Intelligence, United States Senate, on Russian Active Measures Campaigns and Interference in the 2016 U.S. Election, Volume I: Russian Efforts against Election Infrastructure with Additional Views." Washington, DC: Select Committee on Intelligence, United States Senate, 2019.

"Report of the Select Committee on Intelligence, United States Senate, on Russian Active Measures Campaigns and Interference in the 2016 U.S. Election, Volume II: Russia's Use of Social Media and Additional Views." Washington, DC: Select Committee on Intelligence, United States Senate, 2019.

Shearer, Elisa. "Social Media Outpaces Print Newspapers in the U.S. as a News Source." Pew Research Center, December 10, 2018. www.pewresearch.org/fact-tank/2018/12/10/social-media-outpaces-print-newspapers-in-the-u-s-as-a-news-source/.

Shearer, Elisa, and Katerina Eva Matsa. "News Use across Social Media Platforms 2018." Pew Research Center, September 10, 2018. www.journalism.org/2018/09/10/news-use-across-social-media-platforms-2018/.

Shiffrin, Seana Valentine. "Paternalism, Unconscionability Doctrine, and Accommodation." *Philosophy & Public Affairs* 29, no. 3 (2000): 205–250.

Shklar, Judith. "The Liberalism of Fear." In *Liberalism and the Moral Life*, edited by Nancy L. Rosenblum. Cambridge, MA: Harvard University Press, 1989.

Simon, Herbert A. *Models of Man: Social and Rational-Mathematical Essays on Rational Human Behavior in a Social Setting*. 1st ed. New York: Wiley, 1957.

Skeem, Jennifer, John Monahan, and Christopher Lowenkamp. "Gender, Risk Assessment, and Sanctioning: The Cost of Treating Women like Men." *Law and Human Behavior* 40 (September 5, 2016).

Sloan, Robert H., and Richard Warner. "Algorithms and Human Freedom." *Santa Clara High Technology Law Journal* 35, no. 4 (March 13, 2019): 1–34.

Smith, Angela M. "Attributability, Answerability, and Accountability: In Defense of a Unified Account." *Ethics* 112, no. 3 (April 2012): 575–589.

Smith, Michael. "A Constitutivist Theory of Reasons: Its Promise and Parts." *Law, Ethics and Philosophy* 1 (December 1, 2013): 9–30.

Solove, Daniel J. "Privacy Self-Management and the Consent Dilemma." *Harvard Law Review* 126 (2013): 1880–1903.

Sonnad, Nikhil, and Tim Squirrell. "The Alt-Right Is Creating Its Own Dialect. Here's the Dictionary." Quartz. Accessed July 7, 2020. https://qz.com/1092037/the-alt-right-is-creating-its-own-dialect-heres-a-complete-guide/.

Sosa, Ernest. "For the Love of Truth?" In *Virtue Epistemology: Essays on Epistemic Virtue and Responsibility*, edited by Linda Zagzebski and Abrol Fairweather, 49–62. Oxford: Oxford University Press, 2000.

Spears, Andy. "Bias Confirmed – Tennessee Education Report." *VAMboozled!* (blog), 2015. http://tnedreport.com/2016/05/bias-confirmed/.

Squirrell, Tim. "A Definitive Guide to Incels." *Timsquirrell.com* (blog), 2020. www.timsquirrell.com/blog/2018/5/30/a-definitive-guide-to-incels-part-two-the-blackpill-and-vocabulary.

Stoljar, Natalie. "Feminist Perspectives on Autonomy." In *The Stanford Encyclopedia of Philosophy*, edited by Edward N. Zalta, Winter 2018. Metaphysics Research Lab, Stanford University, 2018.

Strauss, Valerie. "D.C. Teacher Tells Chancellor Why IMPACT Evaluation Is Unfair." *Washington Post*, August 16, 2011. www.washingtonpost.com/blogs/answer-sheet/post/dc-teacher-tells-chancellor-why-impact-evaluation-is-unfair/2011/08/15/gIQAoyhBIJ_blog.html.

Strawson, Peter. "Freedom and Resentment." *Proceedings of the British Academy* 48 (1962): 1–25.

Sunstein, Cass R. *#Republic: Divided Democracy in the Age of Social Media*. Princeton; Oxford: Princeton University Press, 2017.

Superson, Anita. "Deformed Desires and Informed Desire Tests." *Hypatia* 20, no. 4 (2005): 109–126.

Susser, Daniel, Beate Roessler, and Helen Nissenbaum. "Online Manipulation: Hidden Influences in a Digital World." *Georgetown Law Technology Review* 4 (2019): 1–45.

Sweeney, Latanya. "Discrimination in Online Ad Delivery." *Communications of the ACM* 56, no. 5 (January 28, 2013): 44–54.

"Only You, Your Doctor, and Many Others May Know." *Technology Science*, September 29, 2015. https://techscience.org/a/2015092903/.

Terry v. Ohio, 392 U.S. 1 (1968).

Turque, Bill. "More than 200 D.C. Teachers Fired." *The Washington Post*, July 15, 2011. www.washingtonpost.com/blogs/dc-schools-insider/post/more-than-200-dc-teachers-fired/2011/07/15/gIQADnTLGI_blog.html.

U.S. Department of Justice. "Report on the Investigation into Russian Interference in the 2016 Presidential Election, Volume I ('Mueller Report')." Washington, DC: U.S. Department of Justice, March 2019.

"Report on the Investigation into Russian Interference in the 2016 Presidential Election, Volume II ('Mueller Report')." Washington, DC: U.S. Department of Justice, March 2019.

U.S. v. Internet Research Agency, LLC, No. 1:18-cr-00032 (U.S. District Court for the District of DC) (Indictment, February 16, 2018) www.justice.gov/file/1035477/download.

Vincent, Nicole A. "A Structured Taxonomy of Responsibility Concepts." In *Moral Responsibility: Beyond Free Will and Determinism*, edited by Nicole A. Vincent, Ibo van de Poel, and Jeroen van den Hoven, 15–35. Library of Ethics and Applied

Philosophy. Dordrecht: Springer Netherlands, 2011. https://doi.org/10.1007/978–94-007–1878-4_2.

Wachter, S., B. D. M. Mittelstadt, and C. Russell. "Counterfactual Explanations without Opening the Black Box: Automated Decisions and the GDPR." *Harvard Journal of Law and Technology* 31, no. 2 (2018): 841–887.

Wachter, Sandra, Brent Mittelstadt, and Luciano Floridi. "Why a Right to Explanation of Automated Decision-Making Does Not Exist in the General Data Protection Regulation." *International Data Privacy Law* 7, no. 2 (May 1, 2017): 76–99.

Wagner, Ben. "Liable, but Not in Control? Ensuring Meaningful Human Agency in Automated Decision-Making Systems." *Policy & Internet* 11, no. 1 (2019): 104–122. https://doi.org/10.1002/poi3.198.

Wagner v. Haslam, 112 F. Supp. 3d 673 (M.D. Tenn. 2015).

Waldman, Ari Ezra. "Power, Process, and Automated Decision-Making." *Fordham Law Review* 88, no. 2 (September 29, 2019): 613–632.

Walsh, Elias, and Dallas Dotter. "Longitudinal Analysis of the Effectiveness of DCPS Teachers." Mathematica Policy Research Reports. Mathematica Policy Research. Accessed April 21, 2018. https://ideas.repec.org/p/mpr/mprres/65770df94dde4573b331ce1cb33a9e07.html.

Weaver, Matthew. "Facebook Scandal: I Am Being Used as Scapegoat – Academic Who Mined Data." The Guardian, March 21, 2018. www.theguardian.com/uk-news/2018/mar/21/facebook-row-i-am-being-used-as-scapegoat-says-academic-aleksandr-kogan-cambridge-analytica.

Weber, Max. *Economy and Society: An Outline of Interpretive Sociology.* University of California Press, 1978.

Wells, Katie J., and Declan Cullen. "The Uber Workplace in Washington, D.C." Kalmanovitz Initiative for Labor and the Working Poor, Georgetown University, 2019.

Whittlestone, Jess, Rune Nyrup, Anna Alexandrova, Kanta Dihal, and Stephen Cave. "*Ethical and Societal Implications of Algorithms, Data, and Artificial Intelligence: A Roadmap for Research.*" London: The Nuffield Foundation, 2019.

Williams, Bernard. "Deciding to Believe." In *Problems of the Self: Philosophical Papers 1956–1972*, edited by Bernard Williams, 136–151. Cambridge: Cambridge University Press, 1973.

Williams, Garrath. "Responsibility as a Virtue." *Ethical Theory and Moral Practice* 11, no. 4 (2008): 455–470.

Wingfield, Nick, Mike Isaac, and Katie Benner. "Google and Facebook Take Aim at Fake News Sites." *The New York Times*, November 14, 2016. www.nytimes.com/2016/11/15/technology/google-will-ban-websites-that-host-fake-news-from-using-its-ad-service.html.

Wisconsin v. Loomis, 881 N.W.2d 749 (Wisconsin Supreme Court 2016).

Wood, Allen W. "Coercion, Manipulation, Exploitation." In *Manipulation: Theory and Practice*, edited by Christian Coons and Michael Weber. Oxford; New York: Oxford University Press, 2014.

World Health Organization. "Ten Health Issues WHO Will Tackle This Year." Accessed July 6, 2020. www.who.int/news-room/feature-stories/ten-threats-to-global-health-in-2019.

Wylie, Christopher. *Mindf*ck: Cambridge Analytica and the Plot to Break America.* New York: Random House, 2019.

Yaffe-Bellany, David. "Equifax Data-Breach Settlement: Get up to $20,000 If You Can Prove Harm." *The New York Times*, July 22, 2019. www.nytimes.com/2019/07/22/business/equi fax-data-breach-claim.html.

Yeung, Karen. "'Hypernudge': Big Data as a Mode of Regulation by Design." *Information, Communication & Society* 20, no. 1 (January 2, 2017): 118–136.

Yu, Persis S., and Sharon M. Dietrich. "Broken Records: How Errors by Criminal Background Checking Companies Harm Workers and Businesses." National Consumer Law Center, April 11, 2012.

Zarsky, Tal. "The Trouble with Algorithmic Decisions: An Analytic Road Map to Examine Efficiency and Fairness in Automated and Opaque Decision Making." *Science, Technology, & Human Values* 41, no. 1 (January 1, 2016): 118–132.

Index

Index

Index   205

Hieronymi, Pamela, 77
Houston Fed of Teachers v. Houston Ind Sch Dist,
   5–6, 7, 45, 59–60, 93–95, 161

IMPACT, 45–47, 53, 54–56
incels, 128–132
Instagram, 179
Internet Research Agency, 16, 178–182, 183, 184

Kant, Immanuel, 25, 47, 48, 50
  the Categorical Imperative, 48
Korsgaard, Christine, 48
Kumar, Rahul, 51–52

legitimacy, 42, 185
  access constraint, 168, 173, 176
  descriptive criteria, 165–166
  disjunctive conception, 169–171
  epistemic criteria, 168–169
  will-based conceptions, 169
legitimation, 85, 173–176, 185
Loomis, Eric, 3–4, 7, 13, 14, 91
loot boxes, 113–114, 116

machine learning, 9–10
  unsupervised learning, 10
manipulation, 116–117
Mill, John Stuart, 48
moral theories
  consequentialist moral theories, 39
  deontological moral theories, 39
  virtue-based moral theories, 39

new media, 119–122
Northpointe, Inc., 3, 4, 60, 61, 62

O'Neil, Cathy, 7, 12
Oshana, Marina, 26, 27, 29–33, 38, 41, 42, 140–141,
  167, 172

Parfit, Derek, 49, 51, 53
  the Consent Principle, 49
paternalism, 117, 122–126
  epistemic paternalism, 42, 121–122, 126–128,
  185, 186
perfectionism, 28
  weak perfectionism, 30
Peter, Fabienne, 168–171
Pettit, Philip, 33, 42, 169
predictive analytics, 9
PredPol, 163–165, 180, 183, 186
Principle of Informational Control, 80–81
Principle of Informed Cognitive Agency, 81

Principle of Informed Practical Agency, 79
ProPublica, 60, 61–64, 145
PublicData.com, 74

Rawls, John, 51, 52, 167–168, 169
Raz, Joseph, 116, 168–169
reactive attitudes, 52
Reasonable Endorsement Test, 52–53, 71, 99,
  168, 185
relative burden, 56–57, 59–60, 61–65, 184
reliability, 54, 184
responsibility, 138–141, 184
stakes, 55, 184
Reddit, 128–129, 133–134
responsibility, 141
  capacity responsibility, 139, 148, 162
  causal responsibility, 139, 146
  role responsibility, 139, 148
responsibility gap, 138, 156–158
right of access, 86–87
right to explanation, 86, 87–90
  counterfactual explanations, 89
  ex ante explanations, 87–88
  ex post explanations, 87–88
  right to object, 90–91
  specific decisions, 87
  specific explanations, 88–89
  system-level explanations, 87
right to object, 86
right to rectification, 86–87

Scanlon, Tim, 51, 52
stop-and-frisk, 33–34
Strong Principle of Informational Control, 81
Strong Principle of Informed Cognitive Agency, 81
Strong Principle of Informed Practical Agency, 79
Sweeney, Latanya, 84–85

Taylor, Catherine, 72, 73–76, 78–81, 88, 115
TVAAS, 5, 6, 58–59, 183, 186
Twitter, 121, 179

Uber, 107–109, 119, 149–152, 160–161

vaccine hesitancy, 121, 123–124
VAMs, 4, 55, 182–183, 188

Wagner, Teresa, 5, 58, 115
Wagner v. Haslam, 4–5, 7, 11, 13, 45, 58–59, 93–95
Wisconsin v. Loomis, 3–4, 7, 11, 13, 45, 60–65,
  91–93, 115, 154–156, 161, 182, 188

YouTube, 111–112, 114, 116, 121, 179

For EU product safety concerns, contact us at Calle de José Abascal, 56–1°, 28003 Madrid, Spain or eugpsr@cambridge.org.